Lecture Notes in Computer Scie

Commenced Publication in 1973
Founding and Former Series Editors:
Gerhard Goos, Juris Hartmanis, and Jan van Leeuwen

Fabrice Kordon   Oleg Sokolsky (Eds.)

Composition of Embedded Systems

Scientific and Industrial Issues

13th Monterey Workshop 2006
Paris, France, October 16-18, 2006
Revised Selected Papers

 Springer

Volume Editors

Fabrice Kordon
Université Pierre et Marie Curie
Laboratoire d'Informatique de Paris 6
Modeling and Verification
4 place Jussieu, 75252 Paris Cedex 05, France
E-mail: Fabrice.Kordon@lip6.fr

Oleg Sokolsky
University of Pennsylvania
Department of Computer and Information Science
3330 Walnut Street, Philadelphia, PA 19104-6389, USA
E-mail: sokolsky@cis.upenn.edu

Library of Congress Control Number: 2007941813

CR Subject Classification (1998): D.1.3, D.2-3, D.4.5, F.3, C.2.1, C.2-4

LNCS Sublibrary: SL 2 – Programming and Software Engineering

ISSN	0302-9743
ISBN-10	3-540-77418-1 Springer Berlin Heidelberg New York
ISBN-13	978-3-540-77418-1 Springer Berlin Heidelberg New York

Springer is a part of Springer Science+Business Media

springer.com

© Springer-Verlag Berlin Heidelberg 2007
Printed in Germany

Typesetting: Camera-ready by author, data conversion by Scientific Publishing Services, Chennai, India
Printed on acid-free paper   SPIN: 12209217   06/3180   5 4 3 2 1 0

Preface

Composition of Embedded Systems:
Scientific and Industrial Issues

The Monterey Workshops series was initiated in 1992 by David Hislop with the purpose of exploring the critical problems associated with cost-effective development of high-quality software systems. During its 14-year history, the Monterey Workshops have brought together scientists that share a common interest in software development research serving practical advances in next-generation software-intensive systems. Each year is dedicated to a particular topic of critical importance. In the past years, workshop topics were "Networked Systems: Realization of Reliable Systems on Unreliable Networked Platforms" (2005 in Laguna Beach, California), "Software Engineering Tools: Compatibility and Integration" (2004 in Vienna), " Engineering for Embedded Systems: From Requirements to Implementation" (2003 in Chicago), "Radical Innovations of Software and Systems Engineering in the Future" (2002 in Venice), "Engineering Automation for Software Intensive System Integration" (2001 in Monterey).

The 14th Monterey Workshop was held in Paris, France, during October 16–18, 2006.

Context of the 2006 Monterey Workshop

Distributed real-time embedded (DRE) systems are notoriously hard to design, implement, and validate. The complexity of a typical system found in many critical applications in civil and military aviation, transportation systems, and medical devices exceeds the capabilities of existing development and verification technologies. Companies spend enormous amounts of time and resources on verification and validation of DRE systems they develop and yet, despite their best efforts, hard-to-find errors show up in deployed products.

More and more, large DRE systems are built from components developed by third-party suppliers in an attempt to reduce development costs. But integration of DRE components presents its own set of problems: components that appear correct in isolation fail to function properly when put together. Research on DRE composition aims to develop techniques for designing DRE components and integrating them into larger systems in such a way that emphasizes safety and reliability of the integrated systems.

The 14th Monterey Workshop on "Composition of Embedded Systems: Scientific and Industrial Issues" focused on new, promising directions for achieving high software and system reliability in DRE systems while minimizing design, verification, and validation efforts and time to market.

All presentations at the workshop were by invitation upon the advice of the Program Committee.

Invited Speakers

Juan Colmenares	University of California at Irvine, USA
David Corman	Boeing, USA
Gregory Haik	Thales, France
Jérôme Hugues	Telecom-Paris, France
Xenofon Koutsoukos	Vanderbilt University, USA
Ingolf Krueger	UC San Diego, USA
Radu Grosu	Stony Brook University, USA
Gabor Karsai	Vanderbilt University, USA
Christoph Kirsch	University of Salzburg, Austria
Fran cois Laroussinie	ENS Cachan, France
Klaus Müller-Glaser	FZI, Germany
Rick Schantz	BBN Technologies, USA
Manuel Rodriguez	Naval Postgraduate School, USA
Roman Obermaisser	TU Vienna, Austria
Fran cois Terrier	CEA-LIST, France
Joseph Sifakis	Verimag, France

Papers included in this volume were selected among the submissions from the workshop's discussions.

Workshop Topics

Our society is increasingly reliant on embedded systems for many critical day-to-day activities. In many application domains, such as automotive and avionics industries, satellite communications, and medical devices, embedded software is the major driving force. Development of embedded software has come to dominate design effort, time, and costs. Despite massive development efforts, software is now a significant cause of failure in embedded devices. Advances in embedded software development technologies are therefore fundamental to the economic success, scientific and technical progress, as well as national security of our society.

Development of embedded software-intensive systems is always a hard task due to a multitude of stringent constraints that these systems have to satisfy, including stringent timing, memory footprint, and other resource requirements. In recent years, the problem has become even more complicated due to the advent of DRE systems, which need to interact with each other in a timely and predictable fashion, while still satisfying their individual requirements. The increased complexity of DRE systems has rendered existing development technologies inadequate for the demands of today's applications.

Composition is a possible approach for conquering the complexity of modern embedded systems design. In this approach, the components of the system can be developed in isolation and then integrated together in a property-preserving way. Compositional development for embedded systems is an active research area, but much remains to be done to keep up with the needs of industry and society.

The workshop discussed a range of challenges in embedded systems design that require further major advances in software and systems composition technology:

- **Model-driven development for DRE systems.** Modeling and model-driven development (MDD) are of particular importance for DRE systems, because of their dependence on continuously evolving environments and strict requirements that need to be specified precisely for testing and verification.
- **Balancing cost and assurance in DRE systems.** High assurance comes at a high cost. System developers need to balance development costs and assurance levels depending on the criticality of particular system aspects. This area has not received enough attention from the research community and system developers lack proper tools to reason about such trade-offs.
- **Domain-specific languages for DRE systems.** Domain-specific languages (DSL) allow designers to represent systems directly using concepts from their application domains. Because of this, models and designs are easier to understand and validate, increasing confidence in the system. Research on DSL has been very active recently, yet many open questions remain, including semantic definitions for DSLs and correctness of model transformations with respect to the language semantics.
- **Composition of real-time components.** Timing and resource constraints, prevalent in DRE system development, make composition much more difficult. Component interfaces that are the basis for system integration now have to expose not only the input and output behaviors of the component, but also its resource demands. Formalisms that are used to reason about composition need to be able to capture the notion of resources and resource scheduling.
- **Fault tolerance for DRE.** Dealing with emergency situations is a major part of the DRE operation. The handling of faults and other abnormal events consumes a major portion of the system development efforts and represents the vast majority of code in a system implementation. At the same time, most model-driven approaches concentrate on the functional aspects of system behavior and the nominal environment.

The papers presented at the workshop and collected in this volume discuss recent advances in addressing the above challenges, and outline directions of future research necessary to conquer them. The papers are organized into the following three groups:

- The first group addresses the problem of MDD for DRE systems. Papers in this group address model-level composition of functional and non-functional properties, as well as correctness of property-preserving model transformations that are key to the MDD process.
- The second group of papers is devoted to software engineering and analysis for component-based DRE systems.
- Finally, the last group of papers discuss component implementation and integration technologies that address the composition on a more concrete level, while making full use of modeling and software engineering approaches considered in the first two groups.

Acknowledgements

We are grateful to the Steering Committee, the Local Organizing Committee, and the invited speakers for making the workshop a success. We acknowledge generous sponsorship from the Army Research Office (David Hislop) and from the National Science Foundation (Helen Gill).

September 2007   Fabrice Kordon
                                                 Oleg Sokolsky

Organization

Executive Committee

Program Chairs	Fabrice Kordon (Université Pierre & Marie Curie, France)
	Oleg Sokolsky (University of Pennsylvania, USA)
Local Organization	Fabrice Kordon (Université Pierre & Marie Curie, France)

Technical Program Committee

Beatrice Berard	Université Paris-Dauphine, France
Valdis Berzins	Naval Postgraduate School, USA
Juan de la Puente	Universidad Politecnica de Madrid, Spain
Gabor Karsai	Vanderbilt Universiy, USA
Insup Lee	Pennsylvania University, USA
Edward Lee	University of California at Berkeley, USA
Tom Maibaum	King's College, London, UK
Joseph Sifakis	Verimag, France
Henny Sipma	Stanford University, USA
Francois Terrier	CEA-LIST, France

Table of Contents

Model Driven Development and Embedded Systems

Software Engineering for Embedded Systems

Composition Technologies

On the Correctness of Model Transformations in the Development of Embedded Systems

Gabor Karsai and Anantha Narayanan

Institute for Software Integrated Systems,
Vanderbilt University,
Nashville TN 37203, USA

Abstract. Model based techniques have become very popular in the development of software for embedded systems, with a variety of tools for
design, simulation and analysis of model based systems being available
(such as Matlab's Simulink [20], the model checking tool NuSMV [4] etc.).
Model transformations usually play a critical role in such model based
development approaches. While the available tools are geared to verify
properties about individual models, the correctness of model transformations is generally not verified. However, errors in the transformation
could present serious problems. Proving a property for a certain source
model becomes irrelevant if an erroneous transformation produces an
incorrect target model. One way to provide assurance about a transformation would be to prove that it preserves certain properties of the
source model (such as reachability) in the target model. In this paper,
we present some general approaches to providing such assurances about
model transformations. We will present some case studies where these
techniques can be applied.

1   Model Based Development of Embedded Systems

Embedded software today is often being developed using model-based techniques. The industry-standard tools for such development are widely available,
and they typically include a visual modeling language (supporting dataflow-
style and statechart-style modeling paradigms), a simulation engine, and a code-
generator that produces embedded code from the diagrams [1,2]. The modeling
languages used are practical, but their semantics is often not defined precisely,
to the level of detail used in case of more traditional languages such as Ada. The
only source for the definition of semantics is often the vendor's documentation.
Other tools (e.g. [3]) provide support for embedded system development through
the UML 2.0 modeling language standard, with highly customizable code generators. The advantages of using these model-based tools are well-known, and widely
publicized by their vendors. The gains in productivity can be clearly measured
in practical applications. The higher-level, domain-specific models that could be
directly executed and then 'compiled' into code are natural for control designers,
and let engineers ignore implementation level details that introduce 'accidental
complexities' in software development.

F. Kordon and O. Sokolsky (Eds.): Monterey Workshop 2006, LNCS 4888, pp. 1–18, 2007.

However such model-based tools often fall short on the side of system verification. System verification in practice means simulating the design using the simulation engine; an activity which cannot be exhaustive, by definition. The model-based development environments allow creating a simulation model of the plant to be controlled, as well as an (executable) model of the controller that controls it, such that integrated simulation studies could be performed. Approaches and tools have also been developed for the simulation of time-domain properties of schedulers, networks, protocols, etc. Simulation of embedded systems as the de facto technique for verification is widely practiced in the industry.

1.1   The Problem with Model-Based Approaches

It is unclear how model-based approaches lend themselves to the certification processes mandatory in critical applications, like aerospace and safety systems. Models offer higher-level abstractions for specifying and designing systems, and -if their semantics is well-defined- can be subjected to rigorous formal, often automated, verification. However, the verification of the models does not necessarily imply the verification of the code generated from the models. Neither does simulation-based testing imply that the generated code will work with the physical environment as desired. Note that existing practical approaches like code reviews and code-level verification fare better, as the subject of the verification is the final artifact, not an abstraction of it. However, automatically generated code could be hard to understand and analyzed in a manual process, thus code reviews are not practical for model-based systems. There have been several efforts in defining the semantics of modeling languages [6], most significantly, the Unified Modeling Language [7]. Such approaches often apply to generic languages such as the UML, and are not tailored to domain specific languages that can vary greatly from application to application. It is also extremely difficult to come up with a semantics for a language that captures all behavior, and is practical to use at the same time.

We should recognize that the crucial ingredient in model-based development of critical embedded software is the correctness of tool-chains that tie modeling, verification, and code generation together. The productivity gains and the expected assurances for the correctness of generated systems of model-based development cannot be reached unless the toolchain used provides some sort of guarantees that the code satisfies the stringent requirements. Figure 1 shows the notional architecture of a model-based development tool-chain.

Note that these toolchains often include non-trivial transformation or translation steps, including the code generator and model translators that connect the design language used (e.g. Statechart [1]) to the analysis 'language' (e.g. SMV [4]), and possibly other model-to-model transformation steps. When these tools are used, it is natural to expect that model-to-model transformations preserve the semantics of the models, verification results computed by analysis tools (e.g. model checkers) are valid for the design models, and the generated code exhibits identical behavior to the one specified by the model. Thus, the correctness of such 'model transformations' is an essential question to answer. Otherwise, for

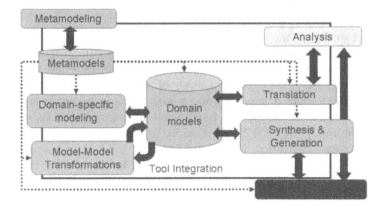

Fig. 1. Notional Architecture of a Model-based Development Toolchain

instance, verification results obtained for the models cannot be carried over to the code generated from the models. In summary, model-based development for embedded systems of the high-consequence category must address the need for verifiable model transformations and code generators that give assurances for the logical consistency of the toolchain.

2 Towards Verified Transformations

Verifying model transformations, in general, is as difficult as verifying a compiler for a high-level language. However, the domain-specific (read: restricted) nature of the modeling languages, and the fact that model transformations can be formally described using high-level constructs (e.g. graph transformation rules [8]) provides an opportunity for establishing the correctness of transformations with a reasonable effort.

One key pragmatic observation is that the correctness may not be necessary in general (i.e. for all properties and for all possible models to be transformed), rather, it is sufficient to establish it for specific cases (i.e. for specific properties and for specific models). This means that the correctness of the model transformation is not proven in general, but a proof is provided for every invocation of that transformation that is valid -only- for the actual model being transformed. In other words, for each instance of the model transformation a certificate is automatically generated that can be used, for example, in a certification process such as [9] and [10]. Thus, the goal is to build such machinery into the model transformation tools, so that the certificates can be automatically produced. In addition, the verification itself must be independent of the domain. In other words, it must not be tied to a single domain specific language, but be applicable to a wide class of such languages. We call this approach 'instance-based verification'. We have developed two early prototypes for such model transformations that we will discuss below.

2.1   Certification Via Bisimilarity

Assume that we have a modeling language that supports a Statechart like notation for modeling. Suppose that we wish to verify reachability properties of such
models. The semantics of Statecharts allow, for example, inter-level transitions
(which are transitions that cut across levels of hierarchy). This makes verification of properties such as reachability non-trivial. One approach to overcome this
difficulty is to transform them into a simplified notation such as Extended Hierarchical Automata (EHA) [12], and then using a model checker such as SPIN
[11] to verify reachability in the model. Note that EHA-s are not isomorphic
to Statecharts, although there exists an algorithm for translating Statecharts
to EHA-s [13]. We have implemented this transformation algorithm using our
graph transformation environment [8].

The problem of verification is formulated as: "Show that the reachability properties determined by the model checker tool on the translated EHA model hold
for the original Statechart model". Such properties are commonly encountered
in model based development, where the models are some form of a transition
system. We have approached this problem by finding a bisimulation [14] between
the source and the target models. The justification for this is that, for the input and the result of the model transformation to be behaviorally equivalent,
the transition systems must be bisimilar. For this purpose, we use the following
definition of bisimulation:

Bisimulation. Given an LTS (S, Λ, $\rightarrow$), a relation R over S is a *bisimulation*
if:

$$(p,\ q) \in R \text{ and } p \xrightarrow{\alpha} p' \text{ implies that}$$
$$\text{there exists a } q' \in S \text{ such that } q \xrightarrow{\alpha} q' \text{ and } (p',\ q') \in R,$$

and conversely,

$$q \xrightarrow{\alpha} q' \text{ implies that}$$
$$\text{there exists a } p' \in S \text{ such that } p \xrightarrow{\alpha} p' \text{ and } (p',\ q') \in R.$$

The instance-based verification approach must generate a 'certificate' that
shows whether a bisimilarity relationship exists. This certification can be produced by:

1. introducing extra steps into the transformation process that build 'links'
   (that trace a relation R) between elements of the input and target models
   of the transformations, and
2. using a simple, linear-time algorithm to check if R is a bisimulation

With a minimal extension to the existing model transformation tool we were
able to generate the required certificate for every run of the translator. Figure 2
describes the process. The changes to the model transformations were straightforward and artificially introduced errors in the transformation were detected by
the bisimilarity checker.

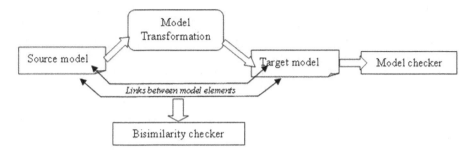

Fig. 2. Checking Bisimilarity to Certify Transformations

2.2 Certification by Semantic Anchoring

In an embedded system development process often a multitude of modeling languages are used. For example, as a design language one might use Stateflow, but as the input language of a code generator one might use the UML-variant of Statecharts. The annoying differences between these languages are not well-known and not easy to discover. Hence, there is a strong need for the formal definition of the semantics of such domain-specific modeling languages. Recent work [15] has developed the concept of *semantic anchoring* that solves the problem in two steps, described below.

1. First, a simple, well-defined and well-understood mathematical framework, called the semantic unit is developed that defines a core semantic idea. A labeled transition system capturing the core behavior of a Finite-State Automaton is an example for a semantic unit. This unit is defined in a formal document, as well as in a formal language, whose underlying semantics is well-known [1]. The description must be parametric, i.e. one should be able to instantiate the definitions with different parameter values (e.g. different number states, different transitions, events, etc.)
2. Second, the semantics of a domain-specific modeling language is defined by the (model) transformation that maps the abstract syntax of the modeling language into a fully configured instance of the semantic unit. This transformation is considered the definition of the DSML.

Now given two modeling languages, with the corresponding definitions of the semantics, how can we show that the model transformation mapping the first language into the second is correct? In our example, given a definition for the semantics of both Stateflow and UML-Statecharts, how can we show that the model translator from Stateflow to UML-Statecharts preserves the model's behavior? The key idea here is that this can be checked by finding a bisimulation on the level of the 'anchored' models, i.e. on the level of the instantiated semantic units (or, *behavior models*).

---

[1] In our work the ASML language has been used that is based on the notion of Abstract State Machines of Gurevich [16].

One difficulty in this approach is that the differences in the languages may result in behavior models that are structurally dissimilar, even though they may model the same observable property. Consider, for instance, the transition systems in Figure 3. Assume that Figure 3(a) represents an automaton, where the dotted, unlabeled states and transitions are not observable by an external observer. To an external observer, the automaton will appear to function identically to the one represented by the transition system in Figure 3(b). Thus, the two automata appear identical to an external observer, even though the inherent transition systems are not bisimilar.

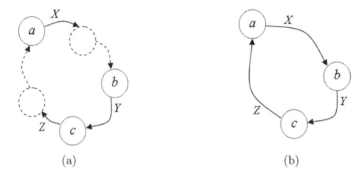

(a)   (b)

Fig. 3. Similar Transition Systems

To address this issue, we turn to the notion of *weak bisimilarity* [17]. Weak bisimulation allows us to weaken the notion of what constitutes a transition, allowing us to set the granularity at which we accept two systems as behaviorally equivalent. In our case, we can simply disregard unobservable states (such as the dashed ones in Figure 3(a)), and define the relation **R** only for the observable states. We then define a transition as going from one observable state to another, by collapsing the dashed transitions appropriately. Using these guidelines, we rephrase our earlier definition of bisimulation, for the special case of weak bisimulation as:

Weak Bisimulation. Given an LTS (S, Λ, $\rightarrow$), a relation R over S is a *weak bisimulation* if:

$$\forall \ (p, q) \in R \text{ and } \forall \alpha \colon p \overset{\alpha}{\Rightarrow} p', \ \exists \ q' \text{ such that } q \overset{\alpha}{\Rightarrow} q' \text{ and } (p', q') \in R,$$

and conversely,

$$\forall \alpha \colon q \overset{\alpha}{\Rightarrow} q', \ \exists \ p' \text{ such that } p \overset{\alpha}{\Rightarrow} p' \text{ and } (p', q') \in R.$$

where p, q, p', q' are all observable states, the transition $\Rightarrow$ is from one observable state to another.

The approach to verifying the transformation is illustrated in Figure 4. The input and the target models of the transformation are 'translated down' into the common semantic framework. This is done by the semantic anchoring steps

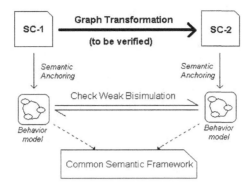

Fig. 4. Framework for verifying behavior preservation

that are assumed to be correct, as they define the semantics of the input and target languages. The lower-level behaviors are linked to the original input and the resulting target models respectively, while maintaining some notion of correspondence between the model elements of the input and the target. The relation **R** is encoded based on these correspondences, between the two transition systems representing the low-level behavior models. We then check if **R** is a weak bisimulation, based on the above definition. This will allow us to conclude if the source and the target models behave identically.

We will now look at some case studies that use the techniques described above, to provide a correctness certification for transformation instances that were successful.

3 Case Study 1: Statechart to EHA Transformation

To illustrate the first approach described above, we describe a transformation from Statecharts to Extended Hybrid Automata (EHA). We wish to analyze a specific property in a Statechart model, namely the property of *reachability*, by transforming it into an EHA model and using a model checker. The *verification* of the transformation consists of assuring whether the source and target models are identical with respect to reachability, for a particular instance of its execution. In other words, we wish to check whether every state that is reachable in the EHA model is also reachable in the Statechart model, and vice-versa.

3.1 Extended Hierarchical Automata

EHA models are composed of one or more *Sequential Automata*, which are non-hierarchical finite automata. The states of a Sequential Automaton (called *Basic States*) may be *refined* into further Sequential Automata, to express hierarchy in a flat notation. A Statechart model can be represented by a Sequential Automaton, with a finite automaton representing the top level states of the Statechart. Compound states in the Statechart must be represented as individual Sequential

Automata, and marked as *refinements* of the corresponding Basic States in the EHA. The entire Statechart can be represented this way, using a set of Sequential Automata and a series of refinements.

Some transitions in the Statechart may cut across levels of hierarchy. Such transitions are said to be inter-level. Transitions in an EHA model, however, are always contained within one Sequential Automaton, and cannot cut across levels of hierarchy. Inter-level transitions my therefore be elevated based on the scope of the transition. An inter-level transition is placed in the Sequential Automaton corresponding to the Statechart state containing it, and is drawn between the Basic States corresponding to the top-most ancestors of the source and target states in the Statechart. The transition in the EHA is also annotated with special attributes called *source restriction* and *target determinator*, which keep track of the actual source and target states of the transition.

3.2   Transformation Steps

The transformation from Statecharts to EHA was specified as a graph transformation, using GReAT [8], based on the approach described in [13]. The basic steps of the transformation are listed below:

1. Every Statechart model is transformed into an EHA model, with one top level Sequential Automaton in the EHA model.
2. For every (primitive or compound) state in the Statechart (except for regions of concurrent states), a corresponding basic state is created in the EHA.
3. For every composite state in the Statechart model, a Sequential Automaton is created in the EHA model, and a "refinement" link is added that connects the Basic State in the EHA corresponding to the state in the Statechart, to the Sequential Automaton in the EHA that it is refined into.
4. All the contained states in the composite state are further transformed by repeating steps (1) and (2). The top level states in the Statechart are added to the top level Sequential Automaton in the EHA.
5. For every non-interlevel transition in the Statechart model a transition is created in the EHA between the Basic States corresponding to the start and end states of the transition in the Statechart model.
6. For every inter-level transition in the Statechart model, we trace the scope of the transition to find the lowest parent state s_P that contains both the source and the target of the transition. A transition is created in the EHA, in the Sequential Automaton corresponding to s_P. The source of the transition in the EHA is the Basic State corresponding to the highest parent of the source in the Statechart that is within s_P, and the target in the EHA is the Basic State corresponding to the highest parent of the target in the Statechart that is within s_P. The transition in the EHA is further annotated, with the *source restriction* attribute set to the basic state corresponding to the actual source in the Statechart, and the *target determinator* set to the basic state corresponding to the actual target in the Statechart.

Figure 5 shows a sample statechart model, and Figure 6 shows the transformed EHA model. There are two inter-level transitions in the Statechart model

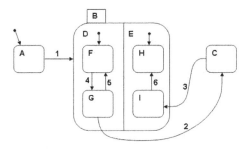

Fig. 5. A sample Statechart model

(namely, *2* and *3*). Their equivalent transitions in the EHA model are annotated with the appropriate *source restriction* and *target determinator*, as shown in the table in Figure 6.

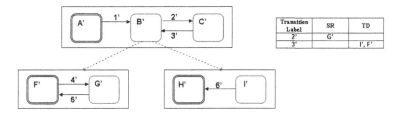

Transition Label	SR	TD
2'	G'	
3'		I', F'

Fig. 6. Sample EHA model

3.3 Verifying the Transformation

We wish to check whether every state that is reachable in the EHA model is also reachable in the Statechart model, and vice-versa. To define the property of reachability in Statecharts, we use the notion of a *state configuration*. A state configuration in a Statechart is a valid set of states that the system can be active in. If a state is part of an active configuration, then all its parents are also part of the active configuration. A transition takes a system from one state configuration to another state configuration. Similarly, a state configuration in an EHA model is a set of Basic States. If a Basic State is part of an active configuration, and is part of a non-top-level Sequential Automaton, then the Basic State that is refined into this Sequential Automaton is also a part of the active configuration.

We perform the verification by treating the models as transition systems between state configurations, and finding a bisimulation relation between them, based on the following steps:

1. Every state configuration S_A in the Statechart model must have an equivalent state configuration S_B in the EHA model. Based on the transformation described above, a Basic State is created in the EHA model for every State in the Statechart. During the transformation process, we use a 'cross-link' to

relate the State in the Statechart model and its corresponding Basic State in the EHA model (as shown in Figure 7), meaning that the two are equivalent. We define that the state configurations S_A and S_B are in $\mathbf{R}$, or $(S_A, S_B) \in \mathbf{R}$, if every State in S_A has an equivalent Basic State in S_B and vice-versa.

2. If for any two equivalent state configurations $(S_A, S_B) \in \mathbf{R}$, there exist transitions $(t\colon S_A \rightarrow S'_A,\ t'\colon S_B \rightarrow S'_B)$ such that S'_A and S'_B are equivalent, then the relation R is a bisimulation.

If the R is a bisimulation, then verifying the EHA model for reachability will be equivalent to verifying the Statechart model for reachability. If not, it means that the models do not behave identically with respect to reachability, and that could be due to an error in the transformation.

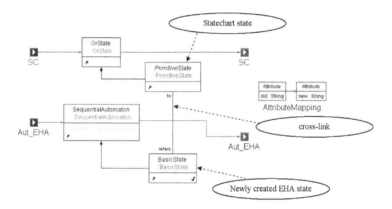

Fig. 7. Sample GReAT rule with cross-link

4   Case Study 2: Transformation between Variants of Statecharts

To illustrate the next approach to verifying transformations, we describe a transformation between two variants of the Statecharts formalism. For the purposes of this case study, we will consider two hypothetical variants, and list out their differences. Their semantics will be described by semantic anchoring.

4.1   Variants of Statecharts

Since the introduction of the original Statecharts formalism [18], many implementation variants have been developed, a number of which have been surveyed in [19]. These variants differ in several subtle features. For this case study, we propose two hypothetical variants, called *SCA* and *SCB*, which differ in certain specific aspects as noted below.

Compositional Semantics. Compositional semantics is the property of a language by which a compound object is completely defined by the semantics of its subcomponents. The presence of inter-level transitions (which cut across levels of hierarchy) in Statecharts violates compositional semantics [19]. If a Statechart allows inter-level transitions, it does not have compositional semantics. In our case study, only SCB will have compositional semantics. In other words, SCA will allow inter-level transitions, while SCB will not.

Inter-level transitions may be 'simulated' in SCB by using special 'self-termination' and 'self-start' states, which act as proxy states for effecting transitions across different hierarchies. To maintain equivalent step semantics while performing such transitions, the proxy states must be *instantaneous* (i.e. executed in the same time step).

Instantaneous States. Instantaneous states are entered and exited within a single time step in the execution of the Statechart. When a system encounters an instantaneous state, it is immediately exited, until a non-instantaneous state is reached. The sequence of transitions leading to the final state is called a 'macro step'. Most common Statechart variants do not allow instantaneous states. In this case study, we will allow only SCB to have instantaneous states.

State References. In some Statecharts variants, triggers may be specified by referencing the activity of other parallel states. For instance, the condition $in(S)$ is true when state S is active, and entering or exiting S will result in events $en(S)$ and $ex(S)$ respectively. Such conditions are called state references. In this case study, we will allow SCA to have state references, but not SCB.

Figure 8 shows an SCA model and an SCB model. The SCB model in this case simulates the behavior of the SCA model. The state D in Figure 8(b) is an instantaneous state that acts as a 'self-termination' state. The transitions T_{21} and T_{22} are fired in a single time step, thus simulating the effect of firing the transition T_2 in Figure 8(a). We would like to note at this point that there may be models that can be described in one Statechart variant that cannot be described in the other. Our objective is not to find a transformation that will transform any SCA model into an SCB model; it is only to check whether a particular SCB model generated by transforming an SCA model is indeed acceptable.

4.2 Semantic Anchoring

We will use non-hierarchical FSMs as the semantic unit to represent the behavior of the Statechart variants, extended to allow instantaneous states. The semantics of the FSM semantic unit is described using AsmL [15]. The semantic anchoring itself is specified using graph transformations, which transform the Statechart model into its semantic unit.

The behavior models generated by the semantic anchoring are shown in Figure 9. States in the FSM semantic models represent valid state configurations in the Statechart model (for instance, the state P_Q_A in Figure 9(a) represents the state configuration containing the states P, Q and A in Figure 8(a)). The state

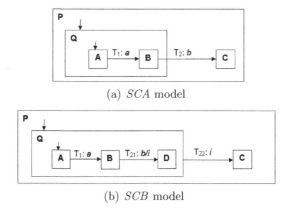

(a) *SCA* model

(b) *SCB* model

Fig. 8. Models of Statechart Variants

P_Q_D in Figure 9(b) is an instantaneous state. Note that the two transition systems are not strictly bisimilar, though they represent similar behaviors as observed by an external observer.

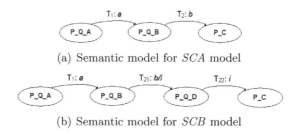

(a) Semantic model for *SCA* model

(b) Semantic model for *SCB* model

Fig. 9. FSM Semantic Models

4.3 Transformation Steps

For this case study, the languages *SCA* and *SCB* were defined in GME, and a transformation from *SCA* to *SCB* was built using GReAT [8]. The main steps in the transformation are listed below:

1. For every state in the *SCA* model, create a state in the *SCB* model, and give it an identical label. This label will later be used to trace the equivalence relation.
2. For every simple transition (with both the source and the destination under a single parent) in the *SCA* model, construct a transition in the *SCB* model between the corresponding states.
3. For every inter-level transition in the *SCA* model, add a self-termination or a self-start state in the *SCB* model, until the source and the destination fall under the same parent, thus constructing a series of transitions in the *SCB* model.

4. If the *SCA* model contains state references, add specially named triggers to the appropriate transitions. For instance, if a trigger *en(S)* is encountered, add a trigger *en_S* in the output, and the action *en_S* to all the transitions into state *S* in the output.

4.4   Verification by Weak Bisimilarity

We consider the behaviors of the two models to be identical if they appear identical to an external observer. Thus, the transition systems representing the behavior need not be strictly bisimilar. We turn to the more practical notion of weak bisimilarity, by carefully redefining what constitutes states and transitions.

We only consider non-instantaneous states, and define transitions to be between non-instantaneous states. Thus, we define a relation **R** between non-instantaneous states of the two transition systems representing the two behavior models. By retaining the state labels during the transformation and the semantic anchoring process, we say that two non-instantaneous states are in **R** if their labels are identical. We then say that **R** is a *weak bisimulation* if:

$$\forall\ (p, q) \in R \text{ and } \forall \alpha: p \overset{\alpha}{\Rightarrow} p',\ \exists\ q' \text{ such that } q \overset{\alpha}{\Rightarrow} q' \text{ and } (p', q') \in R,$$

and conversely,

$$\forall \alpha: q \overset{\alpha}{\Rightarrow} q',\ \exists\ p' \text{ such that } p \overset{\alpha}{\Rightarrow} p' \text{ and } (p', q') \in R.$$

where p, q, p', q' are all non-instantaneous states, the transition $\Rightarrow$ is from one non-instantaneous state to another, and α is the aggregate of the events for the transition, disregarding instantaneous states and actions (The label α constitutes both the cause of a transition and its effect. In our implementation, we represent α as a comma separated list of the events that are the triggers and the actions of the transition. In the case of a weak transition, this list will include all the non-instantaneous events that are the triggers and the actions of the sequence of transitions which constitute the weak transition). According to this definition, the FSM models in Figurers 9(a) and 9(b) are weakly bisimilar. Note that this notion of weak bisimilarity guarantees equivalence of behavior between the two models, for all practical purposes.

5   Case Study 3: Code Generation from Stateflow Models

C code is generated from Stateflow models by converting them to an intermediate form called SFC. SFC provides an abstract representation of C programs, using modeling primitives such as *Functions, FunctionCall, ConditionalBlock* etc. to represent fragments of C code. A straightforward translation can produce the textual C code from the SFC model.

The generated code models the step semantics of the Stateflow diagram [20]. This is achieved primarily by using three types of functions for each state in the Stateflow model: an *enter* function models entry into the state, an *exit* function models leaving the state, and an *exec* function models the step execution of that state if it is in the active configuration for that step. This allows us to, for instance, model a guarded transition as *FunctionCalls* to the appropriate *exit* and *enter* functions, enclosed in a *ConditionalBlock*. Additional statements are generated to complete the model, such as labels for states, variables, and structures to capture context information. The execution of this code simulates the Stateflow model by managing the active state configuration, which is the direct result of how the *enter*, *exit* and *exec* functions are called. The active configuration can thus be mapped on to a finite automaton, which should represent the flattened form of the Stateflow model.

The generation of the SFC model from a Stateflow model is achieved by a graph transformation. Errors in this transformation could generate an incorrect SFC model, which would result in code that may not truly represent the semantics of the original Stateflow model. One way to check if the generated model is indeed correct is to compare the flattened automaton constructed from the state configurations encountered in the C code with the original Stateflow model. If the two are bisimilar, we can conclude that the generated code truly represents the semantics of the Stateflow model for that instance.

The nature of the SFC paradigm allows us to construct the flattened automaton directly from the SFC model, by following some basic steps as outlined below.

5.1   Step 1: Collect the Flattened Active State Configurations

The *exec* function of each state models the step execution for that state. If the state contains sub-states, then it calls the *exec* functions of its active sub-states, and so on, until the leaf states are reached. Thus, tracing a sequence of *exec* function calls to a leaf state will give one active configuration. A function call graph is a graph whose nodes are function signatures, and edges represent potential function calls. A path in this graph represents a sequence of function calls.

Figure 11 shows a portion of a function call graph, restricted to calls between *exec* functions, for the code generated from the Stateflow model in Figure 10 (the

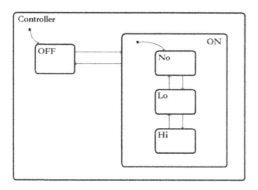

Fig. 10. Sample Stateflow model

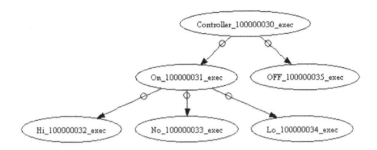

Fig. 11. Function call graph - *exec* functions

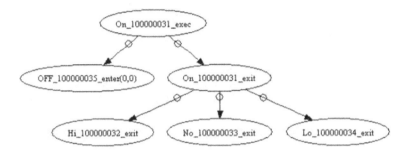

Fig. 12. Function call graph - transitions

function name consists of the name of the state it models in the Stateflow model, followed by a unique id, followed by 'exec' to indicate that it is an exec function). This takes the form of a rooted tree, with the topmost state at the root, and the leaf states as the leaf nodes. Collecting all the states in a path from the root to a leaf node gives one possible active state configuration. The active state configurations in this case are: {Controller, ON, Hi}, {Controller, ON, No}, {Controller, ON, Lo} and {Controller, OFF}. Each of these will correspond to a separate state in the flattened automaton.

5.2   Step 2: Add Transitions to Complete the Finite Automaton

Transitions are implemented by calling the *exit* function of the source state and then the *enter* function of the target state. Both these function calls are placed inside a conditional block in the *exec* function of the source state. This conditional block encodes the triggers and guard conditions. When the source state is active, its *exec* function is called, which checks if the transition can be fired. If it can, then it calls the appropriate *exit* and *enter* functions, which results in a new active configuration. The *exit* function of a state also calls the *exit* functions of its direct sub-states, and the *enter* function of a state also calls the necessary *enter* functions, such as initial sub-states.

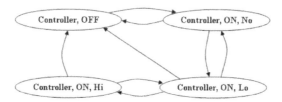

Fig. 13. Flattened automaton from generated code

We once again use the function call graph of the generated C code to determine the transitions in the flattened automaton. Figure 12 shows a section of the call graph, that models the transition from the ON state to the OFF state in Figure 10. The two function calls in the *exec* function of the ON state are enclosed in a conditional block. The *exit* function calls give the state configurations that form the source of the transition, and the *enter* function calls give the state configuration that forms the target of the transition.

In this case, the configurations containing {ON, Hi}, {ON, No} and {ON, Lo} can be the source states of the transition. The target state of the transition is the configuration containing {OFF}. In the flattened automaton, we draw transitions from each of the possible source configurations to the target configuration. In this way, all the possible transitions are created in the flattened automaton. The result is shown in Figure 13. This is the automaton that the generated C code simulates. The check if this represents the semantics of the original Stateflow model, we must check whether the two transition systems are bisimilar.

5.3 Bisimilarity Checking

As we have seen in the first case study, we can generate an EHA representation from the Stateflow model. Figure 14 shows the EHA representation for the Stateflow model in Figure 10. To check for bisimilarity, we first construct a relation **R** mapping each state configuration in the EHA model to its equivalent configuration in the flattened automaton in Figure 13. The transformation from the Stateflow model to the SFC model copies the state labels into the function primitives. This allows us to identify which functions belong to which states. Thus, the labels in the automaton in Figure 13 are derived directly from the Stateflow model. Retaining the state labels in the EHA model allows us to map equivalent state configurations by comparing the labels. After constructing the relation **R**, we check whether **R** is a bisimulation, according to the given definition.

While the function primitives are specific to this implementation, we would like to point out that this example shows that it is possible to obtain an automaton representation from code that is generated to simulate a Statechart model, as an extension of the transformation that generates the code from the Statechart model. This allows us the possibility to establish an assurance about the correctness of the transformation.

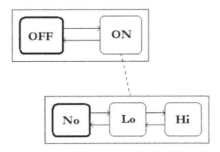

Fig. 14. EHA representation of Stateflow model

6   Summary and Future Work

The model-based development of embedded systems requires transformations on models. Even in simple cases, code generators are needed. For verification, models often need to be translated into the input language of the verification tools. While verification tools can prove properties about models, their results are reliable only if the transformation were correct to begin with. In order to ensure that the embedded system and its code satisfies stringent correctness criteria, it is necessary that the tools used in the development are verified, and all transformations preserve, for example, the salient behavioral properties of the models.

In this paper we introduced the concept of 'instance-based verification' that provides a pragmatic approach to generate a certificate for each transformation executed, and showed some early results for specific model transformations. The three case studies show how this technique can be applied, and address some difficulties that arise in the verification of these transformations. Further research in this area should extend the technique to other properties, e.g. no-cycles in the call graphs of generated code, all variables initialized before use, no index limits violated, and others. Another important extension is the ability to verify transformations that discard or add aspects to the model (such as creating an abstraction of the original model). A strict bisimulation equivalence may not be applicable in such cases, and other coarser forms of equivalence must be explored.

In our approach, we have modified the transformation rules in order to add certain annotations, that will later help us to verify the preservation of certain properties. In the absence of these modifications, it would be a regular model transformation (whose results may not be certifiably correct). We are currently researching techniques by which existing model transformation specifications can automatically be embellished with the ingredients for creating annotations that can be used with a generalized verification framework.

Acknowledgement. This material is based upon work supported by the National Science Foundation under Grant No. 0509098. We would like to thank the anonymous reviewers for their valuable comments and suggestions.

References

1. Matlab, Simulink and Stateflow tools: http://www.mathworks.com
2. Matrix-X tools: http://www.ni.com
3. Rhapsody tools: http://www.ilogix.com
4. The NuSMV tools: http://nusmv.irst.itc.it
5. Formal Verification with SPIN: http://spinroot.com
6. Harel, D., Rumpe, B.: Meaningful Modeling: What's the Semantics of 'Semantics'? Computer 37(10), 64–72 (2004)
7. Evans, A., Lano, K., France, R., Rumpe, B.: Meta-modeling semantics of UML. In: Kilov, H., Rumpe, B., Simmonds, I. (eds.) Behavioral Specifications of Businesses and Systems, Kluwer Academic Publisher, Dordrecht (1999)
8. Agrawal, A., Karsai, G., Neema, S., Shi, F., Vizhanyo, A.: The design of a language for model transformations. Journal Software and Systems Modeling 5(3), 261–288 (2006)
9. Denney, E., Fischer, B.: Certifiable Program Generation. In: Glück, R., Lowry, M. (eds.) GPCE 2005. LNCS, vol. 3676, pp. 17–28. Springer, Heidelberg (2005)
10. Zuck, L., Pnueli, A., Fang, Y., Goldberg, B.: VOC: A Translation Validator for Optimizing Compilers. In: COCV 2002. International Workshop on Compilers Optimization Meets Compiler Verification, ENTCS, vol. 65(2), Elsevier Science, Amsterdam (2002)
11. Holzmann, G.: The model checker SPIN. IEEE Transactions on Software Engineering 23(5), 279–295 (1997)
12. Mikk, E., Lakhnech, Y., Siegel, M.: Hierarchical automata as model for statecharts. In: Shyamasundar, R.K., Euda, K. (eds.) ASIAN 1997. LNCS, vol. 1345, pp. 181–196. Springer, Heidelberg (1997)
13. Varro, D.: A Formal Semantics of UML Statecharts by Model Transition Systems. In: Corradini, A., Ehrig, H., Kreowski, H.-J., Rozenberg, G. (eds.) ICGT 2002. LNCS, vol. 2505, pp. 378–392. Springer, Heidelberg (2002)
14. Sangiorgi, D.: Bisimulation: From the origins to today. In: LICS 2004. Proceedings of the 19th Annual IEEE Symposium on Logic in Computer Science, pp. 298–302. IEEE Computer Society, Los Alamitos (2004)
15. Chen, K., Sztipanovits, J., Abdelwahed, S., Jackson, E.K.: Semantic anchoring with model transformations. In: Hartman, A., Kreische, D. (eds.) ECMDA-FA 2005. LNCS, vol. 3748, pp. 115–129. Springer, Heidelberg (2005)
16. Gurevich, Y.: Specification and Validation Methods. In: Evolving Algebras 1993: Lipari Guide, pp. 9–36. Oxford University Press, Oxford (1993)
17. Harwood, W., Moller, F., Setzer, A.: Weak bisimulation approximants. In: Ésik, Z. (ed.) CSL 2006. LNCS, vol. 4207, Springer, Heidelberg (2006)
18. Harel, D.: Statecharts: A visual formalism for complex systems. Science of Computer Programming 8(3), 231–274 (1987)
19. von der Beeck, M.: A comparison of statecharts variants. In: Langmaack, H., de Roever, W.-P., Vytopil, J. (eds.) ProCoS 1994. LNCS, vol. 863, pp. 128–148. Springer, Heidelberg (1994)
20. Simulink Reference, The Mathworks, Inc. (July 2002)

Supporting System Level Design
of Distributed Real Time Systems
for Automotive Applications

Klaus D. Müller-Glaser[1], Clemens Reichmann[2], and Markus Kuehl[2]

[1] Universitaet Karlsruhe, ITIV, Engesserstrasse 5, 76128 Karlsruhe, Germany
kmg@itiv.uni-karlsruhe.de
[2] Aquintos GmbH, Lammstrass 21, 76133 Karlsruhe, Germany
reichmann@aquintos.com, kuehl@aquintos.com

Abstract. Up to 70 electronic control units (ECU's) serve for safety and comfort functions in a car. Communicating over different bus systems most ECU's perform close loop control functions and reactive functions fulfilling hard real time constraints. Some ECU's controlling on board entertainment/office systems are software intensive, incorporating millions of lines of code. The design of these distributed and networked control units is very complex, the development process is a concurrent engineering process and is distributed between the automotive manufacturer and several suppliers. This requires a strictly controlled design methodology and the intensive use of computer aided engineering tools. The CASE-tool integration platform "GeneralStore" and the "E/E-Concept Tool" for design space exploration supports the design of automotive ECU's, however, GeneralStore is also used for the design of industrial automation systems and biomedical systems.

Keywords: automotive control systems, heterogeneous models, CASE tool integration platform GeneralStore, model transformation, EE-Concept-Tool for design space exploration.

1 Introduction

More than 60 electronic control units (ECU's) serve for safety and comfort functions in a luxury car. Communicating over different bus systems (e.g. CAN class C and B, LIN, MOST, Bluetooth [1]) many ECU's are dealing with close loop control functions as well as reactive functions, they are interfacing to sensors and actuators and have to fulfill safety critical hard real time constraints. The embedded software in such ECU's is relatively small, counting up from a few thousand lines of code to several ten thousands lines of code. The software is running on a standard hardware platform under a real time operating and network management system like OSEK/VDX [2]. Other ECU's controlling the onboard infotainment system (video and audio-entertainment, office in the car with according internet and voice communication, navigation) are really software intensive incorporating already

F. Kordon and O. Sokolsky (Eds.): Monterey Workshop 2006, LNCS 4888, pp. 19–34, 2007.
© Springer-Verlag Berlin Heidelberg 2007

millions of lines of code. All ECU's are connected to the different busses which in turn are connected through a central gateway to enable the communication of all ECU's.

As new functions in future cars require communication to traffic guidance systems, road condition information systems as well as car to car communication, the software intensive infotainment ECU's will be directly coupled to power train and body control ECU's, even forming closed loop control. Thus, the design of these future systems need to combine methodologies and computer aided design tools for reactive systems and closed loop control systems as well as software intensive systems.

The challenge for the design of those distributed and networked control units is to find and define all requirements and constraints, to understand and analyze those manifold interactions between the many control units, the car and the environment (road, weather etc.) in normal as well as stress situations (crash), within a development process which is concurrent and distributed between the automotive manufacturer and several suppliers. This requires a well understood life-cycle model (like the V-model [3]) and a strictly controlled design methodology and using computer aided engineering and design tools to its largest extent.

For the development of closed loop control functions (e.g. power train control) ECU designers prefer graphical methods using data flow diagrams offered by tools like Mathworks Matlab/Simulink [11] or ETAS Ascet-MD [12]. For reactive functions (e.g. body control) designers prefer statechart descriptions offered by e.g. Matlab/Stateflow or I-Logix Statemate [13]. For the software intensive functions in car-infotainment designers prefer the Unified Modeling Language UML [14]. Therefore, the design of the new complex functions which are distributed over many ECU's will require heterogeneous modeling. To support an according model based design methodology we have developed the CASE (Computer Aided Software Engineering) tool integration platform "GeneralStore", which is described in chapter 2 with its meta-modeling and integration aspects as well as simulation and automatic code generation. Chapter 3 discusses model to model transformation and chapter 4 describes the "E/E-Concept Tool" which supports design space exploration for the automotive domain.

2   Case Tool Integration Platform

The integration platform "GeneralStore" is a tool that assists a seamless development process starting with a model and ending with executable code. The integration platform features coupling of subsystems from different modeling domains (see for Figure 1) on model level. From the coupled models it generates a running prototype respectively system by code generation. In addition to object-oriented system modeling for software intensive components in embedded systems, it supports time-discrete and time-continuous modeling concepts. Our approach provides structural and behavioral modeling with front-end tools and simulation/emulation utilizing back-end tools. The CASE-tool chain we present in this chapter further supports concurrent engineering including versioning and configuration management. Utilizing the UML notation for an overall model based system design, the focus of this chapter lies on the coupling of heterogeneous subsystem models and on a new code generation and coupling approach.

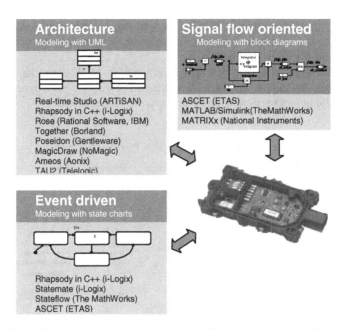

Fig. 1. Tools used for heterogeneous modeling in automotive applications

2.1 Meta Modeling

In our approach the whole system is described as an instance of one particular meta-model in one notation. The related meta-model has to cover all three domains: time-discrete, time-continuous, and software. The Unified Modeling Language is an Object Management Group (OMG) standard [6] which we use as a system notation and meta-model. It is a widely applied industry standard to model object-oriented software. Abstract syntax, well-formed rules, the Object Constraint Language (OCL) and informal semantic descriptions specify UML. As we will point out later, we use this notation to store the overall model while ECU-designers still use those domain adequate modeling languages (e.g. signal flow diagram, state charts, UML, etc.), which fits best to her/his design problem.

The UML specification provides the XML Metadata Interchange format (XMI) [7] to enable easy interchange of meta-data between modeling tools and meta-data repositories in distributed heterogeneous design environments. XMI integrates three key industry standards: the Extensible Markup Language (XML) as a standard of the World Wide Web Consortium W3C [16], the UML, and the Meta Object Facility (MOF) [8], an OMG meta-modeling standard which is used to specify meta-models.

2.2 Integration Platform

The integration platform GeneralStore follows a 3-tier architecture. On the lowest layer (database layer) the commercial object-relational database management system ORACLE respectively MySQL was selected. On the business layer we provide user authentication, transaction management, object versioning and configuration management. GeneralStore uses MOF as its database schema for storing UML artifacts. Inside the database layer an abstraction interface keeps GeneralStore independent from the given database.

While interim objects on the business layer enclose MOF elements, the CASE adaptor stays thin and highly reusable. These interim objects are used to enable object identity to handle object versioning and configuration management.

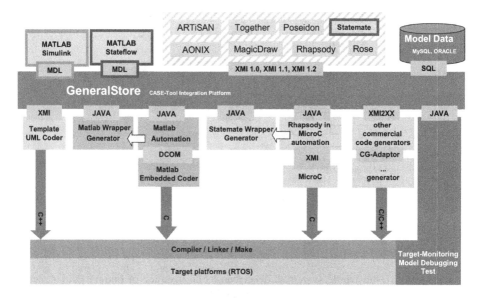

Fig. 2. Integration Platform GeneralStore

The business layer of GeneralStore, the mediator pattern [9], is used to keep the CASE-tool integration simple and its adaptor uniform. The transformations for specific notations supported by CASE-tools are implemented using plug-ins (see top of Figure 2). On the presentation layer GeneralStore provides three principal CASE-tool adapters:

1. MATLAB/Simulink/Stateflow was selected for the control system design domain and the integration is done using the proprietary model file (MDL).

2. Generic and specialized XMI importer/exporter filters of *.xmi files: Here we use XSLT transformations [10] to adopt the tool specific interpretation of the UML and XMI standard. The UML CASE-tools we have chosen are Together (Borland), Poseidon (Gentleware), MagicDraw (No Magic, Inc.), Rhapsody in C++/JAVA (i-Logix), and Rational Rose (IBM). Statemate (i-Logix) was chosen in the time-discrete domain.

3. COM based integration of ARTiSAN Real-Time Studio: This UML CASE-tool was selected because of its focus on embedded real time systems.

All tools, except Statemate, which allows only export of XMI files, are linked to the GeneralStore architecture in a bidirectional way.

The code generation plug-ins (Template Coder, Embedded Coder, and Rhapsody in MicroC) controls the transformation to the source code (Figure 2). Their wrapper generators are automatically building the interface to the UML model.

For model management and CASE-tool control, GeneralStore offers a system hierarchy browser. Since the internal data-model representation of GeneralStore is UML, GeneralStore offers a system browser for all UML artifacts of the current design. A large amount of MOF objects are generated, e.g. an empty model transformed out of Matlab/Simulink already generates 3783 XMI entities because of the many tool internal parameters normally not visible to the user. A simple integrator block needs 405 entities, a basic PID-block can count up to 2786 entities. However, describing many instantiated blocks of the same kind, the XMI entities increase is linear and scales well even to very large designs. The description of an autosampler (robot arm) with closed loop and reactive functions for a chemical analysis system, for example, showed a total of 44239 XMI entities. The description of a complete passenger car for hardware-in-the-loop tests in Matlab/Simulink (>8 Megabyte .mdl file) generated more than 4 million entities. However, today's powerful database systems still perform very well with that amount of data items. For speed up in navigating through a complex design GeneralStore offers design domain specific hierarchy browsers, e.g., a system /subsystem hierarchy view for structural or time-continuous design, or a package hierarchy view for software design.

2.3 Code Generation

There are highly efficient commercial code generators on the market. In safety critical systems certificated code generators have to be used to fulfill the requirements. The GeneralStore platform allows partitioning of the whole system into subsystems. Thus we enable the usage of different domain specific code generators. Each code generator has benefits in specialized application fields.

We follow the Model Driven Architecture (MDA) [14] approach: transforming a Platform Independent Model (PIM) to the Platform Specific Model (PSM).

For control-systems there are commercial code generators like TargetLink (from dSPACE GmbH [17]), Embedded Coder (from Mathworks, Inc.) or ECCO (from ETAS GmbH). In the time-discrete domain we utilize the code generator of Statemate (Rhapsody in MicroC from I-Logix). In the software domain commercial code generators only generate the stubs of the static UML model while behavioral functionality has to be implemented by the software engineer. As we focus on a completely generated executable specification, it is necessary to generate code out of the overall model. Therefore we provide a code generator as a GeneralStore plug-in to enable structural and behavioral code generation directly from a UML model. The body specification is done formally in the Method Definition Language (MeDeLa), which is a high level action language based on Java syntax. It suits the action semantics defined by the OMG since UML version 1.4 as the concrete syntax.

Currently GeneralStore supports Embedded Coder for closed-loop models, Rhapsody in MicroC for state charts, and a template coder for the UML domain (see Figure 2). Our template code generator is using the Velocity engine to generate Java or C++ source code. Velocity is an Apache open source project [18] focused on

HTML code generation. It provides macros, loops, conditions, and callbacks to the data model's business layer. One of its strengths is the speed when rendering.

Using the templates, the structure of the UML model is rendered to code. The behavioral specification is done with MeDeLa. It is transformed to the according Abstract Syntax Tree (AST). Then the AST is traversed as the Velocity template renders each statement or expression. It is possible to access the whole UML model from the template. Up to now, we use class diagrams and state diagrams.

Different domains have interactions, e.g., signal inspection, adoption of control system parameters at runtime, or sending messages between time-discrete and software artifacts. Those interfaces are defined in the different models and the coupling definitions are done in the UML model. The developer of such a subsystem is able to explicitly define which events, signals, data, and parameters can be accessed from the outside (the UML model). After the definition in the specific domain (e.g., closed-loop control system design) is finished the notation is automatically transformed to the UML. For the discrete subsystem domain this works analogously.

The wrapper generator collects all the information about the interface in this model and generates artifacts, which represent the interface in UML. This includes the behavioral part of the access, which is done with MeDeLa. The developer uses the UML template mechanism to specify the general access mechanism for a specific type of interface. This is highly customizable. Thus the code generation provides a highly flexible mechanism for modeling domain interfaces.

2.4 Simulation and Emulation

For early verification on system level and subsystem level simulation as well as emulation is used.

The standard procedure in designing new functions for automotive applications is to build the model with the according tool and simulate that model within that tool (supporting either closed loop control systems, reactive systems or software intensive systems). This works well for the subsystem level where we may have only models of one kind. However, the model of the complete system very often consists of models of different kinds. Simulation of heterogeneous models for closed loop control together with reactive control is supported within several tools e.g. Matlab/Simulink/Stateflow or ETAS Ascet MD). These tools offer synchronized simulation kernels, one for closed loop control to numerically solve systems of ordinary differential equations (calculating physical quantities continuous in value and time), the other kernel to solve boolean equations (quantities discrete in value and time) for reactive systems. Combining these models with UML models is not supported in a single simulation tool. A possible solution is to use and link different tools to carry out co-simulation [20], to use a simulation-backplane [21, 22], or to use GeneralStore to link the code fragments.

In using automatically generated code running on a rapid prototyping hardware platform, emulation complements simulation for verification purposes. Running generated C-code on a target microprocessor platform or even generating VHDL code and synthesizing a hardware implementation of an algorithm to be mapped into an FPGA speeds up execution time by two orders of magnitude compared to simulation.

A very common problem for simulation of automotive applications is due to the use of model libraries of one domain (e.g. closed loop control) but of different tools; most prominent is the use of libraries in Matlab/Simulink and ETAS Ascet MD. Whereas Matlab/Simulink models are used in early system design phases, ASCET MD models may be used later on for models closer to product implementation. So very often a simulation using models out of both tools is required. Here, a tool integration platform like ETAS INTECRIO gives support [23]. INTECRIO is a rapid prototyping environment for electronic control units supporting the specific needs of electronics and software development in the automotive industry. The possible integration of different Behavior Modeling Tools (BMT) allows working with the tool of choice in each project and in each specialized team. Open interfaces and the available BMT Connectors for MATLAB®/Simulink® and ASCET enable a smooth integration of different software functions generated with different BMTs. The resulting software prototype can be tested on a rapid prototyping hardware platform.

Another possible solution is to do a model transformation from one tool to the other tool, e.g. Matlab/Simulink into ASCET MD. The very same problem exists when using UML models built with different UML tools. Thus model to model transformation is another important issue.

3 Model to Model Transformation

The above mentioned reasons ask for model to model transformations, but there are other reasons, too. One of the major problems in the ECU software development process using heterogeneous modelling is an obvious lack in design synchronisation, which means that model data has to be created multiple times to cover the needs of the different design phases (e.g. concept design versus detailed design). Moreover the phase transition between software architecture design (UML notation) and software development (block diagram notation, state-charts) is not continuous as a result of different description languages. This often leads to a design gap between the mentioned design phases. Overall the design gap between different CASE tools or even between different design phases has to be closed to accelerate future developments. A technique to solve this productivity issue is model to model transformation. Established model to model transformations (e.g. model importers to migrate models from different vendor tools) are hard coded today and therefore hardly to maintain as the model often is very complex. We have developed an innovative solution for model-to-model (M2M) transformation to bridge the obvious design gap between different CASE tools.

3.1 Model to Model Transformation Technology

Our model-to-model transformation uses a model-based design approach for the design and construction of transformation rules. This technique to annotate the transformation rules is called M²TOS. It uses the graphical Unified Modelling Language combined with a special action language as a specification language for transformation rules between a source model and a target model. The advantages in using UML for the specification of transformation rules result in a very good readability and maintainability of the transformation rules. An optimising code-generator is used in the M²TOS design process to produce executable and efficient transformation rules without hand-coding at all.

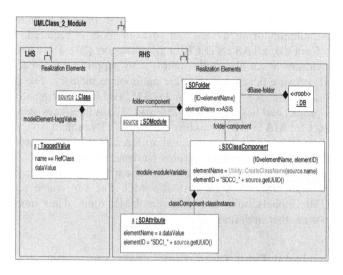

Fig. 3. Transformation Rule specified in UML

In Figure 3 one specific transformation rule is shown. It is separated into a sub-package LHS (left hand side) and RHS (right hand side). LHS is implemented as a search pattern and RHS as a creation pattern that simultaneously parameterises the merge process. The structure of a transformation rule is graphically modelled as a UML Object diagram. The search pattern supports the AND, OR and NOT structures. The attribute values of an object are specified formally in text form by means of the Method Definition Language (MeDeLa). Therefore the expressions are declarative in the search pattern and imperative in the creation pattern. On one hand the transformation rules are grouped in transformation concepts and on the other hand, the rules are organised based on the source meta-model. With both these mechanisms, a clear and easily understandable transformation model can be created. Redundant transformation rules can be avoided by reuse-mechanisms.

3.2 Model to Model Transformation Sequences

In Figure 4 the resulting model-to-model transformation sequence is presented. In the given scenario Mathworks Simulink® is used as a source tool to provide rapid proto-typing models to feed an ASCET® function development for detailed ECU software design. The Simulink models are parsed by an importer of the transformation engine. The transformation engine with the help of the M2M rule-set scans the source model and generates target model artefacts to export to ASCET. The speed of the transformation is of very high performance. Depending on the size of the model and the given CASE tool interface even big models can be transformed under one minute CPU time on a standard PC. In a comparable sequence, a different rule-set implements a M2M transformation between ARTiSAN Studio UML and ASCET.

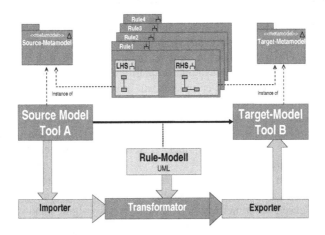

Fig. 4. Structure of the M2M transformation

The available transformation rules for ASCET and Simulink are implemented bidirectional to synchronize models between both CASE tools. This synchronisation technology is very important to ensure that further modifications of transformed models have to be bridged back into a master model or to synchronize development teams using different CASE tools without the need for time-consuming hand-based transformations. This model synchronisation (which also covers the "merge" use case) is implemented with a model versioning technique based on a relational database, to compare an updated model with a previous version of the model. This synchronisation technique ensures that changes in the model will not be lost after repetitive transformation. In any case, a transformation report will be generated.

So far we looked at modeling functionality using heterogeneous models and using different behavior modeling tools. However, this is not enough to evaluate different architectures of distributed ECU's in a car. Design space exploration in early system design phases needs domain specific descriptions of different views onto the system, taking into account not only ECU's but also the mounting spaces and the wiring harness which interconnects them. These aspects build up the electrical/electronic architecture (e/e-architecture) of a car, a large set of metrics is used to analyze alternative architectures.

4   Design Space Exploration

The early concept phases in the development process do have a deep impact on the final e/e-architecture of the vehicle. This impact can be measured in resulting costs for the mass production of e/e-components. The goal of the concept phase therefore is to make the right decision for a specific e/e-architecture under different weighted metrics (costs, quality, reliability etc.) or constraints.

4.1 Requirements for Methods in Early Design Phases

The introduction of methods to improve and formalize early concept phases is a must. The requirements for methods in early concept phases are: a complete formalised description of the e/e-architecture; automated rapid evaluation of the various possible e/e-architectures against defined cost and/or quality metrics. Both requirements can be captured by the introduction of a complete data-model for concept evaluation of e/e-architectures including design domains like Function/Feature Networks (top level description), Function Networks, components networks and finally topology (e.g. wiring harness, mounting locations for ECU components). Combined with a set of properties for each data-model artefact, different e/e-architectures can then be evaluated and compared.

When looking into concepts, the evaluation of different e/e-architectures is nearly as important as their formal description. The assessments to find the "right" architecture are based on numerous metrics that give key figures and qualitative facts for measuring purposes and comparisons between various conceptual alternatives.

Currently, most of these metrics are collected and set together by hand. Often, some data is held in a spread sheet tool like Excel which then allows for calculating some metrics, but still necessary data is to be collected and prepared. This means a time consuming process, which limits today's evaluation to only looking into a few conceptual alternatives focusing on one or two possible vehicle variants. Other metrics can only be estimated by experts, a rather non-objective and non-repeatable basis for drawing decisions. Regarding the actual situation with constraints on time and costs while running into an ever increasing complexity, such manual evaluation is not sufficient anymore.

A prototype for a tool has been developed by DaimlerChrysler (Mercedes-Benz Passenger Car Development and DaimlerChrysler Research & Technology) and by FZI Forschungszentrum Informatik (Research Centre for Information Technology, Department Electronic Systems and Microsystems) in the last three years. After a successful evaluation of the tool prototype at DaimlerChrysler, the tool has been transferred into a commercial product by Aquintos GmbH [24].

4.2 Meta Model for e/e-Architecture

The importance of a formalised meta model for the concept evaluation phase of e/e-architectures is resulting from a need to structure model data (so called concepts), graphics (graphical notation), metrics (cost and quality estimation etc.) and also evaluation results. Benchmarking (e.g. comparison of different e/e concepts) can only be implemented with an e/e-model. The meta model is an automotive domain specific data model to handle the overall concept model of a complex e/e-architecture in the concept phase. The focus of the meta model therefore is on interface data and structural data (e.g. functional architecture). Algorithmic parts are intentionally excluded from the meta model since the algorithmic or state event behaviour of the ECU functions are part of the detailed (fine) development phase following later on. In Figure 5 the different e/e-architecture layers of the meta model are named.

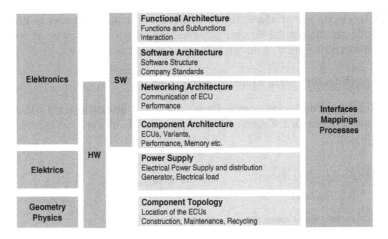

Fig. 5. Architecture Layers available within the E/E-meta model

In general the meta-model is divided into software and hardware model artefacts. From a top-down design approach the functional architecture is an abstract description of which functions the e/e-architecture consists of and how the communication between the functions is established. A function itself is defined as an atomic implementation of an electronic feature (e.g. power window lifter, exterior light, turn signal etc.). From a bottom-up design approach the component architecture, cable harness, networking and power supply are detailed model artefacts in the scope of e/e-architecture hardware. Both hardware and software meta model artefacts are connected with mappings.

Figure 6 shows a topologic schematic of ECU mounting locations inside the body of a passenger car and the resulting wiring harness, this figure also visualizes the need

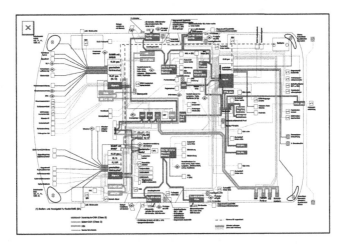

Fig. 6. Topologic schematic of ECU mounting locations, busses and wires

to model the electrical part of a distributed ECU network as the number of ECU's and their location determines the number of wires, the length, the number of connectors required, the overall weight of the wring harness as well as the costs.

4.3 E/E-Architecture Meta Model Construction

The construction of the e/e-meta model was done using the established UML notation. The principal process for the construction of formal meta models was implemented as shown in Figure 7.

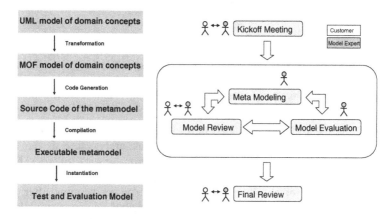

Fig. 7. Development process of the E/E-meta model

Within a kick-off meeting (interview with different automotive experts with knowledge from recent automotive projects like AUTOSAR [5], TITUS etc.) a UML model for the description of e/e-systems was designed. This UML models contains most of the domain concepts to capture information for benchmarking of e/e-architectures. The UML model uses UML classes, associations, properties and packages. This UML model in a second step has been translated into a formal meta model (using the MOF Meta Object Facility notation from the object management group) as mentioned in chapter 2.1. The meta model is a clearly structured version of the UML model from the domain expert interview (extended with model navigation facility) which can be generated automatically to an executable presentation for the use within a CASE tool. The executable meta model is secondly used for the metrics implementation.

4.4 E/E-Architecture Evaluation Metrics

The benchmarking metrics are implemented as executable scripts which navigate within the meta model. For the calculation of estimates necessary properties will be addressed by the metric script. The final design of the meta model is a result of incremental prototype implementations and intensive meta model testing. Actually the e/e-meta model consists of more than 250 meta classes and more than 1000 different meta attributes. The e/e-meta model offers description classes and properties for the following abstraction layers (Figure 8): feature list (which customer features), feature-functions network (abstract function presentation of software and hardware of the e/e-concept with intercommunication), functions network (detailed description of functions with atomic functions and compositions), components network (networking of ECU's and intra-ECU components) and topology (wiring harness, busses, connectors, battery etc.).

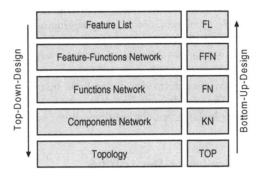

Fig. 8. Abstraction Layers of the Concept Tool Notation

4.5 E/E-Architecture Evaluation

So, the formal description of e/e-architectures in a database now allows for a widely automated evaluation. Once set up, the tool is capable of going repeatedly through various different architecture concepts and producing objective metrics for their comparison. This doesn't only save time, but allows for further investigation of factors that couldn't be taken into account so far.

In an atomised evaluation process, which is supported by a formal database description, it is important to distinguish the two main categories of such metrics: quantitative (e.g. cost, weight, length, number of wires) and qualitative (e.g. reusability, reliability, level of complexity, safety integrity level). Obviously, the quantitative side consists basically of database queries and counting tasks. This remains sufficient as long as all relevant information is already at hand and therefore is included in the databases. However, in the early conceptual stages of a project, several values such as cost and weight have to be estimated. Such estimations can be done by users or automatically be derived by more complex algorithms. In addition, the qualitative side needs more sophisticated algorithms. And, as soon as one requires automated evaluations and comparisons, that summarize the results and use thresholds for flagging, a simple querying is not sufficient any more. With Jython a standardized scripting language is available to the user for independent implementation of any evaluation algorithm. This makes it possible to both program database queries and investigate complex correlations in a similarly straightforward fashion like Excel macros. Furthermore, the results can be attached to the architecture description in the database and be visualized in the editors as either information or colour changes. With seamlessly provided views and editors, that are necessary to support the implementation of algorithms and the back-annotation of the results, the evaluation component is not just a scripting interface but an integral part of the whole tool framework.

4.6 Tool implementation in Cooperation

The complete e/e-concept tool environment was developed in very close cooperation of researchers at DaimlerChrysler and FZI together with the tool users, namely the engineers in passenger car development. Thus the tool is considered to be very user friendly, as the users were involved from the very beginning when defining the API and all dedicated graphical or text editors. However, to build the library of metrics and to evaluate alternative solutions of e/e–architectures was and is completely done by engineers of the OEM, as these libraries hold the proprietary OEM knowledge. More than 100 metrics have been defined so far and will be implemented in according evaluation algorithms. The results so far demonstrate the usefulness of such architecture evaluation tools, however, the results will not be made public due to the proprietary character.

4.7 Current Work: Extension for Test Activities

Despite a high level of process maturity in ECU hardware and software development projects, misunderstandings and errors are hard to avoid due to complexity and development shared between OEM and several suppliers. The seamless integration of test activities into the development process is a required measure to identify problems as early as possible.

Appropriate test methods and tools must be chosen for each development phase. To gain the greatest benefit from testing, activities should already start during the requirements specification phase and accompany the whole development process.

To ensure a maximum efficiency of test activities a seamless test management including an overall test strategy is essential. It avoids test gaps, as well as unwanted test reruns. Professional test engineering as a dedicated part of software and hardware development helps maximizing quality with minimized efforts and costs. Figure 9 shows the goals along the v-model development process.

Already during requirements specification each functional and non functional requirement issue should have an annotation, also formally described in how to validate, verify and test the requirement issue. For early requirements and design reviews a knowledge based rule check can help to detect inconsistent, incomplete and non plausible requirements. The rule checks can be implemented using the LHS-part of the model to model transformation engine as described in chapter 3.1. Based on the formal descriptions first model-in-the-loop tests can be run using simulation, followed by rapid prototyping to prove a solution concept. Rapid prototyping (RP) for automotive ECU's is mainly done by OEM's in three phases (called A, B and C-samples): first concept oriented RP independent of ECU target architecture, then architecture oriented RP, followed by target oriented RP. Then the ECU development is done by a supplier. After delivery of an ECU the OEM performs a hardware-in-the-loop test for a single ECU (component HiL), when all ECU's for a car are available the OEM performs an integration test for these ECU's (integration HiL), finally the

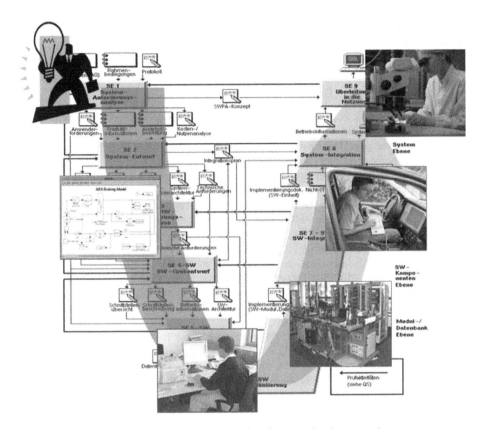

Fig. 9. Supporting test methods and tools along development phases

ECU's are tested in a car during test drives. Finally tests may be repeated for maintenance and repair during the whole life time of the car. Automatic generation of tests, reuse of tests and a seamless test process are current research challenges.

5   Conclusion

To cope with increasing complexity of future e/e-architectures in a car according and different best of point tools are used for modelling and simulation of closed loop control, reactive control and software intensive functions. Tool integration platforms and new tools for early design space explorations of e/e-architectures are required and are currently becoming available commercially. First applications of these tools for the design of next generation cars show promising results but also the need for further research and development of tools especially supporting early system design phases and supporting a seamless design flow from requirements specification to system level modelling, system level simulation, emulation, rapid prototyping, design, analysis, integration, test, application and maintenance. Also, a tight connection to life-cycle product data management systems (PDM) is required.

Domain specific tools will evolve quickly, as evaluating architectures requires taking into account domain specific metrics of high complexity.

References

1. Automotive Busses: http://www.interfacebus.com/Design_Connector_Automotive.html
2. OSEK/VDX homepage: http://www.osek-vdx.org
3. V-Model home-page: http://www.v-modell.iabg.de/vm97.htm#ENGL
4. Polyspace home-page: http://www.polyspace.com
5. Bortolazzi, J.: Systems Engineering for Automotive Electronics. Lecture Notes, Dep. of EEIT, University of Karlsruhe, Germany (2003)
6. Object Management Group: OMG / Unified Modeling Language (UML) V1.5 (2003)
7. Object Management Group: OMG / XML Metadata Inter-change (XMI) V1.2 (2002)
8. Object Management Group: OMG / Meta Object Facility (MOF) V1.4 (2001)
9. Gamma, E., Helm, R., Johnson, R., Vlissides, J.: Design Patterns - Elements of Reusable Object-Oriented Software. Addison-Wesley, Reading (1994)
10. Sussman, D., Kay, M.: XSLT Programmer's Reference. In: WROX (2001)
11. The Mathworks homepage: http://mathworks.com
12. ETAS homepage: http://en.etasgroup.com
13. I-Logix homepage: http://www.ilogix.com
14. UML homepage: http://www.omg.org/gettingstarted/what_is_uml.htm
15. Artisan homepage: http://www.artisansw.com
16. World Wide Web Consortium (W3C): homepage: http://www.w3.com/Consortium
17. Dspace Inc. homepage: http://www.dspaceinc.com/ww/en/inc/home.htm
18. Java based template engine: http://jakarta.apache.org/velocity/
19. Telelogic Inc. homepage: http://www.telelogic.com/
20. Krisp, H., Bruns, J., Eolers, S.: Multi-Domain Simulation for the incremental design of heterogeneous systems. In: ESM 2001. European Simulation Multiconference, pp. S.381–386 (2001)
21. Tanurhan, Y., Schmerler, S., Müller-Glaser, K.: A Backplane Approach for Co-Simulation in High Level System Specification Environments. In: Proceedings of EURODAC 1995 (1995)
22. Schulz, H.M.: Description of EXITE and distributed simulation toolbox. Extessy AG (2002)
23. ETAS INTECRIO Homepage http://en.etasgroup.com/products/intecrio/in_detail.shtml
24. Aquintos GmbH Homepage: http://www.aquintos.com/de/index.php

From MDD to Full Industrial Process: Building Distributed Real-Time Embedded Systems for the High-Integrity Domain

Jérôme Hugues, Laurent Pautet, and Bechir Zalila

GET-Télécom Paris – LTCI-UMR 5141 CNRS
46, rue Barrault, F-75634 Paris CEDEX 13, France
Jerome.Hugues@enst.fr, Laurent.Pautet@enst.fr, Bechir.Zalila@enst.fr

Abstract. From small and very specialized applications, real-time embedded systems are now evolving towards large distributed and interconnected systems. The construction of such systems is becoming increasingly complex, while being put under heavy pressures (economic, mission criticality, time, etc.).

We see a current trend to extend and reuse existing specification and modeling techniques for embedded systems under the "Model Driven Architecture" approach (MDA). Expected benefits range from a better control over the application life-cycle to the integration of performance, analysis or verification tools.

In this paper, we take a very pragmatic position and illustrate how building Distributed Real-Time systems (DRE) for the High-Integrity domain in a Model Driven Development (MDD) process may fail to address core requirements, and why going "back to the basics" of the code and implementation is required to avoid missing the strongest requirements; and avoid a situation in which the MDD fails to deliver its promises.

Our claim is that MDD provides value to the engineering of complex system, if and only if it can take full advantage of the expressive power of the models to help the user in certifying or validating its system. This includes full control of the code generation, validation and verification or testing process.

In the following, we show some limits in current MDD-based DRE projects. We discuss how a careful use of a modeling language like AADL can reduce them, by separating modeling concerns from the underlying execution environment. We then introduce our work in this domain, demonstrating how both a unified modeling approach, combined with precise code generators can provide the user full control and confidence when building its own DRE systems.

1   Introduction

The usage of embedded systems in our daily life is increasing with the use of many electronic appliances, most of which use a computer program inside. They usually fall into the embedded class of systems, meaning their interaction with the user and their constraints (resources, availability, etc.) differ from typical ("desktop") applications.

Besides, economic pressure implied shorter development cycle. For instance, phone suppliers should output a new device every three months. The presence of a bug has a strong economic cost. This implies the development process should follow a stringent engineering methodology.

F. Kordon and O. Sokolsky (Eds.): Monterey Workshop 2006, LNCS 4888, pp. 35–52, 2007.
© Springer-Verlag Berlin Heidelberg 2007

In the mean time, the OMG founded a set of standards to foster the construction of systems. Around the "Model Driven Architecture" (MDA) initiative [OMG03], the model becomes the implementation, backed by the UML as backbone for the modeling language, and CORBA and Object-Oriented languages for the runtime support.

This approach demonstrated its pertinence to develop many business applications. Modeling tools help the developer to formalize its system; validation, model checking and then code generation tools help in validating and building the actual system while reducing manual code writing.

From this success, several specializations of CORBA and UML emerged to address the specific requirements of DRE systems: RT-CORBA (real-time concerns), CORBA/e (downsizing of CORBA for embedded targets), UML/SPT and the MARTE profile, etc. They are presented as foundations for a Model Driven Development (MDD) process, relying on the following postulates: 1) models are the roots of the system, 2) model can be exchanged and processed by different tools, 3) implementation concerns are mitigated: it is assumed a conforming entity will support this process.

Our claim is that these postulates promise too much to the industry; it is likely that one will encounter pitfalls: models inconsistency, tools limitations, performance issues, lack of quality, etc. These pitfalls must be addressed to avoid a situation in which the MDD fails to deliver all its premises, leaving the software engineer with limited tools and techniques, or using costly engineering practice.

In this paper, we discuss Model Driven Development (MDD) at large, and its interaction with other tools, and why we should focus not only on the methodology to be defined for building systems, but also on the run-time entities that best support it.

In the following, we describe one typical occurrence of a MDD process, we then introduce a set of limits in such process. We then present our current work around the definition of an AADL-based toolsuite and conclude with perspectives.

2   MDD in Action: An Analysis

In this section, we introduce a case study that illustrates current trends in building DRE systems following a MDD process.

Defining a DRE system is a complex task that requires many capabilities: system engineering, low-level programming, physics modeling, mission definition, etc. All these skills must be combined to build a complex system such as a GPS or a fleet of UAVs. These skills come from heterogeneous domains (computer science, supervision and planning, mechanics). Models provide the necessary abstraction to exchange information by showing only relevant information.

In [SBK+05], the authors show how relying on models and support tools can suppress many error-prone actions such as code writing, testing and integration.

The process proposed relies on a set of Domain Specific Languages (DSLs), all of which built around meta-models. From these models, a set of rules to generate code that targets the API of the CIAO/TAO/ACE frameworks. These frameworks implement CORBA CCM combined with RT-CORBA and COS Event features.

This case study addresses many issues of DRE systems: compositions of components, configuration, deployment with validation capabilities to ensure QoS requirements can actually be met. Besides, it shows how a large part of a system can be generated from well chosen abstractions, reducing manual coding.

However, this case study also illustrates how complexity issues may impede a MDD process:

- *many dimensions of the problem:* configuration, deployment or definition are each addressed with an ad hoc DSL. This creates many views of the same system. Leading to a huge volume of information to be specified and then understood by the systems engineers.
- *dependency to one platform:* CIAO's configuration model becomes visible at the system modeling level, increasing coupling between the model and its supporting platform. This inversion might reduce portability to different platform.
- *complexity of the process:* as defined, this process involves many software components, built in a long timeframe. This has two costs: development costs to make this process evolve to new models (a fruitful engineering challenge); run-time cost to instantiate all those components.
- *lack analyzability and traceability:* with modeling tools and COTS interleaved, understanding the exact execution path of a request inside the system is challenging. With the use of both code generation and execution framework, ensuring traceability of model entities in the actual code is difficult if not impossible. This decreases the benefits of the whole process, for which the capability to validate, certify the application is the key point.
- *limited optimization:* as a consequence of both complexity and analyzability issues, optimizing the system becomes challenging. Each building block comes with its own "surface" that is difficult to reduce, optimize or analyze with respect to application actual needs: e.g. CORBA POA complexity for simple setup, CORBA COS Notification communication channels, etc. This implied complexity, coming from implementation concerns, greatly impede the use of vertically integrated component-based process on resource-constrained setups.

Each of these issues put a strong limits on the extent of MDD process applied to building DRE systems. However, they are strong requirements of many advanced R&D projects in the space or avionics domain: certification, validation are to be included and enabled in the development process. Resource-aware engineering is also a strong requirement. Therefore, MDD should not only address the construction of the system through a well defined process, but also ensures the quality of the process itself.

In the next section, we list more general limits in defining such process.

3   Challenges in the Definition of a MDD Process for DRE or HI Systems

MDD focuses on the way to combine modeling technologies to ease the construction of complex systems, including DRE. It describes how models can be exchanged between tools to ensure designer's choices are valid and enforced at execution time.

For instance, the MDA working group at the OMG described a set of specifications (technology and tools) to build an integrated environment in which the application is defined, validated and built (e.g. MOF, QVT, etc.).

Hence, a great emphasis is currently set on what to model, and how to use this model. However, key challenges are seldom contemplated:

1. *The accuracy of the model w.r.t. the modeled entities*
   Building a model is a complex task. Every specification (including standards) usually comes with interpretation. These interpretations impede the exploitation of the models, or interoperability between tools. Such interpretation may range from semantics details (e.g. connection between components) to the way one should use the modeling tool by domain experts rather than modeling experts.

2. *The run-time environment*
   The MDA claims that "The model is the implementation". This usually implies an underlying run-time environment (RTE) is defined, and a code generation process from the model to this run-time occurs, mapping model entities onto RTE entities to actually support their execution.

   Building a run-time for DRE systems is a complex task that shall not be underestimated. Functional and non-functional elements, for a large configuration domain make it difficult to have a "one size fits all" architecture. Heterogeneous RTEs shall be defined, all of which built around well-defined patterns that addresses specific needs. By analyzing the model, a specific set of patterns, or a dedicated RTE shall be selected and then configured.

3. *Expressive power of the model*
   Validation or verification tools shall be able to analyze and exploit complete model. Yet, combinatorial explosions, lack of theory for complex assembly of components and tasks, the impossibility to define a specific configuration may reduce the attractive power of MDD.

   Moreover, the model shall not be tainted by the underlying RTE: the impact of configuration parameters from the RTE on the model should be limited to standard elements (e.g. CORBA policies) and not by implementation-defined elements to ensure model's portability.

We note that these challenges are nothing but typical software engineering concerns: Which scheduling theory to apply (RMA, holistic analysis)? How to ensure the code respects this theory (Ravenscar profile, etc.)? How to restrain the code so that it meets these constraints ?

These questions are reworded in MDA vocabulary: Which profile to use? What are the entities of the metamodel? What is the destination of the model transformation process? How to ensure these transformations are correct and preserve the semantics?

MDD aims at defining a canvas in which one can express these concerns, in a set of models that are further exploited for validation or code generation purposes. Yet, building a model shall neither fully hide the design of the underlying verification tools, and RTE; nor neglect them. Code generators and verifications tools belong to the "backend" part of the process: they will turn a model into a running system, validated with respect to domain constraints.

We note that current work around MDD focus on the use of UML, CORBA and Object-Oriented technologies and their extensions for DRE systems. We claim these extensions cannot address a core set of constraints for High-Integrity systems such as:

1. minimalist target environment, for which CORBA and its subsets (like CORBA profile CORBA/e [OMG06]) remains too wide,
2. high-integrity systems, for which object orientation (OO) and dynamic binding does not provide enough information about which piece of code is actually executed [Gas06],
3. hard real time systems, for which QoS is too fuzzy and requires a more formal definition.

Besides, they usually do not cover the full development cycle of the system, leaving verification or testing for future work. By avoiding these difficulties, designers of MDD process can provide cost effective solutions for the average case, but fail to address worst case scenarios.

We note that addressing such scenarios is an interesting challenge to assess MDD viability. First, nothing shall prevent one to address very stringent requirement at the model level, and then generate the appropriate implementation. Second, it is an interesting case study, because we have all the theory to build and assess such system from early requirements down to code generation and evaluation (e.g. WCET, behavior, stack check, ...) and therefore to fully automate the process, from model definition to validation, verification and then from code generation to execution.

Therefore, we claim one could focus on DRE in a hard real time set up to assess a full MDD process, providing both a modeling and a runtime environments; and then to extend it to wider configurations, more difficult to analyze or optimize.

We also note this imposes some "co-design" between the modeling environment and the supporting run-time environment, e.g. to specify configuration, code generation strategies. Such interactions should be taken into account, but reduced to avoid tainting the model with implementation-specific concerns, and preserve model portability.

Such process has already been defined in the context of SCADE [Hal93]. SCADE is a complete modeling and model processing environment. It supports the synchronous language paradigm to model complex high integrity systems. It supports model verification, design-by-contract and provides a certified code generator. However, the code generated is highly dedicated to the SCADE language itself, this reduces its use in wide system that mixes programming languages.

In [BV05], the authors state that generating code minimizes the risk of several semantic breaches when translating the model towards code. The manual coding exposes the developer to these breaches. They propose some guidelines to generate Ravenscar compliant Ada 95 code from a real-time profile for UML. However, this approach is highly specific and misses many features for more general DRE systems, like distribution, resource management.

Thus, a more generic MDE-based process is to be defined. In the following, we aim at defining such architecture

4   An Ideal Model-Driven Suite for DRE Systems

In the previous sections, we listed both CORBA-CCM (and its implementations) and SCADE as complete implementations of a MDE process. However, they are limited in that they integrate in a vertical way many technologies, but fail to go down to fully optimized and fine-tuned code.

In this section, we list requirements for a highly tailorable MDE process, and detail why we should go back to some basics of software engineering to restore balance between modeling and actual code. Then, we present building blocks we are developing to address them.

From the previous sections, we note that the key blocking factors for developing a MDE suite for DRE systems are mostly the high interleaving factor between the models, the modeling process and the exploitation of the models down to code generation.

By carefully separating each level, one might enable finer grained modeling and assembling of software building blocks to build the full system. We list the following requirements to enable such separation of concerns:

- Select a modeling formalism (UML, AADL, components, etc) used to describe the building blocks of the system, their interconnection. This formalism should only capture the static or the dynamic semantics of the system, without any strong reference to the implementation of the underlying run-time environment. This allows for the definition of multiple independent RTEs;
- Select a run-time environment to support the semantics of the above-defined blocks, selected after a complete analysis of the system;
- Define a mapping between blocks and a model processing tool (model checker, schedulability analyzer, code generator).

By allowing separation of concerns between these three layers, one would be in-line with full MDE, allowing model exchanges between tools, while allowing much flexibility in the way the model is used.

Therefore, selecting a run-time environment may become a late binding issue, providing the model and this environment are compatible.

In the following, we illustrate how the *Architecture Analysis and Description Language* (AADL) can serve as a basis for the implementation of this ideal process. We first describe its key features, and then how to use them in a complete process, in the context of High-Integrity process for building DRE systems.

5   An Overview of the AADL

AADL (*Architecture Analysis and Description Language*) [SAE04] aims at describing DRE systems by assembling blocks separately developed.

The AADL allows for the description of both software and hardware parts of a system. It focuses on the definition of clear block interfaces, and separates the implementations from these interfaces. It can be expressed using graphical and textual syntaxes.

An AADL model can incorporate non-architectural elements: embedded or real-time characteristics of the components (execution time, memory footprint...), behavioral descriptions, etc. Hence it is possible to use AADL as a backbone to describe all the aspects of a system.

An AADL description is made of *components*. The AADL standard defines software components (data, threads, thread groups, subprograms, processes), execution platform components (memory, buses, processors, devices) and hybrid components (systems). Components model well identified elements of the actual architecture. *Subprograms* model procedures like in C or Ada. *Threads* model the active part of an application (such as POSIX threads). *Processes* are memory spaces that contain the *threads*. *Thread groups* are used to create a hierarchy among threads. *Processors* model microprocessors and a minimal operating system (mainly a scheduler). *Memories* model hard disks, RAMs, etc. *Buses* model all kinds of networks, wires, etc. *Devices* model sensors, etc. Unlike other components, *systems* do not represent anything concrete; they actually create building blocks to help structure the description.

Component declarations have to be instantiated into subcomponents of other components in order to model an architecture. At the top-level, a system contains all the component instances. Most components can have subcomponents, so that an AADL description is hierarchical. A complete AADL description must provide a top-level system that will contain the other components, thus providing the root of the architecture tree. The architecture in itself is the instantiation of this system.

The interface of a component is a *component type*. It provides *features* (e.g. communication ports). Components communicate one with another by *connecting* their features. To a given component type correspond zero or several implementations. Each of them describe the internals of the components: subcomponents, connections between those subcomponents, etc. An implementation of a thread or a subprogram can specify *call sequences* to other subprograms, thus describing the execution flows in the architecture. There can be multiple implementations of a given component type, so it is possible to select the actual components to put into the architecture, without having to change the other components, this provides a convenient approach to configure applications from a repository of existing entities.

The AADL defines the notion of *properties* that can be attached to most elements (components, connections, features, etc.). Properties are attributes that specify constraints or characteristics that apply to the elements of the architecture: clock frequency of a processor, execution time of a thread, bandwidth of a bus, etc. Some standard properties are defined; but it is possible to define one's own properties.

Figure 1 presents a simple AADL model that depicts two threads: one periodic (GNC, "guidance navigation control"; one sporadic (TMTC, "telemetry/telecommand")

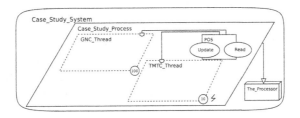

Fig. 1. The GNC/TMTC AADL case study

that interact to read and update a shared variable (POS, "position"). Such system models for instance a satellite guidance system.

Let us note the model depicted in figure 1 is only the high-level view of the system, additional elements can be added to detail the signature of methods that apply on POS, the deployment of each element onto a physical architecture, worst case execution time (WCET) of each element, etc.

Projects such as OSATE [SAE06] define modeling environments to build AADL models, using the Eclipse platform.

As a companion tool, we have developed the Ocarina tool-suite [VZ06] to process AADL models and generate code from this models, targeting a particular RTE. This allows one to develop, configure and deploy distributed systems.

6   Using AADL in an Ideal MDE Process

In the previous section, we presented the AADL, insisting on its static semantics (types and entities). We now reflect on the usage of this language in a complete process.

AADL defines both entities (component types for software and hardware), but also their semantics. This semantics embodies typical behavioral and interaction patterns for High-Integrity systems. It does not prescribe a precise run-time. Therefore, from the AADL standard, multiple run-time may be defined, targeting different application domains (High-Integrity, Real-Time, Fault-Tolerant, deeply embedded, ...).

We want to select as many as possible independent layers of technology.

Without loss of generality, we chose the AADL as a core modeling language to support the different steps of system construction, from early prototypes to final implementation. Supported entities and extensible property sets allow one to build full models and adapt them to the application context. Furthermore, analysis tool can process the models to assess its viability, point out potential problems, and complete the specification when possible (full resource dimensioning, execution metrics).

We have developed the Ocarina tool-suite [VZ06] to process AADL models and allow the developer to develop, configure and deploy distributed systems. Ocarina offers scheduling analysis capabilities, connection with formal verification tools, and more notably code generation to Ada 2005.

Ocarina provides a "front-end" for processing models that describe systems. Then, several "back-ends" allow one to exploit these models and target a specific run-time environment.

These elements are independent from the underlying distribution middleware. We propose two middleware environments to support different families of requirements, also developed by our team:

1. QoS-based: using the schizophrenic middleware PolyORB [VHPK04]. This middleware provides support for typical QoS policies, supporting CORBA (and extensions such as RT-CORBA and FT-CORBA), OMG DDS and a neutral core middleware. This setup allows support for many QoS policies (concurrency runtime, scheduling policies, fault tolerance, protocol and transport configuration, etc.) at a reasonable footprint cost. Besides, it is amenable to formal verification techniques: its core components have been modeled and verified with Petri Nets.

2. High-Integrity edition: using a reduced distribution runtime built for Ravenscar Ada kernels. This setup allows the construction of distributed high-integrity applications that is compliant with development standards from the space industry.

These two middleware implementations propose various levels of configuration and services to address model constraints. This enables the precise construction of application from a common set of AADL properties.

By carefully separating application properties, isolated in AADL properties, from the underlying RTE, we avoid tainting the model with implementation-specific elements and preserve model portability. This also allows one to support new RTEs, for new targets, different code generation strategies, etc.

Let us note that the choice of a particular RTE is driven not by the model itself, through the use of specific features or properties. It is driven by the result of its analysis. Depending on this analysis, the most compatible RTE would be selected given memory constraints, real-time schedules, hardware support, etc.

Therefore, we propose multiple RTE compatible with one unique high-level modeling entity, each of which support a different range of constraints, from DRE to distributed High-Integrity systems, with tools to assess their functional and non-functional properties. This addresses the requirements we listed in the section 4.

In the following, we show how the complete chain has been implemented in the context of High-Integrity systems.

7   From AADL Models to DHI Systems

In this section, we illustrate how an AADL model is sufficient to detail the deployment view of the application: nodes, processors, network buses, tasks on each node; properties refine the type of tasks (periodicity, priority) and the source code associated to each processing task.

We define our distribution model as a set of caller/callee tuples that interact through asynchronous messages. This model is supported by an AADL architectural model that defines the location of each node, and the payload of the message exchanged as a method name plus additional parameters. This model is simple enough for being analyzed by most scheduling algorithms while reducing pessimism in the context of an holistic analysis [GGH00]. Yet, it is powerful enough to model various systems inspired by our research partners.

From a system's AADL description, we first compute required resources, then generate code for each logical node (figure 1). We review the elements that implement this distribution model, detailing their function, the corresponding design pattern and how they are computed from the AADL model. Being a static description of a DRE systems, AADL allows optimizations that reduce the complexity of the code:

- **Naming table:** They are used to store location information on the entities that interact. Each table lists one entry per remote node that can be reached, and one entry per opened communication channel on this node. We build one table per node, computed from the topology of the interactions described in the AADL model. It is indexed by an enumeration affecting one tag per logical node reachable from this node, resulting in $O(1)$ access time to communication handlers (e.g. sockets structures, SpaceWire stacks, ethernet addresses, etc).

- **Marshallers:** They handle type conversion between network streams and actual request data in node's CPU representation. They are derived from subprograms interface, which describe the structure of data to be exchanged. This is computed beforehand from the AADL models, as for CORBA IDL. Resulting code is in $O(\texttt{sizeof (payload)})$ complexity. This code relies on application provided buffers, we describe this point later.

- **Stubs and skels:** They handle the construction and analysis of network messages. It is notionally equivalent to CORBA stubs and skeletons, but reduced to asynchronous oneway request management. Stubs transform a request for an interaction into a network stream, skels do the reverse operation. Both elements are built from AADL components interface and actual interaction between threads, a stub/skel tuple is built only if a remote interaction occurs, otherwise local communication is done using local message boxes. We exploit this knowledge to have $O(\texttt{sizeof (payload)})$ components: a request is a discriminated record, its translation is of linear complexity.

- **Protocol instances:** They are asynchronous communication channels, configured from the deployment information stored in the AADL model. AADL lets the designer express the buses between nodes, the protocol and the threads that access it. All these information are analyzed to configure the exact protocol instances required to allow communication between application entities. They are set up at node start up time. The complexity of the action performed by these instances depends on the underlying transport low layer. Its analysis depends on deployment information (e.g. TDMA, CAN bus, SpaceWire, etc.).

- **Concurrent objects:** They handle the execution logic of the node. We build one task per cyclic or sporadic tasks (corresponding to client-side activity); plus one task per protocol handler to process incoming requests on behalf of an AADL server component. Subsequent tasks are built for the management of the transport low layer. Finally, we build one protected object (mutex-like entities) to allow for communication between tasks. Let us note all these objects strictly follow the Ravenscar profile, ensuring code analyzability using RMA and Holistic analysis.

The generated code provides a framework that will call directly user code when necessary. This relieves the user from the necessity to know an extensive API, and allows a finer control of the behavior of the system that is under the sole responsibility of the code generation patterns. Current code generator targets an Ada 2005 runtime, current ongoing work considers targeting a C runtime.

We note that generating code to configure these entities reduces the need for a large middleware API. Hence, buffers, tasks, naming tables are allocated directly from the application models. This enables a finer control on the code structure, reducing the need for complex structures to register application entities such as CORBA COS Naming, and the hand writing of error prone setup code (e.g. DDS policies). Usually, these API defines some level of protection to defend against concurrent accesses, use memory allocation, all of which goes against the core requirements of HI systems. Besides, those can be discarded by carefully analyzing the model that is a transcription of the application requirements and design plan.

In the following section, we present our current implementation work, and how model processing actually reduces memory footprint while providing interesting code features for HI systems.

8   An Integrated MDE Toolsuite for DHI Systems

In this section, we detail our model processing chain, built around PolyORB-HI, Ocarina and companion tools; and assess it on one complete example.

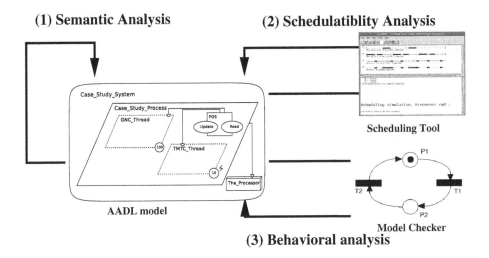

Fig. 2. Exploiting AADL models

8.1   Assessing an AADL Model

AADL models support both code generation and model analysis. Analysis can range from simple semantic analysis to more sophisticated one such as schedulability analysis, model checking of the behavior of the nodes, etc.

In this section, we show how such analysis can be conducted using our AADL model processing suite (figure 2).

Semantic analysis is performed using our AADL compiler Ocarina. Ocarina verifies that the given AADL model is conforming to the AADL standard and that some additional restrictions are respected:

- All event or data ports are connected,
- All threads are either periodic or sporadic,
- All shared data use a concurrent access protocol that bounds priority inversion (e.g. the Priority Ceiling Protocol mandated by the Ravenscar profile).

AADL defines a standard execution semantics, this allows us to go further and assess the system is meaningful, and can run prior to its generation and execution. We allow both schedulability analysis and model checking to assess node liveness.

Schedulability analysis is performed using Cheddar [SLTM04]. Cheddar is an Ada 2005 framework that provides tools and library to check if AADL threads will meet their deadline at execution time. Cheddar uses the Ocarina [VZ06] libraries to analyze the AADL models.

From an AADL model, a model of interacting tasks is computed. Tasks can interact either locally sharing data through protected object (or mutex), or remotely through a communication bus. The first allows for traditional Rate Monotonic Analysis, while the second requires advanced techniques such as Holistic analysis. Cheddar supports both; this enables one to check one's architecture can run within expected bounds.

Checking of the behavior of the nodes is performed by transforming the AADL model into a Petri net [HKPV07] and then by performing formal verification on the resulting Petri net. The transformation into Petri net is performed using a Petri net generator module provided by Ocarina. It maps the behavioral pattern of each AADL entity onto a Petri subnets that are then weaved to form the model of a complete system.

The formal verification (absence of deadlocks, causality analysis through temporal logic formulae ...) is performed using the CPN-AMI Petri Net modeling and model checking environment [MT].

For each interaction pattern expressed in the AADL model (interacting tasks, message sent, ...), we build the corresponding Petri Nets and assemble them to build one model representing the whole system. From this model, we can either explore its state space and look for deadlock (state from which no progress is possible), look for inconsistent state or test for more complex timed logical formulas (such as if event $\mathcal{E}$ holds, then output O is always emitted).

These analyses allow one to fully assess system viability prior to its execution on the target. If required, the model can be refined to correct the behavior, adjust WCET, etc.

8.2   Generating Executable Code

We use code generation facilities in Ocarina to semantically analyze the AADL model, compute required resources and generate code conforming to HI restrictions.

First, the model is built by the application designer, he maps its application entities onto a hardware architecture. Then, this architecture is tested for completeness and soundness, any mismatch in the configuration is reported by the analysis tool (e.g. lack of connection from an object). Consequently, model processing occurs, and code is generated from this AADL model, following a precise set of mapping rules. Finally, code can be compiled and run on the target.

Code generation relies on patterns presented in section 7 inherited from previous work on code generation from Ravenscar [BV05] and classical design patterns for distribution such as the Broker [BMR$^+$96], constrained to remove all dynamic behavior supported by the minimal middleware for HI systems: PolyORB-HI.

We named this middleware "PolyORB-HI" as a follow up to the PolyORB project we develop [VHPK04]. It shares many common architectural notions while using a different code base.

Like PolyORB, PolyORB-HI is a "schizophrenic middleware". Schizophrenic middleware [QKP01] are built on isolated elements that embody key steps in request processing, allowing for finer configuration of each blocks. We identified seven steps in request processing, each of which is defined as one fundamental service. Services are generic components for which an general implementation is provided. Developers may provide an alternate implementation. Each middleware instance is one coherent assembling of these entities. Instances can support standard specifications like CORBA or DDS, or application-specific middleware for embedded targets.

PolyORB-HI strictly follows all restrictions we defined in the previous part. It is developed in Ada 2005 [ISO06]. It is compliant with both the Ravenscar profile and the High Integrity System restrictions (Annexes D and H of the Ada 2005 standard). Let us note that most restrictions are enforced at compile time (no dispatching, no floating point, no allocator, etc). This simply yet efficiently enforces the absence of unwanted features used by the middleware, increasing the confidence in the code generated while limiting its complexity. Code generated by Ocarina follows the same compilation restrictions.

User code is also tested for consistency with the above restrictions. To ensure user code does no impact scheduling (and thus threatens asserted properties), we ensure at compile-time it uses no tasking constructs (tasks and protected objects) by positioning the corresponding restrictions on its packages. This is done using the native Ada `pragma Restrictions` mechanisms.

9   Case Study

In this section, we illustrate on a case study the benefits of this approach to fully build a HI system. This case study has been provided by our partners from the IST-ASSERT project.

9.1   Scenario

The figure 3 shows the software view of our case study. This model holds three nodes, each is a spacecraft with different roles:

1. SC_1 is a leader spacecraft that contains a periodic thread which sends its position to SC_2 and SC_3.
2. SC_2 and SC_3 are follower spacecraft. They receive the position sent by SC_1 with a sporadic thread (`Receiver_Thread`), update their own position and store it in a local protected object. A second thread in these two spacecraft reads periodically the position value from the local protected object, and "watches and reports" all elements at that position (e.g. earth observation, etc...).

This model gathers typical elements from Distributed High Integrity (D-HI) systems, with a set of periodic tasks devoted to the processing of incoming orders

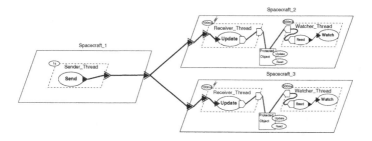

Fig. 3. Software view of the MPC case study

(Watcher_Thread), buffers to store these orders (*Protected Object*) and sporadic threads to exchange data (Receiver_Thread). These entities work at different rates, and should all respect their deadlines so that the Watcher_Thread can process all observation orders in due time.

The software view only represents how the processing is distributed onto different entities (threads) and gathered as AADL processes to form partitions. The next step is to map this view onto a physical hardware view, so that CPU resources can be affected to each node.

The figure 4 is a graphical representation of the deployment view of the system. It only shows the global architecture of the application (number of nodes, their mapping to hardware components). It indicates that each partition is bound to a specific CPU, and how the communication between partitions occurs, using different buses. The details of each node will also be described using AADL.

These two views are expressed using the same modeling notation, they can be merged to form the complete system: interacting entities in the software view represent the processing logic of the system, whereas the hardware view completes the system deployment information by allocating resources.

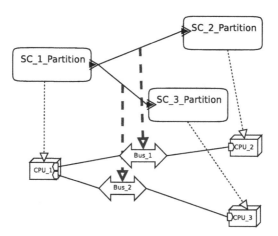

Fig. 4. Deployment view of the MPC case study

From this combined view, a set of analyses can be conducted, in conformance with the process we propose.

9.2 Schedulability Analysis and Model Checking

The case study we retained is simple enough to be analyzed by these tools. Let us note that intermediate models (Cheddar or Petri Nets) are of similar in size and complexity to the initial AADL model. This implies the model transformations we proposed do not add parasite complexity to these intermediate models.

9.3 Generated Code

A prototype of PolyORB-HI, running on both ERC32 and LEON2 targets has been built. These processors are used by the European Space Agency for its next generation of embedded systems (satellites, vehicles, etc...). Thanks to Ada 95 portability, the same code can also be tested on native targets, or on other boards, such as PowerPC-based. This makes the prototyping of embedded system easier since we can test them on native platform before embedding them on their corresponding hardware. In this section, we study the footprint of the code generated on LEON2 targets.

Table 1 summarizes the code size for the node SC_2 of our case study. It that combines periodic and sporadic threads, data components and a SpaceWire interface to receive inbound messages. We display both the actual lines of code (SLOCs) and the size of the binary objects. The used compiler is the GNAT for LEON 1.3 Ada 95 compiler. All tests were done in local, using the tsim simulator for LEON, emulating a $50Mhz$ processor. The SpaceWire interface is simulated in tsim as an I/O module bound to the LEON processor.

The code generation strategy we retained maps AADL constructs onto Ada 95 equivalent ones so that there exists traceability between the AADL model and the corresponding Ada 95 source code: e.g. between AADL threads and Ada 95 tasks, AADL data component and Ada 95 records or protected objects. Such strategy reduces the need for a large API, and eases code review after generation.

The total size of the executable, combining real-time kernel, middleware and the application, is $576kB$, using the GNAT for LEON 1.3 compiler. It fits the requirements from minimal embedded systems, and is clearly under the typical memory range for API-based middleware such as nORB or microORB, which are above $1MB$ for a complete system, including full OS support.

Given the development process we retained, most code is automatically generated from the AADL model. The code in the middleware handles simple and low-level actions: messages, protocol, transport. Generated code adds tasking constructs required to execute the application and enables interaction between entities: transport handler, application activities, advanced marshallers, naming tables, etc...

The code generation strategy we chose accounts for a large part of the distribution aspects of the application: it includes the elaboration of tasks and protected objects, the allocation of dedicated memory area, stubs and skeletons, marshallers and naming table. Finally, the runtime accounts for another large part of the size of the application.

Table 1. Footprint for the SC_2 node

Component	SLOCs	.o size (bytes)
Application	89	8852
Generated code	961	66804
Middleware	1068	32957
Ada Run-Time + drivers	N/A	$\approx 541Kb$

9.4   Assessment of the Process

From the AADL model, we are capable of generating both, information that the model is sound and the corresponding executable, ready to run on LEON2 boards.

We demonstrate how to exploit one AADL model and user-provided code for some processing functions. AADL serves both as a documentation of the system (requirements expression, functional and non functional properties, topology of the system can be expressed in one model) and as a template to validate it and generate its implementation: it preserves system design.

Therefore, we have an immediate benefit from an engineering point of view: the developer can focus on its system architecture. The complete tool suite ensures it is correct, and handles the configuration of all code-level entities. This suppresses many manual code writing, a tedious and error-prone process underlined by well-known software failures in the space domain like the Ariane V maiden flight. It also tremendously reduce the development cycle and allow one to go faster from the prototyping phase to the design of the final system.

All these analyses have been tested successfully on significant examples submitted by industrial partners in the context of the IST-ASSERT project.

10   Conclusions

Model Driven Development is an appealing evolution of software engineering, by proposing a paradigm shift from traditional programming to model and code generation. However, we note it may promise too much and fail to deliver sufficient guarantees for specific domains such as DRE, for very constrained targets.

We claim that some limitations do not lie in the process itself, but in the way it is implemented: the distance between the models and the supporting runtime environment can introduce parasite complexity (runtime overhead, heavy language constructs, etc.). Therefore, it is often necessary to stop modeling activities to go back to the basics of implementation, reducing modeling efforts.

We propose a toolsuite built around the AADL to promote system modeling at the architecture-level. This modeling approach makes it possible to reason at different abstraction levels, from system overview down to implementation concerns. This helps selecting the most precise runtime entities when required.

We proposed two different supporting environment for DRE systems, one based on QoS policies, supporting CORBA and its real-time extensions, DDS, etc.; another supporting High-Integrity constraints. Besides, our toolsuite integrates schedulability analysis and formal verification tools to assess system's viability.

We validated our approach on significant examples provided in the context of the IST-ASSERT project, and detailed some of the outcomes of this project.

Current work focuses on the extension of the Ocarina toolsuite towards other application properties, including fault-tolerance, proof (a-la PVS) and the enforcement of wider application properties to configure the underlying runtime. We are also working on a *C* runtime to support the same level of functions, for other application targets like RTEMS and VxWorks.

Acknowledgement. The authors thank F. Singhoff from the Cheddar project and the members of the IST-ASSERT project for their feedback on earlier version of this work. This work is partially funded by the IST-ASSERT project.

References

[BMR+96] Buschmann, F., Meunier, R., Rohnert, H., Sommerlad, P., Stal, M.: Pattern-Oriented Software Architecture: A System of Patterns. John Wiley & Sons, New York (1996)

[BV05]   Bordin, M., Vardanega, T.: Automated Model-Based Generation of Ravenscar-Compliant Source Code. In: ECRTS 2005. Proceedings of the 17th Euromicro Conference on Real-Time Systems, pp. 59–67. IEEE Computer Society, Washington (2005)

[Gas06]   Gasperoni, F.: Safety, security, and object-oriented programming. SIGBED Rev. 3(4), 15–26 (2006)

[GGH00]   García, J.J.G., Gutiérrez, J.C.P., Harbour, M.G.: Schedulability analysis of distributed hard real-time systems with multiple- event synchronization. In: Proceedings of 12th Euromicro Conference on Real-Time Systems, pp. 15–24. IEEE Computer Society Press, Los Alamitos (2000)

[Hal93]   Halbwachs, N.: A tutorial of Lustre (1993)

[HKPV07] Hugues, J., Kordon, F., Pautet, L., Vergnaud, T.: A Factory To Design and Build Tailorable and Verifiable Middleware. In: Kordon, F., Sztipanovits, J. (eds.) Monterey Workshop 2005. LNCS, vol. 4322, pp. 121–142. Springer, Heidelberg (2007)

[ISO06]   ISO/IEC 8652:2007(E) Ed. 3. Annotated Ada 2005 Language Reference Manual. Technical report (2006)

[MT]   MoVe-Team. CPN-AMI, http://www.lip6.fr/cpn-ami

[OMG03]   OMG. MDA Guide v1.01. OMG (2003)

[OMG06]   OMG. Common Object Request Broker - for embedded. OMG (MAY 2006) Draft Adopted specification ptc/06-05-01

[QKP01]   Quinot, T., Kordon, F., Pautet, L.: From functional to architectural analysis of a middleware supporting interoperability across heterogeneous distribution models. In: DOA 2001. Proceedings of the 3rd International Symposium on Distributed Objects and Applications, IEEE Computer Society Press, Los Alamitos (2001)

[SAE04]   SAE. Architecture Analysis & Design Language (AS5506) (September 2004), available at http://www.sae.org

[SAE06]   SAE. Open Source AADL Tool Environment. Technical report, SAE (2006)

[SBK+05] Schmidt, D.C., Balasubramanian, K., Krishna, A.S., Turkay, E., Gokhale, A.: Model Driven Engineering for Distributed Real-time Embedded Systems. In: Model-Driven Development of distributed Real-Time and Embedded Systems, pp. 31–60. Hermes Publishing (2005)

[SLTM04]   Singhoff, F., Legrand, J., Tchamnda, L.N., Marcé, L.: Cheddar: a Flexible Real Time Scheduling Framework. ACM Ada Letters 24(4), 1–8 (2004)
[VHPK04]   Vergnaud, T., Hugues, J., Pautet, L., Kordon, F.: PolyORB: a schizophrenic middleware to build versatile reliable distributed applications. In: Llamosí, A., Strohmeier, A. (eds.) Ada-Europe 2004. LNCS, vol. 3063, pp. 106–119. Springer, Heidelberg (2004)
[VZ06]   Vergnaud, T., Zalila, B.: Ocarina: a Compiler for the AADL. Technical report, Télécom Paris (2006), available at http://aadl.enst.fr

Model-Based Failure Management for Distributed Reactive Systems

Vina Ermagan, Ingolf Krüger, and Massimiliano Menarini

University of California, San Diego
9500 Gilman Drive, Mail Code 0404, La Jolla, CA 92093-0404, USA
{vermagan,ikrueger,mmenarini}@ucsd.edu
http://sosa.ucsd.edu

Abstract. Failure management is key to the development of safety-critical, distributed, reactive systems common in such applications as avionics, automotive, and sensor/actuator networks. Specific challenges to effective failure management include (i) developing an understanding of the application domain so as to define what constitutes a failure; (ii) disentangling failure management concepts at design and runtime; and (iii) detecting and mitigating failures at the level of systems-of-systems integration. In this paper, we address (i) and (ii) by developing a failure ontology for logical and deployment architectures, respectively, including a mapping between the two. This ontology is based on the interaction patterns (or services) defining the component interplay in a distributed system. We address (iii) by defining detectors and mitigators at the service/interaction level – we discuss how to derive detectors for a significant subset of the failure ontology directly from the interaction patterns. We demonstrate the utility of our techniques using a large scale oceanographic sensor/actuator network.

Keywords: Failure Management, Distributed Systems, Ontology, Reactive Systems.

1 Introduction

Failures can cause serious harm in many application domains. In domains such as avionics, automotive, and plant control, lives often depend on the correct functionality of software systems. One of the most challenging tasks of system developers is to ensure that the system both delivers the expected functionalities and is resilient to failures. We advocate the use of a combination of elements from Model Driven Architecture (MDA) [1] and Service-Oriented Architectures (SOA) to disentangle functional aspects of system behavior from the treatment of failures.

The basic building block of our approach is the service. Services capture interaction patterns between system entities. Our approach leverages the interaction descriptions captured by services to identify, at run time, deviations from the specified behavior. An ontology guides the identification of failures and the activation of additional services that mitigate the effects of such failures.

F. Kordon and O. Sokolsky (Eds.): Monterey Workshop 2006, LNCS 4888, pp. 53–74, 2007.

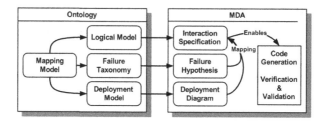

Fig. 1. Model-based failure-management approach

Figure 1 outlines the model-based failure management approach we propose. The figure shows the two main elements of our approach. We leverage an ontology, encompassing a failure taxonomy, service oriented models, deployment models and the mapping between them, to inform an MDA approach. We enrich the logical and deployment models typical of any MDA with a failure hypothesis. This additional artifact, based on the failure ontology, captures what physical and logical entities can fail in a system. It also provides a formal basis to reason about system correctness in presence of failures.

Our SOA models are based on hierarchically composed interaction models, extending the service notion used, for example, in Web services [2]. Addressing quality of service of end-to-end properties becomes easier because the interactions of different nodes are the main modeling entities in our specification language. In our approach, the key mechanism to deal with failures is decoupling *Unmanaged Services* and *Managed Services*. *Unmanaged Services* are responsible for providing the required functionalities, while *Managed Services* enable the detection of failures and the implementation of mitigation strategies that avoid, or recover from, failures.

A service-oriented process using the failure taxonomy requires devising two special types of Services: Detectors and Mitigators (similar to the detector/corrector approach taken by Arora et al. in [3]). Detectors compare the communication patterns captured in the service specification with the ones observable in the running system; they apply mitigation strategies when a behavior is detected that does not match the specification. Mitigators are services that modify the interaction pattern of the system so as to recover from failure conditions.

In prior work we have applied these ideas in the context of the automotive domain [4]. Here, we generalize and extend this work to a wider range of application domains, including sensor networks. Furthermore, we present first ideas towards the derivation of detectors and mitigators from interaction specifications.

Outline: The remainder of the paper is structured as follows. In Section 2, we describe a case study extracted from the domain of oceanographic sensor networks, which we use as a running example throughout this paper. In Section 3, we present the failure taxonomy. In Section 4, we present the relationship between the ontology and the interaction-based specification of services. In Section 5, we discuss two patterns that generate detectors for two important types of failures: absence of expected behaviors and occurrence of unexpected behaviors.

Section 6 addresses the applicability of the approach and limitations of the proposed solutions. Section 7 covers the related work. Section 8 provides concluding remarks.

2   A Case Study

The proposed approach for creating failsafe systems can be tailored to target various embedded, distributed reactive systems. Examples of application domains are automotive, avionics, plant control, and wireless sensor networks. In this paper, we target a large federated sensor network system where low-power devices connected via slow wireless network links interact with more powerful computation devices connected to traditional wired networks. The example is inspired by requirements for the domain of global ocean observatories, namely the federated Ocean Research Interactive Observatory Networks (ORION) program, for which a conceptual architecture study is available at [5]. We limit ourselves to a small subset of ORION's goals, namely the development of an infrastructure for marine observation allowing scientists to share the control of sensor networks deployed on the ocean floor.

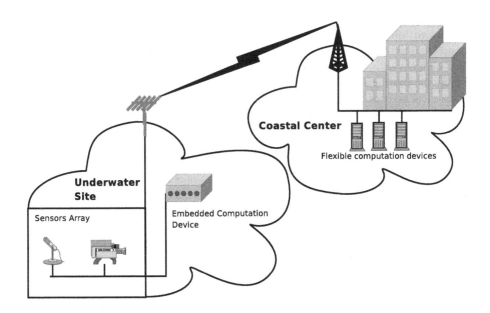

Fig. 2. Underwater sensor case study from ORION

To demonstrate our approach we introduce the simple case study of Figure 2. The setup includes two sites: an underwater site and a coastal center. The underwater site has a sensor array consisting of one audio and one video sensor. These sensors are controlled by a low-power embedded computation unit and can communicate to the coastal center via a slow and unreliable wireless link. The components of the underwater observatory site are connected via a traditional wired network that provides reliable communication between the embedded processing unit, the sensors array and the wireless communication subsystem. The coastal center communicates with the underwater site via a wireless transmitter; the rest of the components (including various powerful computers for scientific computation and workstations for scientists to interact with the system) are connected by a wired network.

In this paper, we will focus on a single use case that allows us to discuss how to deal with failures. The goal of our system is to take pictures of whales. The use case proceeds as follows: the underwater microphone detects whale sounds and activates the camera when a whale is nearby. The camera takes pictures. Image processing software processes the images to detect if the picture with reasonable probability contains a whale. If so, the picture is compressed and sent to the surface for further analysis. The more powerful image detection software running on the mainland computers can then determine whether the animal in the picture is indeed a whale. If so, it instructs the underwater station to send more pictures of it. In the current paper, we are not interested in how the image or sound detection algorithms work; instead, we focus on how to detect and address possible failures in the system.

Figure 3 shows the interactions that must be carried out by system components to fulfill the use case outlined above. The graphical language used to define the interactions is based on Message Sequence Charts (MSC) [6,7,8]. An MSC defines the relevant sequences of *messages* (represented by labeled arrows) among the interacting *roles*. Roles are represented as vertical axes in our MSC notation. The MSC syntax we use should be fairly self-explanatory, especially to readers familiar with UML2 [8]. In particular, we support labeled boxes in our MSCs indicating alternatives and unbounded repetitions. High-level MSCs (HMSCs) indicate sequences of, alternatives between and repetitions of services in two-dimensional graphs – the nodes of the graph are references to MSCs, to be substituted by their respective interaction specifications. HMSCs can be translated into basic MSCs without loss of information [7].

A number of extensions to the standard MSCs warrant explanation [9,10]. First, we take each axis to represent a *role* rather than a class, object, or component. The mapping from roles to components is a design step in our approach. Second, we use an operator called *join* [7,9], which we use extensively to compose *overlapping* service specifications. We call two services *overlapping* if their interaction scenarios share at least two roles and at least one message between shared roles. The join operator will *synchronize* the services on their shared messages, and otherwise result in an arbitrary *interleaving* of the non-shared messages of its operands. Join is a powerful operator for separating an overall service into interacting sub-services.

Our use case scenario is captured by four MSC graphs. Figures 3(b) through 3(d) show three interactions defining the "ValidatePicture", "StopCamera" and "TakePictureUnderwater" services, respectively. Figure 3(d) shows the use of

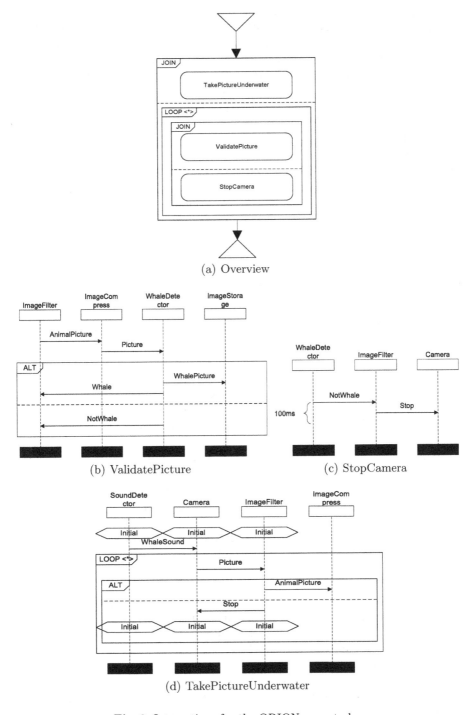

Fig. 3. Interactions for the ORION case study

both unbounded repetition (outer box labeled "LOOP") and nondeterministic alternatives (inner box labeled "ALT"). Note how the services depicted in these three figures overlap. Figure 3(a) captures the composition of the other three by using the join operator. Consider, for instance, the *AnimalPicture* messages in Figures 3(b) and 3(d). The use of the join operator forces the ValidatePicture interaction to start only when TakePictureUnderwater has identified that an animal is in the picture and the picture has been sent to the *Image Compress* role.

The behavior prescribed by the four graphs of Figure 3 is the following. The *ValidatePicture* MSC Figure 3(b) prescribes that the component playing the role *Image Filter* sends a message containing the image of an Animal (*AnimalPicture*) to the component playing the *Image Compress* role. This picture is then compressed and sent trough the slow unreliable link to the *Whale Detector* program on the shore facility. The system activity can now proceed in two ways: either the *Whale Detector* recognizes that the picture contains a Whale, in which case it sends it to the *Image Storage* role to be archived and return a *Whale* message to the *Image Filter* role, or it detects that the image does not contain a whale, in which case it returns a *NotWhale* message to the *Image Filter*. The *StopCamera* MSC (Figure 3(c)) is very simple. It mandates that a NotWhale message sent from *Whale Detector* to *Image Filter* is followed by a *Stop* message sent to the *Camera*. The brace in the MSC defines a deadline for the interaction of 100 milliseconds. The other MSC, showing the initiation of the picture-taking activity, is *TakePictureUnderwater* (Figure 3(d)). The *Sound Detector* sends a *WhaleSound* message to the *Camera*. From this point a loop is initiated in which the *Camera* sends Pictures to the *Image Filter*. Two alternatives are possible: the image filter sends an *AnimalPicture* message to *Image Compress* or it sends a *Stop* to *Camera*. When camera receives a *Stop* message it exits the loop and stops taking pictures.

Figure 3(a) depicts the *Overview* HMSC. It joins the three MSCs previously described. The join operator prescribes the parallel execution of the joined MSCs synchronizing on common messages. For example, because the *AnimalPicture* message between roles *Image Filter* and *Image Compress* is encountered in both *ValidatePicture* and *TakePictureUnderwater*, and they are joined, only one instance of *Animal Picture* will be exchanged and the other messages defined in *ValidatePicture* must follow the *AnimalPicture* message defined in *TakePicture-Underwater*.

The interactions of Figure 3 outline the expected behavior of the system without any consideration for failures. In other words, Figure 3 contains the "sunny-day scenarios". This is a good starting point for understanding regular system functionality; the next step is to also gain an understanding of what entities in the domain can fail and how these failures should be dealt with. Failures, of course, happen at runtime rather than in the domain model itself. Therefore, the steps required for failure analysis are (i) mapping the logical roles expressed in the interaction to runtime entities, and (ii) defining a failure hypothesis that formalizes our assumption about what can and cannot fail in the system. In the following sections, we will analyze this case study for possible failures and provide the required steps for failure management.

3   Failure Taxonomy

Failure management is particularly effective if it is performed throughout the development process[11] – rather than, as often happens, as an afterthought. To raise awareness of failures already from the very early phases of the software and systems engineering process, including requirements gathering, a comprehensive taxonomy for failures and failure management entities is essential. Failure taxonomy is a domain specific concept [11]. In previous work, we have developed a general failure taxonomy for the automotive domain [4]. Here we extend this ontology to address failure management in distributed reactive systems. Furthermore, we discuss a domain-specific failure model for sensor networks, as the case study of this paper.

Figure 4 shows the extended failure taxonomy using UML2 class diagram notation[8]. It captures the relationships between failures and our means for detecting and managing them. The central entity of this taxonomy is a *Failure*. A *Failure* has one or more *Cause*s and one or more *Effect*s.

A failure *Cause* can be due to either a software problem, *Software Failure*, or a hardware problem, *Hardware Failure*, and is very dependent on the application domain. In Figure 5, we have captured several of the elements that can fail in our application domain, and we have identified the types of failures they can

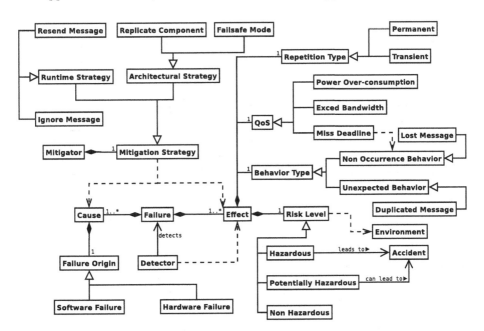

Fig. 4. Failure ontology

cause. *Hardware Failures* can be due to failing *Sensors, Actuators, Wireless* and *Wired Networks*, and *Computation Units. Software Failures* are due to bugs in *Programs* that run on the *Computation Units.*

In Figure 4, an *Effect* is the observable result of a failure occurrence. A *Detector* can detect the occurrence of a *Failure* based on its *Effect.* This relation binds the detector to the observable results of failures. Therefore, it is important to define what type of *Effects* a failure can have, and to leverage them to create *Detectors.*

We have identified four key aspects of the *Effect.* First, the *Risk Level* identifies the degree of hazard a particular failure can cause. Based on this assessment it is possible to decide if the failure can be ignored or not. The three main risk levels are *Hazardous, Potentially Hazardous,* and *Non Hazardous.* A *Hazardous* failure always leads to an *Accident,* while a *Potentially Hazardous* failure can lead to an *Accident* given some specific conditions. *Non Hazardous* failures never lead to accidents. An *Accident* is an unwanted event with *serious consequences.* The definition of a *serious consequence* depends on the specific domain. In our simple example, we could define it as an event that requires somebody to physically access the underwater site. Therefore, the occurrence of a failure that completely disables the software running on an embedded computation device would be an accident. In a domain such as avionics, an accident could be an event that causes loss of lives. It is important to notice that the assessment of risk depends on the *Environment.* If the embedded device was running in the scientist's office instead of underwater, the need to access it to restart the system in the event of a software failure would not have the same consequences, and would not probably be considered an accident.

Another important aspect of the failure *Effect* is the *Behavior Type* of the failure. The *Failure* can either cause the system to present an *Unexpected Behavior* or a *Non Occurrence Behavior*[12]. An *Unexpected Behavior* is the occurrence

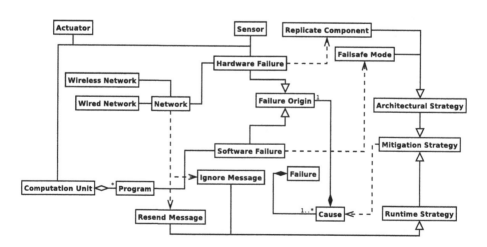

Fig. 5. Domain failures

of an event that was not supposed to happen. One instance of an *Unexpected Behavior* is a duplicated message; another is the power-intake of a network node being outside of the specified range. *Non Occurrence Behavior* is defined by the absence of an event that was supposed to happen. A lost message in a communication protocol is an example of such behavior.

It is important to realize that it is often impossible to identify the correct behavior type of a failure's *Effect* without additional information about the failure *Cause*. If the sequence of messages Ma, Mb is expected by a role A, and the role receives Mb as a first message, it can be either that message Ma was lost, or a wrong message Mb was sent instead of Ma. A lost message would be an instance of *Non Occurrence Behavior*, and a wrong message would be an instance of *Unexpected Behavior*. The importance of this classification is that it allows us to capture two detection strategies. *Unexpected Behavior* can be detected by an observer that has only a specification of the sequence of events that can happen in a correct system. On the other hand, detecting a *Non Occurrence Behavior* often requires the introduction of the concept of time.

The third aspect of an *Effect* is the *Quality of Service*. Sometimes the only observable result of a failure is the degradation in the *Quality of Service* properties of the system. Three types of *Quality of Service Effects* can be identified. *Bandwidth Exceeding*, *Missing Deadlines*, and *Power Over-consumption*. *Bandwidth Exceeding* happens when sensors send too many requests over the network, or when, for example, they send too much data at too high a frequency. *Missing Deadline* happens when, because of some failure, the system has slowed down, and it can not meet the timing constraints any more. For instance, when a highly loaded node in a network breaks down, the load might be distributed over the neighboring nodes, which could lead to an overload of the neighbors, and hence a slowdown in several nodes. Finally, *Power Over-consumption* happens when a node's power consumption exceeds the expected limit. This is particularly important in systems such as the one introduced in the case study, or in the sensor networks domain, where accessing nodes for battery replacement is very costly, and hence, it is very important that nodes remain power-efficient.

The last aspect of an *Effect* is the *Repetition Type*. We deem the *Effect* to be either *Permanent* or *Transient*. Classic examples of a *Permanent* failure are total hardware failures – such as total failures of sensors, program crashes, or deadlocks. The *Transient* repetition type can arise from transient hardware problems such as flipped bits during communication due to unexpected noise from the *Environment*, or race conditions in concurrent programs.

When a failure is detected, the system needs to mitigate it. This is done by following certain *Mitigation Strategies*. The *Mitigation Strategy* we must apply to deal with failures depends both on the failures' *Effect*s and *Cause*s. We identify two main strategies: *Runtime Strategy* and *Architectural Strategy*. When a duplicated message is detected at runtime, *Ignore Message* can be one *Runtime Mitigation Strategy*. Similarly, when a message loss is detected, *Resend Message* is a candidate *Runtime Mitigation Strategy*. *Replicate Component* and *Failsafe Mode* are typical *Architectural Strategies*. In our case study, if we assume that the embedded computation unit hardware in the underwater site can break down, and we still want to be able to guarantee the functionality of the system without the need to dive in and change the unit, we must use the *Replicate Component* strategy and provide a backup computation unit. To deal with the possible loss of a message on the wireless link between the two sites, we can apply the *Resent Message* strategy. We must introduce an acknowledgment message for each transmission and resend the message until one party gets an acknowledgment from the other.

4   Services

Implementing distributed reactive systems is a complicated and error-prone task. Model Driven Architectures [1,13,14] and Service-Oriented Architectures (*SOA*) have been proposed as a solution to tackle the complexity of such systems. Failures in distributed systems happen not only at a level internal to the components, but also, and more severely, they happen across the interactions of the integrated components. Hence, failures are mainly crosscutting issues that must be addressed in an end-to-end manner. Service-oriented design is specifically suited for addressing failures, because *Services* are by nature crosscutting concerns of the system. In previous work, we have discussed our service-oriented approach for design and development of distributed reactive systems [15,4]. We concentrate on the modeling of services themselves, rather than deployment concerns such as service publishing, discovery and binding – these aspects of service-oriented architectures are covered extensively in the literature [2].

In the following, we briefly describe our model for service-oriented design for distributed reactive systems. Then we introduce our interaction-based model for *Services*.

4.1   Failure Aware Service Model

In our approach, distributed reactive systems are captured as a collection of *Services*. Intuitively, the system has a number of *Services*, each providing one or more system functionalities. *Services* can have *Detectors* and *Mitigators* in order to manage the *Failures* that are identified within each *Service*. In the following, we will describe each entity in more detail.

The main entity of the model is the notion of *Service*. A *Service* is defined by a series of interactions providing some system functionality. A *Service* can be a *Composite Service* or a *Basic Service*. Every *Composite Service* is composed of a number of sub-*Services* interacting with each other to provide a more general *Service*. Each of the sub-*Services* can be simple or composite on their own, thereby allowing the model to provide a hierarchy of services to tackle the complexity of distributed systems.

Figure 3 illustrates the application of the *Service* model to our case study. Three *Basic Services* each capture part of the defined system functionality: taking the picture under water, validating the picture, and stopping the Camera.

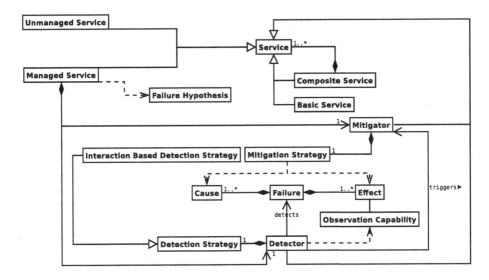

Fig. 6. Models of services

They are shown in parts $(b) - (d)$, and Figure $3-(a)$ illustrates the *Composite Service* integrating the three *Basic Services*.

Services are either *Managed Services* or *Unmanaged Services*. This categorization is orthogonal to services being *Composite* or *Simple*, meaning that every *Composite Service* or *Basic Service* can be either *Managed* or *Unmanaged*. *Unmanaged Services* define system behavior without considering failures, while *Managed Services* are critical concerns of the systems that require failure management.

Managed Services are a type of *Services* and, therefore, they can also be a component of a *Composite Service*. In particular, it is possible to have *Managed Services* that are composed of other *Managed Services*. Each one of them will have a *Detector* and a *Mitigator* that will address failures at its level. Using this schema, by hierarchically composing simpler services in more complex ones and by adding Detectors and Mitigators to the various component services, it is possible to achieve a fine level of granularity in managing failures.

One specific *Service* is a *Detector*. A *Detector* is responsible for monitoring the *Managed Services* it is associated with, and detecting the eventual occurrence of a failure. The *Detector* detects the possible occurrence of a failure based on a *Detection Strategy*. One possible *Detection Strategy* is detection based on *Interactions*. In the next section, we will elaborate further on our model for *Services* and *Interactions*.

Upon occurrence of a *Failure*, the corresponding *Detector* detects the failure by observing its *Effects*. For instance, an unreliable communication medium might loose a message. The effect of this failure is that the recipient would not receive the expected message. A common mechanism for detecting failures is using timeouts. Time is captured in the model in the form of *Deadlines*.

An *Effect* of a failure could be missing a *Deadline*. Each asserted *Deadline* is associated with a *Detector* that is responsible for monitoring that *Deadline*. Note that every failure has one or more *Causes* as well as some *Effects*. The cause of the above failure can be an unreliable communication medium. Note that the same *Effect*, namely not receiving the expected message, might have another *Cause*, such as failure of the sender, rather than the communication channel. Although the *Detector* will detect a failure based on its *Effects*, it might also be able to identify the failure's *Cause* by storing information about the state of the different participating roles, or contained sub-*Services*.

Each *Detector* is associated with a corresponding *Mitigator*. Upon detection of a failure, the *Detector* activates the corresponding *Mitigator* responsible for managing that specific failure. A *Mitigator* is another specific *Service* that is responsible for resolving the faulty state in order to maintain the safety of the system. A *Mitigator* applies its corresponding *Mitigation Strategy* to resolve the faulty state. *Mitigation Strategies* describe what should be done when a specific type of failure happens. Typical *Mitigation Strategies* are replication, changing the mode to a more restricted operation mode, resending in case of a message loss, or ignoring the message in case of a message duplicate. Following the strategy pattern, decoupling the definition of the mitigation strategy from the entity that applies it provides flexibility to the model by allowing future changes to the strategy that is applicable to a specific failure without the need to make any additional modifications to other elements in the system.

This model, allows us to compose a predefined *Unmanaged Service* with a *Detector* and its associated *Mitigator* in order to add failure management to it, creating a *Composite Managed Service*. If multiple failures are identified in one Service, it will be wrapped in multiple layers of *Detectors* and *Mitigators*. This capability provides a seamless means to manage the failures that are found in further iterations of the design/development process, without redefining the existing *Services*.

Note that defining the failure management entities as part of the model is highly encouraged; this captures the possible failures in the system at the very early stages of the design process, specifically during requirements gathering. However, capturing all the possible failures and their detecting and mitigating solutions in the first iteration of the design/development process is not necessary for designing a failsafe system, as it is not usually even possible.

In order to illustrate the application of the *Detectors* and *Mitigators*, consider our case study again. The underwater equipment must work in a very energy efficient manner, and so a critical system function is to make sure that if there is no whale in the pictures taken by the Camera, picture-taking stops right away. Since the wireless communication between the Underwater Site and the Coastal Center is unreliable and might lose messages, there exists the chance that the Whale Detector may decide that there are no whales in the picture and send this message to the Image Filter, but the message may get lost. Waiting for the Camera to take another picture, passing it through the Image Filter and Image Compressor, and resending it would waste energy. In addition, if the response

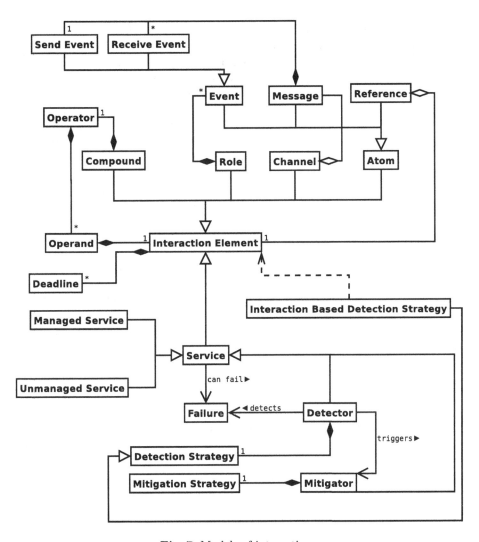

Fig. 7. Models of interactions

of the Whale Detector would be lost several times in a row, the picture taking process would be repeated multiple times before stopping; more energy would be wasted. Note that it also might be the case that the Whale Detector service itself might fail, resulting in no reply to the Underwater Site whatsoever. Hence, sending a Stop message to the Camera in case there is no reply from the Whale Detector is critical.

One way to express this critical requirement is to enforce a time constraint, say 1 second, on the interval between sending the Animal Picture message by the Image Filter and the receipt of the Whale/Not Whale message from the Whale Detector. A *Detector* is then added to the Validate Picture Service. The *Detector* monitors the communications of the Image Filter Service. If the *Detector* observes the transmission of the Animal Picture message by the Image Filter, but the Whale/Not Whale message was not received within 1 second, then a Failure is detected. When the Failure is detected, the *Detector* sends a message to the corresponding *Mitigator*, triggering it to resolve the situation. One possible mitigation is for the *Mitigator* to act on behalf of the ValidatePicture service and to inject a Stop message into the system so that it is delivered to the Camera. Note that if the Image Filter Software or the mapped hardware is assumed to be unreliable as well, we should also enforce a time constraint, say 10 milliseconds, between receipt of a Not Whale message from the Whale Detector and the transmission of the Stop message to the Camera. If the *Detector* detects a failure for this time constraint, again it activates the corresponding *Mitigator*, which sends the Stop message. Note that the communication between the entities of the Underwater Site is considered a wired and reliable communication, and hence, observing the sending of the Stop message assures that the Camera receives it.

One other interesting point in this model is that the Detector can also occasionally detect the Cause of the failure. For instance, the *Detector* can distinguish between the failure of the Image Filter and the failure of the wireless connection or the Coastal Center. If the Picture Message is received by the Image filter, but the Animal picture is not sent within the 1 second interval, then the cause of the failure can be assumed to be the Image Filter. This is also the case if the Not Whale message is received, but the Stop message is not sent within the 10 ms interval.

One final entity of the service model is the *Failure Hypothesis*. In order to verify that a system is fail-safe, we need to make some assumptions and restrictions on how it can fail. Of course there is no way to reason about a system where all pieces of hardware in that system might fail at the same time. A *Failure Hypothesis* captures how the system is assumed to be able to fail while still remaining safe. This information is captured in the form of a *Failure Hypothesis* based on the failure taxonomy presented in the previous section. A *Failure Hypothesis* identifies the entities in the system that can fail. Hence, every *Managed Service* is associated with a *Failure Hypothesis*. A *Failure Hypothesis* is also known by and has an impact on both the *Managed Service*'s *Detector* and *Mitigator*. In our case study, the fact that the Wireless connection might lose messages is part of the *Failure Hypothesis*. If the Image Filter is assumed to be able to fail, then this information is also part of the *Failure Hypothesis*.

4.2   Interaction Model

In this section, we briefly discuss our interaction model for *Services*. A more elaborate explanation of this model can be found in [4]. As illustrated in Figure 7, a *Service* provides a specified functionality, as defined by the interaction of its *Roles*. Hence, a *Service* is captured as a composite *Interaction Element*. This expresses the close relationship we see between services and their defining interaction patterns; it also makes the interaction patterns accessible to defining failure detectors and mitigators.

An *Interaction Element* can be a *Role*, a *Channel*, an *Atom*, or a *Compound*. In an interaction, a *Role* represents the participation of a system entity in an interaction pattern. An *Atom* can be a *Message*, an *Event*, or a *Reference* to another *Service*. An *Event* is either a *Send Event* or a *Receive Event*. *Compound* interaction elements consist of a number of *Interaction Elements* composed by *Operators*. Instances of *Operators* are *Sequence, Loop, Alternative, Parallel* and *Join*, representing sequential composition, repetition, choice, parallel and join composition, respectively.

Note that this interaction model abstracts away from concrete notations – in this text we have used MSCs based on this interaction model to specify the services of our case study in Figure 3. The interaction model can also easily be married with the UML2 sequence diagram and state machine model [8].

5 Deriving Detectors

In the previous section, we identified two distinct types of behavior for failure *Effects*: *Unexpected Behavior* and *Non Occurrence Behavior*. The importance of this classification is evident when we try to devise detectors able to deal with failures that present such effects. From the MSC-based specification of the interaction behavior, it is possible to automatically create two types of detectors, each able to identify one type of failure effect.

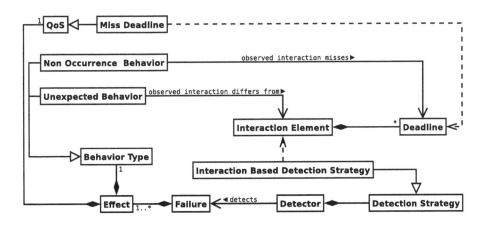

Fig. 8. Relation between detectors, deadlines and effects

Because our specification is based on interactions, failures making the system violate its specification can be identified by observing how the real communication deviates from the expected one. In Figure 8, we have captured the relationship between the failure effects on the system behavior and the interaction elements in an *Interaction Based Detection Strategy*. The *Interaction Element* defines a communication pattern that must be carried out between elements of the system. At run-time it is possible to observe the actual interactions and determine if they deviate from the specified ones.

By their very nature MSCs define causal relationships between messages exchanged. To enable the definition of QoS properties (and in particular of timing properties), we enrich the model by assigning to each interaction element a deadline property that mandates a maximum execution time for the whole interaction[16]. Deadline attributes allow for specification of end-to-end QoS properties. With this addition, we are able to automatically obtain from the specification the two types of detectors we need to identify failures that present either types of effect.

To detect *Unexpected Behaviors*, we can create an observer that analyzes all messages exchanged as part of an interaction fragment and compares the observation to the definition of the corresponding *Interaction Element*. In particular, we are interested in identifying failures at the granularity of Roles. Therefore, each lifeline in the specification MSC identifies the interaction fragment that must be observed.

In previous work, [17,16] we have devised an algorithm that is able to synthesize a state machine for each lifeline in an MSC, capturing the communication behavior of the corresponding role. The input into this algorithm is a set of MSCs such as the one given in Figure 3; we make a closed-world assumption with respect to the interaction sequences that occur in the system under consideration. We derive an automaton for an individual role specification from a given set of MSCs by successively applying four transformation steps: 1. *projection* of the given MSCs onto the role of interest, 2. *state insertion*, i.e. adding missing start and end states before and after every interaction pattern, 3. *transformation* into an automaton by identifying the MSCs as transition paths, and by adding intermediate states accordingly, and 4. *optimization* of the resulting automata. This synthesis algorithm [18] works fully automatically for *causal* MSCs [19], and can handle choice, repetition, concurrency/interleaving and join [7]. Because the algorithm is based on syntactic manipulation of the given MSCs it is oblivious to the underlying MSC semantics – as long as the semantics of the target component model matches the one used for the MSCs serving as input to the algorithm.

Figure 9 shows the state machine obtained by applying the outlined algorithm to the MSC specification for the Camera role. Starting in state _js0_, when a whaleSound is received, the camera takes the picture and sends it to the Image Filter. The camera keeps sending until it receives a Stop signal and returns to its initial state. If the camera is broken and does *not* stop sending pictures when the stop message is received, we would observe a message Picture when the camera is in state _js0_. This would be identified by the system as an *Unexpected Behavior* failure.

Thus, to detect failures, a state machine is run in parallel with the code for each role in the system. For each message sent or received by the role, the state machine takes the transition labeled with the corresponding message name. For a given type of observed message, if it is not possible to find any transition from

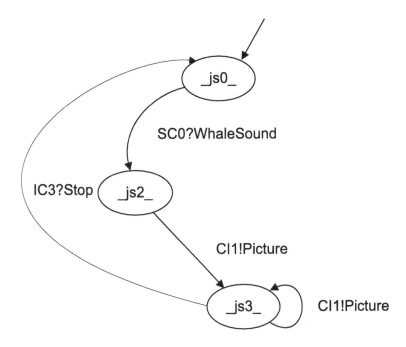

Fig. 9. State machine for the detector of the Camera role

the current automaton state, then a failure is detected. In particular, if the error is in an outgoing message of a role under observation, the role is considered to have failed, and appropriate mitigators are activated.

In general, detecting *Non Occurrence Behavior* requires more information; the simple causal relationship between messages is not enough. In fact, the MSCs in our interaction specification are used to describe purely asynchronous communication patterns. In this scenario, if a communication channel fails, receipt of a message could be delayed forever and may never trigger failure detection. To address this, we have then enriched our model with the *Deadline* entity, which introduces the concept of time into the model. With this addition, we are able to specify QoS requirements that are time-related and to detect failures whose effect is a *Non Occurrence Behavior*. The detector is still based on the observation of messages exchanged. In this case, however, a watchdog timer is activated when an *Interaction Element* message is observed, and it has a timeout defined by the *Deadline* value. When the *Interaction Element*'s last message is observed, the watchdog is deactivated. If the watchdog fires, a *Non Occurrence Behavior* failure is detected.

6   Discussion

The failure management approach we have presented in this paper associates the notion of failures with the interaction patterns that define services. This is particularly suitable in the context of systems of systems integration challenges – here many failures occur and have to be managed at the level of sub-system interplay.

The ontology we have developed effectively constitutes a requirements gathering language for failures throughout the software and systems engineering process – this language can be used informally, or can be translated into formal analysis frameworks supporting test and verification. One possible application for the ontology is to translate it into a set of spreadsheets that are populated and tracked by engineers throughout the development process; this would introduce a structured yet flexible approach to capturing failure management knowledge into the requirements engineering life-cycle. The ontology itself is designed to allow refinement and tailoring to domains other than the one explicitly explored in this text – in many cases this is simply a matter of defining specific failure causes and effects, as well as the corresponding mapping from logical to runtime entities.

The presented approach gives rise to a rich set of research questions. The first issue is in the generation of state machines from message sequence charts. Services (captured by the interactions) are partial specifications of the system. However, in order for the generated state machine to be able to detect *Unexpected Behavior* failures, it must specify the complete communication behavior of each role. Therefore, we must use MSCs to capture a complete specification of the system communication. One way to weaken this requirement is to monitor only a subset of the messages exchanged by each role. This would allow the creation of a partial specification where messages not specified in an MSC are not monitored for failure detection.

Another problem in the creation of *Unexpected Behavior* monitors is that, in general, a nondeterministic state machine can have multiple identically-labeled outgoing transitions from a given state. A state machine of this kind would operate an internal choice that is not detectable by observing the communication during an execution of the system. Without additional information on the internal state of the system, we would have to deal with it by delaying the inference of the chosen transition to the moment where the right choice can be identified – a strategy known as angelic nondeterminism[20]. From the observation point of message traces we have chosen, there is always an equivalent automaton where the next state is unequivocally defined by the observed messages. We then can simply run such an automaton in parallel to the role, as described in the previous section.

Another interesting discussion point is how to plug detectors and mitigators into the service architecture without changing the original unmanaged service interaction descriptions. In fact, we want to have *Detectors* observing the interactions without needing to change the original services. Broadcasting communication infrastructures could enable the transparent integration of detectors. Unfortunately, mitigators are harder to integrate. Sometimes, in fact, there is the need to completely change the message routing policy in order to apply a mitigation strategy. We are currently experimenting with using an enterprise service bus (ESB [21]) based architecture to implement managed services – in fact, ESB provides complete decoupling between routing policies and communicating entities. This is left as future work.

Future work will also investigate how to deal with timing issues in detecting *Non Occurrence Behavior* failures. In particular, research should be conducted into the implementation of a global deadline detection clock that spans distributed entities. Especially for tight QoS timing constraints, detectors and mitigators that are physically separate from the services they manage can introduce unacceptable delays, making failure management impossible. On the other hand, in order for our approach to failure management to work, the probability of detector and mitigator failure must be decoupled from the probability of the failure of the service they apply to. Limitations to the presented approach and options for dealing with those issues will be analyzed in a forthcoming paper.

7 Related Work

Various approaches to failure management have been proposed in the literature. For instance, Fault Tolerant CORBA [22] is an OMG standard for a fault tolerant middleware. Its aim is to provide a transparent framework for dealing with failing objects in CORBA-based applications. This standard has been analyzed and implemented in several research projects (for example, [23]). Similarities with our approach can be found in the concept of fault detectors and recovery services. However, their detectors use heartbeat messages or polling an is_alive method to detect faults. Our approach generalizes this idea and allows us to detect not only crash or deadlock failures, but, in general, unexpected and nonoccurrence behavior failures. Also, the mitigation strategy in our case is more flexible. While FT-CORBA allows only object replication, we can accommodate a much wider set of mitigation strategies [12]. Finally, not relying on heartbeat messages to detect failures, but being able to analyze the normal flow of messages exchanged, our detectors can be deployed on systems where there are tight constraints on communication resources.

Our *Detectors* and *Mitigators* are closely related to the detector and corrector used in [3] by Arora and Kulkarni to achieve failure tolerance. Similarly to our approach they add components to the system in a stepwise manner to address different failures. The main difference is that our work focuses on interactions and gives a global view of the failure as a violation of an end-to-end property, while the work in [3] defines programs as sets of variables and actions operating on variables.

The concept of a *failure hypothesis* needed to enable verification of the system safety is also not new. In [24], for example, a fault model capturing the permitted fault behavior of a physical system is expressed as a separate model called *fault impact*. In our case the failure hypothesis has a larger scope and can encompass also software failures. Moreover we use a different specification technique (MSCs as opposed to Petri nets).

In creating mitigators we can leverage standard techniques for failure management. For example, we plan to leverage techniques similar to N-Version Programming [25] to reduce the risk of implementation errors. The mitigation strategy when a malfunction is detected could be to switch to a reduced functionality safe mode version of the code that probably doesn't contain the error. Moreover, our detectors are generated from the model and contain different code than the handmade implementations in the system. It would also be interesting to extend our model to combine it with architectural reconfiguration approaches such as the one presented in [26,27]. Another technique that could be used in our system is a software black box-like approach. In [28], the authors assign features to modules and add hooks to record procedure calls. They then use a decoder to interpret the collected data and debug eventual errors. In our approach, we start from the model. Moreover we don't need hooks because messages can be spoofed from a communication channel. Also, we already detect failures with detectors, so we can easily provide a software black box that records useful data during execution. In such a scenario, programmers could receive data on failures from running systems and further improve product quality during the lifetime of the system.

8   Conclusion

In this paper, we have presented a model-based approach to failure management. Our models define services by means of interaction patterns – this allows us, in particular, to address failures at the systems-of-systems integration level.

The proposed solution for failure management is based on a failure ontology for the application domain. This ontology disentangles logical architecture from deployment and runtime aspects; this allows us to lift failure management from being an implementation afterthought to *all* phases of the software and systems engineering process. We use the ontology to identify additional services called *Detectors* and *Mitigators* that are in charge of identifying failures and recovering from them. Both detectors and mitigators are associated with *Strategies* we can tailor to specific failure causes and effects. Detectors and Mitigators wrap "unmanaged" into "managed" services. This is useful for extending specifications of "sunny-day scenarios" to take failures into account, without having to alter the original scenarios. This results in a low barrier for introducing the failure management approach. Managed services are hierarchical, which allows us to introduce detectors and mitigators at any level of abstraction/detail.

We have also presented two patterns for deriving *Detectors* from interaction specifications. This technique addresses both unexpected and missing behaviors. Its limitations are in the treatment of missing behaviors when no deadlines are specified, as well as in failures that do not represent themselves at the level of interactions. Introducing time as an explicit modeling concept together with classical architectural strategies such as redundancy, heart-beats and watch-dogs helps alleviate this limitation.

There is ample opportunity for future research. In particular, the coupling of the proposed approach with architectural and design patterns for failure management has the potential for enabling the design of a comprehensive methodological failure management framework that covers the entire software and systems engineering process.

Acknowledgments. Our work was partially supported by NSF grants CCF-0702791 and OCE/GEO #0427924, as well as by funds from the California Institute for Telecommunications and Information Technology (Calit2). The authors are grateful to the organizers and participants of the Monterey workshop 2006 for highly valuable discussion on this subject. We thank Barry Demchak and the reviewers for their insightful comments on this manuscript.

References

1. Mellor, S., Clark, A., Futagami, T.: Special Issue on Model-Driven Development. In: IEEE Software, vol. 20(5), IEEE, Los Alamitos (2003)
2. W3C: Web services architecture (2004),
   http://www.w3.org/TR/2004/NOTE-ws-arch-20040211
3. Arora, A., Kulkarni, S.S.: Component based design of multitolerant systems. IEEE Transactions on Software Engineering 24 (1998)
4. Ermagan, V., Krüger, I., Menarini, M., Mizutani, J.I., Oguchi, K., Weir, D.: Towards Model-Based Failure-Management for Automotive Software. In: Proceedings of the ICSE 2007 Workshop on Software Engineering for Automotive Systems (SEAS) (2007)
5. CI Conceptual Architecture Design Team: Orion cyberinfrastructure conceptual architecture, www.orionprogram.org/advisory/committees/ciarch/default.html
6. ITU-TS: Recommendation Z.120: Message Sequence Chart (MSC) (2004)
7. Krüger, I.H.: Distributed System Design with Message Sequence Charts. PhD thesis, Technische Universität München (2000)
8. OMG: UML 2.1.1 Superstructure Specification. Number formal/07-02-03. OMG (2007)
9. Krüger, I.H.: Capturing Overlapping, Triggered, and Preemptive Collaborations Using MSCs. In: Pezzé, M. (ed.) FASE 2003. LNCS, vol. 2621, pp. 387–402. Springer, Heidelberg (2003)
10. Krüger, I.H., Mathew, R.: Systematic Development and Exploration of Service-Oriented Software Architectures. In: Proceedings of the 4th Working IEEE/IFIP Conference on Software Architecture (WICSA), pp. 177–187. IEEE, Los Alamitos (2004)
11. Leveson, N.G.: Safeware: system safety and computers. ACM Press, New York (1995)
12. Putman, J.: Architecting With Rm-Odp. Prentice-Hall, Englewood Cliffs (2000)
13. Gilliers, F., Kordon, F., Regep, D.: A Model Based Development Approach for Distributed Embedded Systems. In: Wirsing, M., Knapp, A., Balsamo, S. (eds.) RISSEF 2002. LNCS, vol. 2941, pp. 137–151. Springer, Heidelberg (2004)
14. Jackson, E.K., Sztipanovits, J.: Corrected through Construction: A Model-based Approach to Embedded Systems Reality. In: 13th Annual IEEE International Symposium and Workshop on Engineering of Computer Based Systems, IEEE, Los Alamitos (2006)

15. Krüger, I., Meisinger, M., Menarini, M.: Applying Service-Oriented Development to Complex System: a BART case study. In: Kordon, F., Sztipanovits, J. (eds.) Monterey Workshop 2005. LNCS, vol. 4322, Springer, Heidelberg (2007)
16. Ahluwalia, J., Krüger, I.H., Phillips, W., Meisinger, M.: Model-based run-time monitoring of end-to-end deadlines. In: EMSOFT 2005. 5th ACM international conference on Embedded Software, ACM Press, New York (2005)
17. Krüger, I.H., Mathew, R.: Component synthesis from service specifications. In: Leue, S., Systä, T.J. (eds.) Scenarios: Models, Transformations and Tools. LNCS, vol. 3466, Springer, Heidelberg (2005)
18. Krüger, I., Grosu, R., Scholz, P., Broy, M.: From mscs to statecharts. In: Rammig, F.J. (ed.) Distributed and Parallel Embedded Systems, pp. 61–71. Kluwer Academic Publishers, Dordrecht (1999)
19. Finkbeiner, B., Krüger, I.: Using message sequence charts for component-based formal verification. In: Specification and Verification of Component Based Systems (SAVCBS), Iowa State University Workshop at OOPSLA (2001)
20. Back, R., von Wright, J.: Combining Angels, Demons and Miracles in Program Specifications. TCS 100(2), 365–383 (1992)
21. Krüger, I., Meisinger, M., Menarini, M., Pasco, S.: Rapid Systems of Systems Integration - Combining an Architecture-Centric Approach with Enterprise Service Bus Infrastructure. In: 2006 IEEE International Conference on Information Reuse and Integration (IRI 2006), IEEE Systems, Man, and Cybernetics Society, pp. 51–56 (2006)
22. OMG: Fault Tolerant CORBA. vol. formal/04-03-21. OMG (2004)
23. Baldoni, R., Marchetti, C., Virgillito, A., Zito, F.: Failure management for ft-corba applications. In: WORDS 2001. Proceedings of the Sixth International Workshop on Object-Oriented Real-Time Dependable Systems, IEEE, Los Alamitos (2001)
24. Völzer, H.: Verifying fault tolerance of distributed algorithms formally – an example. In: Proceedings of the International Conference on Application of Concurrency to System Design, IEEE, Los Alamitos (1998)
25. Chen, L., Avizienis, A.: N-Version Programming: A Fault-Tolerance Approach to Reliability of Software Operation. In: Proc. 8th IEEE Int. Symp. on Fault-Tolerant Computing (FTCS-8), pp. 3–9 (1978)
26. Giese, H., Henkler, S.: Architecture-driven platform independent deterministic replay for distributed hard real-time systems. In: Proceedings of the ISSTA 2006 workshop on Role of software architecture for testing and analysis, pp. 28–38 (2006)
27. Tichy, M., Schilling, D., Giese, H.: Design of self-managing dependable systems with UML and fault tolerance patterns. In: Proceedings of the 1st ACM SIGSOFT workshop on Self-managed systems, pp. 105–109 (2004)
28. Elbaum, S., Munson, J.: Software Black Box: an Alternative Mechanism for Failure Analysis. In: International Symposium on Software Reliability Engineering, pp. 365–376 (2000)

A Methodology and Supporting Tools for the Development of Component-Based Embedded Systems

Marc Poulhiès[1,2], Jacques Pulou[2], Christophe Rippert[1], and Joseph Sifakis[1]

[1] VERIMAG
[2] France Telecom R&D
{poulhies, rippert, sifakis}@imag.fr, jacques.pulou@orange-ftgroup.com

Abstract. The paper presents a methodology and supporting tools for developing component-based embedded systems running on resource-limited hardware platforms. The methodology combines two complementary component frameworks in an integrated tool chain: BIP and THINK. BIP is a framework for model-based development including a language for the description of heterogeneous systems, as well as associated simulation and verification tools. THINK is a software component framework for the generation of small-footprint embedded systems. The tool chain allows generation, from system models described in BIP, of a set of functionally equivalent THINK components. From these and libraries including OS services for a given hardware platform, a minimal system can be generated. We illustrate the results by modeling and implementing a software MPEG encoder on an iPod.

1 Introduction

Embedded systems development is subject to strong requirements for optimality in the use of resources, and correctness with respect to non-functional properties, as well as requirements for time-to-market and low cost through reuse and easy customization.

We need holistic methodologies and supporting tools for all development activities from application software to implementation. The methodologies should be component-based to ease code reuse, modularity, reconfiguration and allow implementations having a minimal footprint by only including the necessary services. Components allow abstractions for structuring code according to a logical separation of concerns. For early design error detection, application of validation and analysis techniques is essential, especially to guarantee non-functional properties. Finally, the methodologies should rely on automated implementation techniques that, for a given hardware platform, make the best possible use of its characteristics and include only strictly necessary OS services.

Model-based development techniques aim at bridging the gap between application software and its implementation by allowing predictability and guidance through analysis of global models of the system under development. They offer in

F. Kordon and O. Sokolsky (Eds.): Monterey Workshop 2006, LNCS 4888, pp. 75–96, 2007.

principle, domain-specific abstractions independent of programming languages and implementation choices. Nevertheless, they rely on system component models, which drastically differ from software component models used for operating systems and middleware [1,2,3]. For system description, components should encompass real-time behavior, rich interfaces and a notion of composition for natural description of heterogeneous interaction and computation. In contrast, software components allow structuring and reuse of functions and associated data. They use point-to-point interaction (*e.g.* function calls) through binding interface specifications.

We present a fully component-based methodology and supporting tools for the development of real-time embedded systems. The methodology combines two complementary component frameworks in an integrated tool chain: BIP [4,5] and THINK [6] (see Figure 1). BIP is a framework for model-based development including a language for the description of heterogeneous real-time systems, as well as associated simulation and verification tools. THINK is a software component framework for the generation of small-footprint embedded systems. Our tool chain allows generation, from system models described in BIP, of a set of functionally equivalent THINK components. From these and libraries including OS services, a minimal system is generated for a given hardware platform.

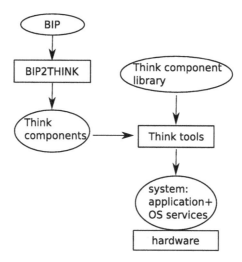

Fig. 1. The BIP to THINK tool-chain

The paper deals with the integration of component-based approaches used at the two ends of the development chain. Usually, model-based techniques focus on system description and analysis while they provide limited or very specific support for component-based implementation. For instance, tools supporting heterogeneous description, such as Ptolemy [7] or Metropolis [8], do not address implementation issues. Others, such as MetaH [9], Giotto [10] or ROOM [11], rely on given models of computation and provide support for specific implementations.

Component-based techniques for operating systems and middleware lack analysis capabilities [1]. This motivates work on modeling middleware and operating systems, for instance to evaluate performance and validate configuration mechanisms as in [12]. However, such works typically use a standard system architecture with all system services located in the kernel, and providing no support for applications to control the behavior of low-level services. This requires modeling the kernel in order to validate its runtime behavior, a very difficult task considering the complexity of standard kernels.

In contrast, THINK is based on the exokernel paradigm [13] leading to minimal solutions involving only the strictly necessary services. Using this paradigm permits to move all the critical services (such as scheduling for instance) into the application space, where they can be validated with the applications. This leaves only very basic functionalities into the nano-kernel, which can be tested separately to guarantee their proper runtime behavior. THINK is a mature exokernel technology which has been successfully used to generate implementations for very constrained platforms such as smart cards [14], AVR (ATmega 2561, 8bits microprocessor, 8Kb RAM, 256Kb FLASH) as well as ARM platforms (32Mb RAM, 64Mb FLASH).

Our work integrates heterogeneous system modeling and analysis with a general component-based implementation techniques. In this respect, it has similar objectives with the work around nesC/TOSSIM/TinyOS environment for the development of wireless sensor networks [15,16,17]. This framework has a more narrow application scope and the integration between programming, simulation and implementation tools is much stronger. However, in contrast with TinyOS, THINK preserves the components as runtime entities, permitting dynamic reconfiguration or component replacement. Our work has also some similarities with VEST [18]. However, VEST relies upon a thread-based model, whereas neither BIP nor THINK adopt any specific behavioral model.

The paper is organized as follows. Section 2 presents the BIP component framework used to model the behavior and structure of systems. Section 3 describes the THINK framework which provides the library and tool chain used to generate system implementations. The generation tool used to translate a BIP description to a THINK system is presented in Section 4. A quantitative evaluation of the results on a software MPEG encoder is presented in Section 5.

2   The BIP Component Model

BIP[5,19] (*Behavior, Interaction, Priority*) is a framework for modeling heterogeneous real-time components. BIP supports a methodology for building components from:

- *atomic* components, a class of components with behavior specified as a set of transitions and having empty interaction and priority layers. Triggers of transitions include *ports* which are action names used for synchronization.
- *connectors* used to specify possible interaction patterns between ports of atomic components.

– *priority relations* used to select amongst possible interactions according to conditions depending on the state of the integrated atomic components.

The application of this methodology leads to layered components (see fig 2). The lower layer describes the behavior of a component as a set of atomic components; the intermediate layer includes connectors describing interactions between transitions of the layer underneath; the upper layer consists of a set of priority rules used to describe scheduling policies for interactions.

This methodology allows a clear separation between behavior and structure of a system (interactions and priorities).

The implementation of the BIP component framework includes a language for hierarchical component modeling, and a code generator for an execution platform on Linux. The execution platform allows simulation as well as exhaustive state space enumeration. The generated models can be validated by using techniques available in Verimag's IF toolset [20,21].

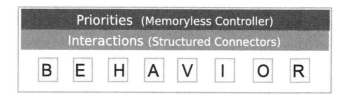

Fig. 2. Layered component model

We provide a description of the main features of the BIP language.

2.1 Atomic Components

An atomic component consists of:

– A set of *ports* $P = \{p_1 \ldots p_n\}$. Ports are action names used for synchronization with other components.
– A set of *control states* $S = \{s_1 \ldots s_k\}$. Control states denote locations at which the components await for synchronization.
– A set of *variables* V used to store (local) data.
– A set of transitions modeling atomic computation steps. A transition is a tuple of the form (s_1, p, g_p, f_p, s_2), representing a step from control state s_1 to s_2. It can be executed if the guard (boolean condition on V) g_p is true and some interaction including port p is offered. Its execution is an atomic sequence of two microsteps:
  1. an interaction including p which involves synchronization between components with possible exchange of data, followed by
  2. an internal computation specified by the function f_p on V. That is, if v is a valuation of V after the interaction, then $f_p(v)$ is the new valuation when the transition is completed.

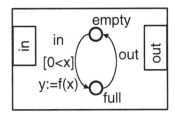

Fig. 3. An atomic component

Figure 3 shows an atomic reactive component with two ports *in*, *out*, variables
x, y, and control states *empty*, *full*. At control state *empty*, the transition
labeled *in* is possible if $0 < x$. Interactions through *in* may modify the variable
x . They are immediately followed by the computation of a new value for y. From
control state *full*, the transition labeled *out* can occur. The omission of guard
and function for this transition means that the associated guard is *true* and the
internal computation microstep is empty. The syntax for atomic components in
BIP is the following:

atom::=
    component *component_id*
        port [**complete** | **incomplete**] *port_id*⁺
        [**data** *type_id data_id*⁺]
        behavior
        {**state** *state_id*
            {**on** *port_id* [**provided** *guard*]
            [**do** *statement*] **to** *state_id*}⁺}⁺
        end
    end

That is, an atomic component consists of a declaration followed by the definition
of its behavior. Declaration consists of ports and data. Ports are identifiers and
have attributes complete and incomplete whose meaning will be explained in 2.2.
For data basic C types can be used. In the behavior, *guard* and *statement* are
C expressions and statements respectively. We assume that these are adequately
restricted to respect the atomicity assumption for transitions e.g. no side effects,
guaranteed termination.

    Behavior is defined by a set of transitions. The keyword **state** is followed by a
control state and the list of outgoing transitions from this state. Each transition
is labelled by a port identifier followed by its guard, function and a target state.

    The BIP description of the reactive component of figure 3 is:

component *Reactive*
    port *in*, *out*
    data int x, y
    behavior

```
      state empty
         on in provided 0 < x do y:=f(x) to full
      state full
         on out to empty
   end
end
```

The following example shows an atomic component modeling the control of a simple preemptable task:

```
component Task
   port complete awake,begin,finish
   port incomplete preempt, resume
   behavior
      state IDLE
         on awake to WAIT
      state WAIT
         on begin to EXECUTE
      state EXECUTE
         on finish to IDLE
         on preempt to SUSPEND
      state SUSPEND
         on resume to EXECUTE
   end
end
```

The component has four control states called IDLE, WAIT, EXECUTE and SUSPEND, five ports called awake, begin, finish, preempt and resume. The ports have attributes *complete* and *incomplete* which characterize the way they synchronize with other ports to form *interactions* (see next section).

2.2   Connectors and Interactions

Components are built from a set of atomic components with disjoint sets of names for ports, control states, variables and transitions.

Notation: We simplify the notation for sets of ports in the following manner. We write $p_1|p_2|p_3|p_4$ for the set $\{p_1, p_2, p_3, p_4\}$ by considering that singletons are composed by using the associative and commutative operation $|$.

A connector γ is a set of ports of atomic components which can be involved in an interaction. We assume that connectors contain at most one port from each atomic component. An interaction of γ is any non empty subset of this set. For example, if p_1, p_2, p_3 are ports of distinct atomic components, then the connector $\gamma = p_1|p_2|p_3$ has seven interactions: $p_1, p_2, p_3, p_1|p_2, p_1|p_3, p_2|p_3, p_1|p_2|p_3$. Each non trivial interaction i.e., interaction with more than one port, represents a synchronization between transitions labeled with its ports.

Following results in [22], we introduce a typing mechanism to specify the *feasible* interactions of a connector γ, in particular to express the following two basic modes of synchronization:

- Strong synchronization or rendezvous, when the only feasible interaction of γ is the maximal one, i.e., it contains all the ports of γ.
- Weak synchronization or broadcast, when feasible interactions are all those containing a particular port which initiates the broadcast. That is, if $\gamma = p_1|p_2|p_3$ and the broadcast is initiated by p_1, then the feasible interactions are $p_1, p_1|p_2, p_1|p_3, p_1|p_2|p_3$.

A system run is a sequence of feasible interactions.

The typing mechanism distinguishes between *complete* and *incomplete* interactions with the following restriction: All the interactions containing some *complete* interaction are complete; dually, all the interactions contained in incomplete interactions are incomplete. An interaction of a connector is *feasible* if it is complete or if it is maximal.

Preservation of completeness by inclusion of interactions allows a simple characterization of interaction types. It is sufficient, for a connector γ to give the set of its minimal complete interactions. For example, if $\gamma = p_1|p_2|p_3|p_4$ and the minimal complete interactions are p_1 and $p_2|p_3$, then the set of the feasible interactions are p_1, $p_2|p_3$, $p_1|p_4$, $p_2|p_3|p_4$, $p_1|p_2|p_3$, $p_1|p_2|p_3|p_4$.

If the set of the complete interactions of a connector is empty, that is all its interactions are incomplete, then synchronization is by rendezvous: the only feasible interaction involves all the ports of the connector (this is the maximal incomplete interaction of the connector), see figure 4(a). Broadcast through a port p_1 triggering transitions labeled by ports $p_2, \ldots, p_n$ can be specified by taking p_1 as the only minimal complete interaction.

The syntax for connectors is the following:

interaction ::= *port_id*$^+$
connector::=
    connector *conn_id* = *port_id*$^+$
    [**complete** = interaction$^+$]
    [**behavior**
        {**on** interaction [**provided** *guard*] [**do** *statement*]}$^+$
    end]

That is, a connector description includes its set of ports followed by the optional list of its minimal complete interactions and its behavior. If the list of the minimal complete interactions is omitted, then this is considered to be empty. Connectors may have behavior specified as for transitions, by a set of guarded commands associated with feasible interactions. If $\alpha = p_1|p_2|...|p_n$ is a feasible interaction then its behavior is described by a statement of the form: **on** α **provided** G_α **do** F_α, where G_α and F_α are respectively a guard and a statement representing a function on the variables of the components involved in the interaction. As for atomic components, guards and statements are C expressions and statements respectively.

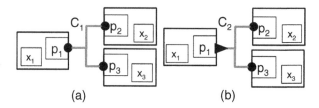

Fig. 4. Interaction types

The execution of α is possible if G_α is *true*. It atomically changes the global valuation v of the synchronized components to $F_\alpha(v)$.

We use a graphical notation for connectors in the form of trees.

We denote an incomplete singleton interaction by a bullet on the corresponding port and an incomplete singleton interaction by a triangle. A generalisation of this notation is possible to describe hierarchical connectors [23]. For example, consider the connector C_1 described below:

connector $C_1 = p_1|p_2|p_3$
behavior
    on $p_1|p_2|p_3$ **provided** $\neg(x_1 = x_2 = x_3)$
    do $x_1, x_2, x_3 := \text{MAX}(x_1, x_2, x_3)$
end

It represents a strong synchronization between p_1, p_2 and p_3 which is graphically represented in figure 4(a), where the singleton incomplete interactions p_1, p_2, p_3 are marked by bullets. The behavior for the interaction $p_1|p_2|p_3$ involves a data transfer between the interacting components: the variables x_i are assigned the maximum of their values if they are not equal.

The following connector describes a broadcast initiated by p_1. The corresponding graphical representation is shown in fig 4(b).

connector $C_2 = p_1|p_2|p_3$
complete $= p_1$
behavior
    on p_1 **do** skip
    on $p_1|p_2$ **do** $x_2 := x_1$
    on $p_1|p_3$ **do** $x_3 := x_1$
    on $p_1|p_2|p_3$ **do** $x_2, x_3 := x_1$
end

This connector describes transfer of value from x_1 to x_2 and x_3.

Notice that contrary to other formalisms, BIP does not allow explicit distinction between inputs and outputs. For simple data flow relations, variables can be interpreted as inputs or outputs. For instance, x_1 is an output and x_2, x_3 are inputs in C_2.

2.3   Priorities

Given a system of interacting components, priorities are used to filter interactions amongst the feasible ones depending on given conditions. The syntax for priorities is the following:

priority::=
     priority *priority_id* [**if** *cond*] interaction < interaction

That is, priorities are a set of rules, each consisting of an ordered pair of interactions associated with a condition (*cond*). The condition is a boolean expression in C on the variables of the components involved in the interactions. When the condition holds and both interactions are enabled, only the higher one is possible. Conditions can be omitted for static priorities.

Notation: We simplify the notation for repetitive rules. It is possible to have a set of interactions instead of a single interaction in the previous pair. All the interactions in the left hand side set have a lower priority than all the interactions in the right hand side set.

The *System* example given in section 2.4 illustrates the use of priorities.

2.4   Compound Components

A compound component allows defining new components from existing sub-components (atoms or compounds) by creating their instances, specifying the connectors between them and the priorities. The syntax of a compound component is defined by:

compound::=
     component *component_id*
          {**contains** *type_id* {*instance_id*[*parameters*]}$^+$}$^+$
          [connector$^+$]
          [priority$^+$]
     end

The instances can have parameters providing initial values to their variables through a named association.

An example of a compound component named *System* is shown in figure 5. It is the serial connection of three reactive components, defined as:

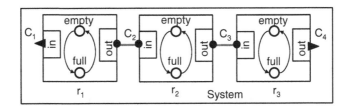

Fig. 5. A compound component

component $System$
   contains $Reactive$ r_1, r_2, r_3
   connector $C_1 = r_1.in$
   complete $= r_1.in$
   connector $C_2 = r_1.out|r_2.in$
   behavior
      on $r_1.out|r_2.in$ **do** $r_2.x := r_1.y$
   end
   connector $C_3 = r_2.out|r_3.in$
   behavior
      on $r_2.out|r_3.in$ **do** $r_3.x := r_2.y$
   end
   connector $C_4 = r_3.out$
   complete $= r3.out$
   priority P_1 $r_1.in < r_2.out|r_3.in$
   priority P_2 $r_1.in < r_3.out$
   priority P_3 $r_1.out|r_2.in < r_3.out$
end

We use priorities to enforce a causal order of execution as follows: once there is an in through C_1, the data are processed and propagated sequentially, finally producing an out through C_4 before a new in occurs through C_1. This is achieved by a priority order which is the inverse of the causal order.

The following example shows a compound component obtained by composition of three instances `task1`, `task2` and `task3` of the atomic component `Task`, given in the previous example in section 2.1.

component $FPPS$
   contains $Task$ $task1$, $task2$, $task3$
   connector $beg1 = task1.begin, task2.preempt,task3.preempt$
   connector $beg2 = task2.begin, task1.preempt,task3.preempt$
   connector $beg3 = task3.begin, task1.preempt,task2.preempt$
   connector $fin1\_res2 = task1.finish, task2.resume$
   connector $fin1\_res3 = task1.finish, task3.resume$
   connector $fin2\_res1 = task2.finish, task1.resume$
   connector $fin2\_res3 = task2.finish, task3.resume$
   connector $fin3\_res1 = task3.finish, task1.resume$
   connector $fin3\_res2 = task3.finish, task2.resume$
   priority
// Priorities are shown below
end

The connectors are used to enforce mutual exclusion, that is, at most one task can be in state `EXECUTE`. For example, the connector `begi` is used to force preemption by `taski` of the other tasks when they are at state `EXECUTE`. The connector `fini_resj`$(i \neq j)$ is used to resume preempted tasks when `taski` finishes. It is easy to check mutual exclusion between tasks in the compound component.

We show below the three types of rules used to enforce decreasing priorities between the tasks.Rules $\texttt{beg}i\_j(i \neq j)$ for beginning tasks of higher priority. Rules $\texttt{beg}i\texttt{pre}j$ to avoid preemption of tasks of higher priority. Finally, the rule $\texttt{fin1\_2\_3}$ ensures that when both **task2** and **task3** are suspended, **task2** will resume.

priority // resume task2 if both task3 and
// task2 are suspended
priority fin1_2_3 $task1.finish|task3.resume < task1.finish|task2.resume$
// do not start 3 if 1 is ready
priority beg1_3 $task3.begin, task3.begin|task1.preempt, task3.begin|task2.preempt$
     $< task1.begin$
// do not start 2 if 1 is ready
priority beg1_2 $task2.begin, task2.begin|task1.preempt, task2.begin|task3.preempt$
     $< task1.begin$
// do not start 3 if 2 is ready
priority beg2_3 $task3.begin, task3.begin|task2.preempt, task3.begin|task1.preempt$
     $< task2.begin$
// do not start 2 if 1 is executing
priority beg2pre1 $task2.begin|task1.preempt < task1.preempt$
// do not start 3 if 1 is executing
priority beg3pre1 $task3.begin|task1.preempt < task1.preempt$
// do not start 3 if 2 is executing
priority beg3pre2 $task3.begin|task2.preempt < task2.preempt$

2.5   Implementation

The implementation of the BIP framework (see figure 6) includes a frontend for editing and parsing BIP programs, and a dedicated platform for the validation of models. The execution platform (BIP/Linux Platform on fig. 6) consists of an Engine and software infrastructure for executing the models. It directly implements BIP's operational semantics in the following manner:

At a given control state, an atomic component waits for interactions through the ports of the transitions enabled at that state. The Engine has access to the connectors and the priority rules of the compound components. When all the atomic components are waiting for interaction, the Engine:

1. computes the possible interactions;
2. filters by using priority rules the possible interactions by considering only the maximal ones according to the priority orders;
3. chooses and executes one maximal interaction. The execution may involve transfer of data between the interacting components. These are notified at the end of the transfer to continue the execution of their interacting transitions.

The platform allows state space exploration and provides access to the model-checking tools of the IF toolset [20,21]. It generates a finite state model that is

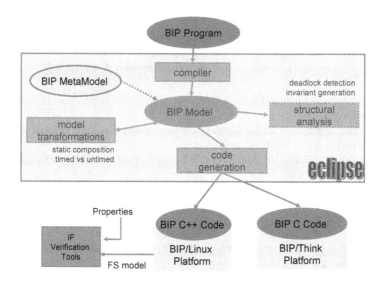

Fig. 6. BIP Framework

fed to the IF tools permitting to validate BIP models and ensure that they meet properties such as deadlock-freedom, state invariants and schedulability.

For instance, it is easy to check that the FPPS example is deadlock-free. For schedulability analysis, a timed BIP model is needed. It can be obtained by adding timing constraints (*e.g.* enforcing periodicity of the awake port and worst case execution times on the finish port) to the system model. Timing constraints are expressed in BIP by using variables modeling clocks following the hybrid automata paradigm [24]. More information about modeling real-time systems in BIP can be found at [19].

3   The Think Framework

THINK[6,25] (*THink Is Not a Kernel*) is a software framework for the development of small-footprint embedded systems. It includes a programming model, a library of operating system abstractions, and a set of tools dedicated to automatize the configuration and building processes.

THINK is an implementation of the Fractal component model [26]. Fractal has been implemented on various software platforms (Java [27], .Net, C++ [28], etc.) and for various uses (middlewares, multimedia applications, aspect-oriented programming, etc.). THINK is a C/assembly implementation of Fractal aiming as easing the development of low-footprint embedded systems. Fractal is a hierarchical component model which advocates design patterns, such as separation of concerns for instance, to reduce development and maintenance costs of complex software systems. A component in Fractal consists of two parts: a functional core which implements the service provided by the component, and a control layer used to manage the component itself and implement non-functional properties. Fractal programming model is based on the *export-bind* design pattern, which guarantees the flexibility of the composition and permits to develop modular implementations of system services. Components in Fractal can be dynamically reconfigured or replaced due to the separation between the functional part of a component and its control interface [29]. This programming model is a major asset compared to similar system-building tools such as the OSKit [30] for instance, as it permits to manage components as runtime entities which can be easily reconfigurated or replaced.

THINK includes a library of standard system abstractions optimized for various embedded platforms (ARM, PowerPC, Xscale, AVR, etc) that can be used to build minimal systems suitable for execution on severely constrained hardware platforms. THINK includes both platform-independent services (*i.e.* memory manager, TCP/IP stack, file-systems, etc.) and services depending on the characteristics of the underlying hardware (*i.e.* MMU manager, NIC and IDE drivers, etc.). The modularity of the Fractal component model permits to link only the required services, without having to manage cross-dependencies between modules as this is often the case in monolithic kernels. This flexibility is a major asset with respect to traditional embedded operating systems which typically include all the system services that could possibly be used by applications, resulting in a major waste of memory for embedded applications. THINK is thus especially well suited for resource-limited embedded systems as it permits to build dedicated runtime environments including only the system abstractions needed by the embedded applications.

THINK offers various tools easing the configuration and building of the system. The structure of the system is described using an Architecture Description Language (ADL) that permits to specify which component must be included in the system and the static links between the components. An Interface Description Language is used to describe the services implemented by the components and how they can interact. A generation chain takes these descriptions and automatically generates a minimal system composed of the applications, the selected system services and the software framework needed to make them interact.

4   The BIP to Think Compiler

We developed a compiler which generates THINK components from BIP source code, as well as the glue code needed to bind them (C and ADL source files). Figure 7 depicts the translation process, which preserves the structure of BIP models. Atomic components are translated into THINK components. For each connector a THINK component is generated. Priorities are implemented by using a specific THINK component. Finally, an Engine component is used to implement the operational semantics of BIP. Checking the correctness of the translation can be decomposed into two steps:

- checking the correctness of each individual translation for atomic components, connectors and priorities. These translations are simple expansions of the BIP code which are easy to check.
- checking correctness of the Engine which is the only active component. The Engine implements the semantics in the form of a simple automaton (see figure 8).

Bellow, we illustrate the method by using the FPPS example.

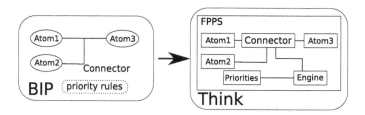

Fig. 7. The BIP to THINK translation process

4.1 Atomic Components

Each BIP atomic component is mapped into a THINK component. Each data variable of an atomic BIP component is translated into an interface (Data) exported by the corresponding primitive THINK component. The interface consists in two simple methods get and set.

Similarly, each port of an atomic BIP component is translated into an interface (Port) with 2 main methods: isSynced, to evaluate the guard of the transition associated with this port, and execute, to compute the function of this transition. We provide below the code generated for the port begin and the transition from state WAIT to EXECUTE:

```
#define TASK_EXECUTE 3

// self variable is the Task component
//   instance reference used to access
//   bound interfaces and component's
//   variables
_enter_state_EXECUTE (Taskdata *self) {
  reset_ports(self);
  self->finish_port = 1;
  self->preempt_port = 1;
  self->state = TASK_EXECUTE;
}

_begin_execute (Taskdata *self){
  if (self->state == TASK_WAIT){
    _enter_state_EXECUTE(self);
  }
}
```

Notice that when a state is entered (method _enter_state_EXECUTE here), the variables associated with ports (finish_port and preempt_port, ...) are reset (*i.e.* set to 0) and only the variables associated with the ports that can be enabled (*ie.* the port labels an outgoing transition from present state and its guard (if any) evaluates to true) are toggled. Interactions eligible for execution must have their port variables set to 1.

4.2 Connector Components

Each connector of a BIP description is translated into a THINK component. This component is bound to the Port interface of each port of the connector and exports a Connector interface. If the connector has guarded commands, it is also bound to the Data interface of each involved variable.

The connector component computes the feasible interactions of the connector and triggers the execution of a maximal one, when it is needed. This is implemented by using 2 methods:

- execute which executes one maximal feasible interaction of the connector and returns false if there is no feasible interaction;
- isLegal which tests whether there is at least one feasible interaction to execute.

A connector component can also inhibit some interaction so as to respect priorities (see 4.3). This is implemented by 2 methods:

- inhibit(id) method which marks the id interaction as not eligible
- the isInteractionLegal(id) that tests whether or not the id interaction is feasible.

We provide below the isLegal and execute methods for a connector connecting port begin of the component task1, and ports preempt of components task2 and task3. The compiler is able to statically compute the maximum interaction and stores it in the MAX_INT macro. The example below shows a *broadcast* synchronization used when the first task begins (connector beg1):

```
// max interaction code
#define MAX_INT 0x0007
// connector local port coding
#define TASK1_BEGIN   0x1
#define TASK2_PREEMPT 0x2
#define TASK3_PREEMPT 0x4

// self variable is the connector component
//   instance reference
bool isLegal(beg1data *self) {
// this mask has 1 bit for each port
  self->port_mask = 0;
//ask if task1.begin is synced or not
  if(CALL(self->task1_begin, isSynced)){
```

```
    self->port_mask  |= TASK1_BEGIN;
  }
  if(CALL(self->task2_preempt, isSynced)){
    self->port_mask  |= TASK2_PREEMPT;
  }
  if(CALL(self->task3_preempt, isSynced)){
    self->port_mask  |= TASK3_PREEMPT;
  }
// legal iff begin port synced
  return (self->port_mask & TASK1_BEGIN);
}

bool execute(beg1data *self){
// if begin not synced, nothing to execute
  if (!(self->port_mask & TASK1_BEGIN)) {
    return 1;
  }
//notify all synced ports
  if (self->port_mask & TASK1_BEGIN){
    CALL(self->task1_begin, execute);
  }
  if (self->port_mask & TASK2_PREEMPT){
    CALL(self->task2_preempt, execute);
  }
  if (self->port_mask & TASK3_PREEMPT){
    CALL(self->task3_preempt, execute);
  }
  return 0;
}
```

4.3   The Priority Component

All BIP priority rules are implemented into a single THINK component. This
component is bound to the Connector interface of each involved connector and
to the Data interface of each variable used in the guards. It exports a simple
Priority interface which includes the method apply. This method sequentially
applies all the priority rules in the system. For example, one relation of the BIP
priority rule beg1_3 from the previous example is translated into:

```
// beg3 : task3.begin, task2.preempt
//       < beg1 : task1.begin

// self variable is the priority component
// instance reference

// guard is empty
guard = 1;
// low prio connector : beg2
cn_low = self->beg2;
```

```
// high prio connector : beg1
cn_high = self->beg1;
iid_low = BEG2_TASK2_BEGIN |
  BEG2_TASK3_PREEMPT ;
// high prio inter. id (iid)
iid_high = BEG1_TASK1_BEGIN ;

// ask high prio connector if it is legal
// and inhibit inter on lower prio connector
// if needed
if (guard && CALL(cn_high,
 isInteractionLegal, iid_high))
  CALL(cn_low, inhibit, iid_low);
```

4.4   The Engine

The `Engine` component implements the BIP Engine using a THINK component. It contains the entry point of the system generated by THINK and is responsible for scheduling the computation. It runs an infinite loop (see figure 8) choosing one maximal feasible interaction out of all possible ones and executing it. The Engine first builds a list of connectors for which at least one interaction is feasible (using the `isLegal` method for connectors), then it asks the priority component to apply priorities (using the `apply` method). Finally, it chooses a connector from the previous list and executes it (using the `execute` method of the connector).

4.5   Deployment

Figure 9 shows the architecture generated for `FPPS` after it has been deployed (running). For the sake of clarity, only one connector component is represented.

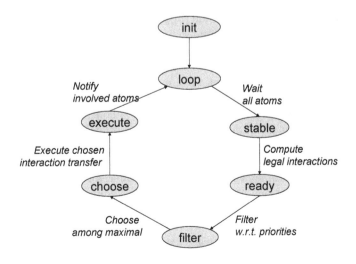

Fig. 8. Engine's loop

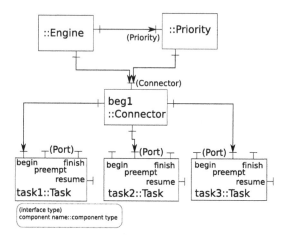

Fig. 9. The generated system after deployment

The FPPS example described in BIP in the previous section includes three tasks running in mutual exclusion. This property has been validated on the BIP code using model-checking tools. The correctness of the translation process ensures that mutual exclusion between the three tasks is respected in the code generated by the BIP2Think compiler.

5   Evaluation

To illustrate our methodology and evaluate the performances and memory-footprint of the generated system, we considered a software MPEG encoder. We started from monolithic legacy C code (approx. 7000 lines of code). We used BIP as a programming model for componentizing the C code so as to reveal causality dependencies between functions. This led to a BIP model consisting of 20 components and 34 connectors. A high-level decomposition of the BIP encoder model in shown below. Bullets represent incomplete ports and thick lines represent buffered connections (*i.e* 2 connectors with a buffer component in the middle).

We used scheduling policies proposed in [31] to control the execution of the model so as to respect given deadlines and optimize quality. The BIP to THINK compiler produces 56 components. The resulting code is 6300 lines of C code and 1000 lines of ADL code.

We generated an implementation of the encoder for an Apple iPod Video on which we only used one of the two ARM cores running at 80Mhz. The test consists in the encoding of 2 different videos.

To estimate the overhead added by the BIP componentization, we compare the generated encoder system against a monolithic implementation derived from the original encoder source code (*i.e.* without BIP or THINK). Results are given on Figures 11 and 12.

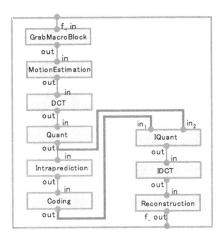

Fig. 10. BIP encoder model

Resolution	Length	Encoding time	Speed
(in pixels)	(in frames)	(in seconds)	(in fps)
320×240	40	500	0.08
64×48	161	77	2

Fig. 11. Performances on the iPod Video for the BIP+THINK encoder

Resolution	Length	Encoding time	Speed
(in pixels)	(in frames)	(in seconds)	(in fps)
320×240	40	200	0.203
64×48	161	37	4.3

Fig. 12. Performances on the iPod Video for the monolithic encoder

The overall encoding frame rate seems reasonable given the low CPU frequency and memory bandwidth of the iPod. Figure 12 shows an overhead in performance of roughly 100% for the BIP+THINK version. This is reasonably good considering that our compiler is still in an early stage of development and has no optimization features. A more detailed analysis of the overheads by profiling, shows that this is due for approximately 66% to execution of connectors and for 33% to execution of priority rules. These can be reduced by code optimization. One possible optimization is to replace the priority component and take into account priorities at compile time by restricting the guards of the atomic components. This solution is more efficient but less modular as it is not possible to incrementally modify priorities. A similar optimization can be applied for connectors. It is possible, by using BIP's operational semantics, to replace two components by a single product component. The execution of connectors between composed components becomes an internal transition of the product component. This avoids communication overheard but also leads to a less modular solution.

The system size (including the video encoder) is 300Kb for the BIP+THINK and 216Kb for the monolithic version which results in a 38% overhead in size. For comparison, a regular iPod linux kernel weights more than 1Mb without any application code.

6   Conclusion and Future Work

We presented a methodology and tools for the design, validation and implementation of component-based systems. The methodology integrates two existing component frameworks: one for high-level system description and analysis, the other for component-based execution and reconfiguration. BIP allows high-level system descriptions which can be simulated and validated on a workstation before being deployed on the target embedded platform. THINK offers a large library of system services, already optimized for embedded hardware platforms, to produce a minimal system, based on the modularity of the library and compilation chain.

Integration is through a transformation preserving not only the semantics but also the structure of the system model. The implementation includes a set of components for scheduling, interconnect and functionality, which can be dynamically reconfigured. Rigorous operational semantics of BIP allows application of state-of-the-art validation techniques on system models for checking properties such as deadlock-freedom, state invariants and schedulability. Model validation implies validation of the implementation, provided that the tool chain and the low-level services included in the system are correct. This is ensured by the systematic approach used in the translator which maps BIP concepts directly into THINK components, and by the simplicity of the nano-kernel which includes only basic services, due to the exokernel architecture.

Bare-machine implementation is particularly appropriate for embedded systems. It allows tailored, lightweight, low-overhead solutions and precise control of execution timing. Another advantage is validation of the implementation which may be problematic when legacy operating systems are used. Faithfully modeling the underlying execution mechanisms for a given operating system is non-trivial.

Future work concerning the BIP to THINK translator includes support for external events, such as interrupts or I/O. This type of events are currently supported by THINK and can be modeled in BIP as external ports. Another work direction is the optimization of bindings in the THINK framework, in order to keep the flexibility of the export-bind design pattern without enduring the cost of going through a proxy each time an inter-component method invocation is executed.

Acknowledgments

We would like to thank Ananda Basu, Jacques Combaz and Loïc Strus for contributing to the work presented in this paper.

References

1. Friedrich, L., Stankovic, J., Humphrey, M., Marley, M., Haskins, J.: A Survey of Configurable, Component-Based Operating Systems for Embedded Applications. IEEE Micro 21(3), 54–68 (2001)
2. Object Management Group: The CORBA Component Model Specification v4.0 (April 2006)
3. Microsoft Corporation: COM: Component Object Model Technologies http://www.microsoft.com/com/
4. Sifakis, J.: A Framework for Component-based Construction. In: Proceedings of the International Conference on Software Engineering and Formal Methods (September 2005)
5. Basu, A., Bozga, M., Sifakis, J.: Modeling Heterogeneous Real-Time Components in BIP. In: 4th IEEE International Conference International Conference on Software Engineering and Formal Methods (September 2006)
6. Fassino, J.P., Stefani, J.B., Lawall, J., Muller, G.: THINK: A Software Framework for Component-based Operating System Kernels. In: Proceedings of the Usenix Annual Technical Conference (June 2002)
7. Eker, J., Janneck, J.W., Lee, E.A., Liu, J., Liu, X., Ludvig, J., Neuendorffer, S., Sachs, S., Xiong, Y.: Taming Heterogeneity: The Ptolemy Approach. Proceedings of the IEEE 91(1), 127–144 (2003)
8. Balarin, F., Watanabe, Y., Hsieh, H., Lavagno, L., Passerone, C., Sangiovanni-Vincentelli, A.L.: Metropolis: An Integrated Electronic System Design Environment. IEEE Computer 36(4), 45–52 (2003)
9. Vestal, S.: Formal Verification of the MetaH Executive Using Linear Hybrid Automata. In: IEEE Real Time Technology and Applications Symposium, pp. 134–144 (June 2000)
10. Henzinger, T.A., Kirsch, C.M., Sanvido, M.A.A., Pree, W.: From Control Models to Real-Time Code using Giotto. IEEE Control Systems Magazine 23(1), 50–64 (2003)
11. Selic, B.: Real-Time Object-Oriented Modeling (ROOM). In: IEEE Real Time Technology and Applications Symposium (June 1996)
12. Subramonian, V., Gill, C.D., Sanchez, C., Sipma, H.B.: Reusable Models for Timing and Liveness Analysis of Middleware for Distributed Real-Time Embedded Systems. In: Proceedings of the 6th Conference on Embedded Software (October 2006)
13. Engler, D.R., Kaashoek, M.F., O'Toole, J.: Exokernel: An Operating System Architecture for Application-Level Resource Management. In: Proceedings of the 15th ACM Symposium on Operating Systems Principles (December 1995)
14. Deville, D., Galland, A., Grimaud, G., Jean, S.: Smart Card operating systems: Past, Present and Future. In: Proceedings of the 5th NORDU/USENIX Conference (February 2003)

15. Hill, J., Szewczyk, R., Woo, A., Hollar, S., Culler, D., Pister, K.: System Architecture Directions for Network Sensors. In: Proceedings of the 9th ACM Conference on Architectural Support for Programming Languages and Operating Systems (November 2000)
16. Levis, P., Lee, N., Welsh, M., Culler, D.E.: TOSSIM: Accurate and Scalable Simulation of Entire TinyOS Applications. In: ACM SenSys, pp. 126–137 (November 2003)
17. Gay, D., Levis, P., von Behren, R., Welsh, M., Brewer, E., Culler, D.: The nesC Language: A Holistic Approach to Networked Embedded Systems. In: Proceedings of the ACM Conference on Programming Language Design and Implementation (June 2003)
18. Stankovic, J.A., Zhu, R., Poornalingam, R., Lu, C., Yu, Z., Humphrey, M., Ellis, B.: VEST: An Aspect-Based Composition Tool for Real-Time Systems. In: Proceedings of the 9th IEEE Real-Time and Embedded Technology and Applications Symposium (May 2003)
19. BIP: http://www-verimag.imag.fr/~async/BIP/bip.html
20. Bozga, M., Graf, S., Ober, I., Ober, I., Sifakis, J.: The IF Toolset. In: School on Formal Methods for the Design of Computer, Communication and Software Systems (September 2004)
21. Bozga, M., Graf, S., Mounier, L.: IF-2.0: A Validation Environment for Component-Based Real-Time Systems. In: Brinksma, E., Larsen, K.G. (eds.) CAV 2002. LNCS, vol. 2404, pp. 343–348. Springer, Heidelberg (2002)
22. Gößler, G., Sifakis, J.: Composition for component-based modeling. Sci. Comput. Program 55(1-3), 161–183 (2005)
23. Bliudze, S., Sifakis, J.: The algebra of connectors: structuring interaction in bip. In: EMSOFT 2007. Proceedings of the 7th ACM & IEEE international conference on Embedded software, pp. 11–20. ACM Press, New York (2007)
24. Alur, R., Courcoubetis, C., Halbwachs, N., Henzinger, T.A., Ho, P.H., Nicollin, X., Olivero, A., Sifakis, J., Yovine, S.: The Algorithmic Analysis of Hybrid Systems. Theor. Comput. Sci. 138(1), 3–34 (1995)
25. Think: http://think.objectweb.org/
26. Fractal: http://fractal.objectweb.org/
27. Bruneton, E., Coupaye, T., Leclercq, M., Quéma, V., Stefani, J.B.: The Fractal Component Model and Its Support in Java. Software Practice and Experience, special issue on Experiences with Auto-adaptive and Reconfigurable Systems 36(11–12), 1257–1284 (2006)
28. Layaïda, O., Hagimont, D.: Plasma: A component-based framework for building self-adaptive applications. In: Proceedings of the Conference on Embedded Multimedia Processing and Communications (January 2005)
29. Polakovic, J., Özcan, A.E., Stefani, J.B.: Building Reconfigurable Component-Based OS with THINK. In: Euromicro Conference on Software Engineering and Advanced Applications (September 2006)
30. Ford, B., Back, G., Benson, G., Lepreau, J., Lin, A., Shivers, O.: The Flux OSKit: A Substrate for OS and Language Research. In: Proceedings of the 16th ACM Symposium on Operating Systems Principles (October 1997)
31. Combaz, J., Fernandez, J.C., Lepley, T., Sifakis, J.: QoS Control for Optimality and Safety. In: Proceedings of the 5th Conference on Embedded Software (September 2005)

Industrial Challenges in the Composition of Embedded Systems

David Corman and James Paunicka

The Boeing Company, P.O. Box 516,
St. Louis, MO. 63166
{David.E.Corman, James.L.Paunicka}@Boeing.com

Abstract. This paper describes a wide range of challenges faced by system designers in developing embedded and networked embedded systems (today's Cyber Physical Systems – CPS). These challenges derive from the complexity of the environment that the systems will need to operate in, coupled with emerging needs to continually increase system capabilities. Environmental complexities include the operation of systems in System-of-Systems (SoS) environments. System complexities posing challenges in embedded systems composition include the ever-increasing desire for on-board vehicle autonomy, and requirements for multiple safety criticalities co-existing within a software suite embedded in a vehicle. These complexity issues are driving dramatic increases in sizes of embedded real-time vehicle software loads. This brings concomitant increases in software development timelines and difficulty in system composition, verification, validation, and certification. The software engineering challenges are daunting, resulting in software being an ever increasing cost and schedule driver in emerging new system developments.

Keywords: embedded real-time systems, systems composition, certification, validation, Cyber Physical Systems.

1 Summary

Emerging techniques in embedded systems development are benefiting from a number of current research areas, such as composability, model-driven development, and techniques in Verification and Validation (V&V) and certification, etc. System attributes, such as autonomy and operation in a System of Systems (SoS) context, provide significant challenges to the systems developer, but also provide interesting opportunities to the research community.

As one of the premier global aerospace companies, the Boeing Company works in a rich set of application areas that will benefit from research focused on composition of real-time embedded systems in multiple domains:

- Air (manned and unmanned, commercial and military)
- Space (ultra high-reliability applications)
- Land (e.g., Future Combat Systems – networked system of systems)

F. Kordon and O. Sokolsky (Eds.): Monterey Workshop 2006, LNCS 4888, pp. 97–110, 2007.
© Springer-Verlag Berlin Heidelberg 2007

Our goal, as systems developers at Boeing, is to transition the best software, techniques and tools from this emerging research by applying them to our current and next-generation of products.

Fig. 1 highlights characteristics of our next generation system developments. Today's systems primarily were developed in a world in which the systems operate individually. They are statically configured with limited capability to adapt to the dynamic environment. Demands on higher system performance and lower system cost are driving next generation systems to be highly networked and highly dynamic in nature. Systems will operate as part of a system of systems with roles that may change as the situation dictates. This will include on-line system customization including on-line code generation. Systems will operate in heterogeneous environments supporting both autonomous behavior and ad-hoc collaborations. As we move from hard wired network environments to a wireless world, systems will be required to exhibit fault-tolerant behaviors that can account for unreliable networks. Moreover, systems will need to be designed to exhibit "predictably safe" behaviors in an uncertain environment. Additionally, design artifacts must be available to support system level verification and validation.

- **Dynamicism**
  - System of systems with changing participants
  - Changing modalities of individual systems
  - On-line code generation
- **Heterogeneity**
  - System of systems
  - Heterogeneous/federated networks
  - Heterogeneous collaborations
    - Ad hoc coalitions
  - COTS/GOTS components in an overall system
- **Fault Tolerance**
  - Unreliable networks
  - High confidence
  - Mission effectiveness in the presence of failures
  - IVHM
- **Scalability**
  - Massive data flows
  - Systems of many systems
  - Ever larger end systems
- **Certification and V & V**

Fig. 1. Pervasive Industrial Strength Challenges in the Composition of Embedded Systems

System complexity is outstripping our capability to affordably develop and compose the next generation of real-time embedded systems. Virtually all new developments will be focused on component-based systems. Most are highly dynamic and require some level of dependable performance. All can benefit greatly from additional research.

This paper describes the wide range of challenges facing designers in composing and developing embedded and networked embedded systems and presents a number of technology development successes aimed at meeting these challenges in efforts that culminated in live flight demonstration on relevant tactical platforms.

2 Embedded System Challenges

Fig. 2 highlights some of the embedded system challenges for today's systems. We use as an example a high performance tactical fighter. The system is characterized by multiple system processors that support the diversity of functions required to both fly and operate effectively. These include embedded processors required for both mission critical (e.g., mission processing) and flight critical activities (e.g., flight control). Traditionally, much of processing was statically controlled with processor resources scheduled on a periodic basis. Processing typically was hard real-time for activities that need to be complete within a frame. In the future, mission processing will include software real-time tasks such as download of imagery that will be soft real-time. Scheduling algorithms will be dynamic and adaptive to the mission state. Additional avionics capabilities including new sensors provide potential to dramatically improve performance. These gains will only be harvested if the system is made more responsive to the dynamic operating environment. This includes support for real-time re-tasking, mission adaptation, mission re-planning in a networked SoS environment that includes smart weapons, autonomous Unmanned Aerial vehicles (UAVs), mixed-initiative control, and collaborative operation.

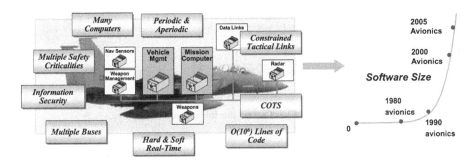

Fig. 2. Embedded System Technology Challenges

System complexities posing challenges in embedded systems composition include:

- Ever-increasing desire for on-board vehicle autonomy, including real-time on-board re-routing in response to dynamic mission conditions and autonomous reactions to various contingencies,
- Requirements for multiple safety criticalities co-existing within a software suite embedded in a vehicle,
- Multi-level security requirements in on-board software,
- Network-centric participation mandating use of constrained legacy data links required for interoperability with existing platforms.

The above complexity issues and drivers are resulting in dramatic increases in the sizes of embedded real-time vehicle software loads. This complexity is reflected in code size estimates for modern fighters such as Joint Strike Fighter predicted by United States Congressional Budget Office to be on the order of 18M lines of code

[1]. This contrasts with today's typical software loads on the order of 1M lines. This, of course, brings concomitant increases in software development timelines and difficulty in system composition, verification, validation, and certification. The software engineering challenges are daunting, resulting in software being an ever increasing cost and schedule driver in emerging new system developments.

2.1 Dynamic Operation in a Networked SoS Environment

Dynamic system behavior requirements can stem from operational issues such as reaction to on-board contingencies, execution of incoming human directives, and participation of platforms in a net-centric environment, including participation in swarms and other cooperative multi-vehicle missions. Implementation of on-board software that can react to these dynamic conditions is supported by a variety of techniques such as mixing of hard and soft real-time tasks, active resource management and dynamic scheduling, and support for software component reconfiguration at system mode changes.

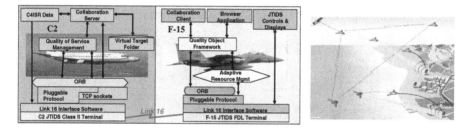

Fig. 3. WSOA First Generation Interoperability Bridge

Boeing demonstrated a first generation solution to the challenge of Dynamic Operation in a SoS Environment in the Weapon System Open Architecture (WSOA) demonstration, Fig. 3. From a technology perspective, WSOA challenges were: 1) Applying Quality of Service (QoS) technology to make optimal use of available bandwidth; 2) Adaptive management of processor resources across the network; 3) Dynamic scheduling to incorporate hard and soft real-time processes [2]. WSOA also introduced the use of a pluggable CORBA protocol above Link 16 along with a new interoperability layer. This protocol layer was used for QoS negotiation and C2-Fighter "tactical net-meeting". On an operational level, WSOA flight demonstrated collaborative real-time mission re-planning and imagery transmission over Link 16 between an F-15 and a surrogate AWACS platform. WSOA demonstration was highly successful and showed that significant utility was achieved as a result of adaptive resource management and dynamic scheduling. [15] provides a tutorial description of the technologies employed in WSOA. The right hand side of Figure 3 highlights the challenges involved in multiple UAV collaboration. The figure was extracted from the DARPA MICA Public Release presentation [16]. Major challenges facing the designer were to develop mixed initiative control of UAV teams including collaborative strategies and tactics for these teams under the supervision of

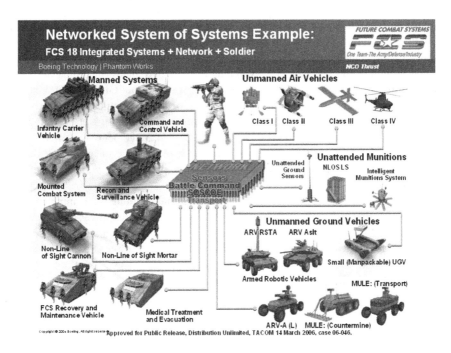

Fig. 4. FCS Networked System of Systems

a single human operator, with adjustable autonomy determining the degree of human authority desired or required during task execution. Although an important first step, the WSOA architecture could not approach answering the true networked SoS challenge posed by today's operational environment with hundreds of interacting systems. Networking challenges include integration of systems within a larger SoS context, including considerations for heterogeneous / federated networks, incorporation of legacy fielded systems, being able to operate with inherently unreliable networks, and making optimum use of data links of various bandwidth capabilities (e.g., wireless, satellite, etc.).

Probably the most complex example of system of system behavior is exhibited by the Future Combat System (FCS). FCS will network 18 separate platform types – 8 manned ground vehicles, 4 unmanned air vehicles, 6 unmanned ground vehicles – with soldiers, unattended ground sensors and munitions, Fig. 4. According to the General Accountability Office [17], FCS is developing a first-of-a-kind network that will entail development of unprecedented capabilities— including: 1) On-the-move communications, high-speed data transmission, dramatically increased bandwidth and simultaneous voice, data and video; 2) The simultaneous design and integration of 18 major weapon systems or platforms within strict size and weight limitations; 3) Maturation and integration into a system of systems of at least 53 technologies that are considered critical to achieving FCS'critical performance capabilities.

Multi-entity embedded systems challenges deal with effective utilization of multiple, sometimes-cooperating vehicles to accomplish an objective. This includes being able to accommodate a heterogeneous mix of vehicles. Challenges include resource and task allocation for vehicles in the population and issues associated with deconflicted dynamic responses to changes in the battlespace.

Information management will play an ever increasing role in SoS operation as massive amounts of data become available from netted platforms for war fighter exploitation [20]. Entities such as the Global Information Grid (GIG) hold the promise of enabling flexible and timely delivery of critical battlespace information from a mix of airborne assets that collect information to war fighters needing that information [21]. Various aspects of information management will help make intelligent use of finite communications bandwidth in the face of an almost infinite amount of data that would be available from airborne platforms (e.g., use of metadata to support information brokering).

Information assurance and security impose additional challenges. Tamper-resistant avionics software is also needed [22, 27]. To support the dynamic system behaviors and coalition environments that are prevalent today, a new paradigm in security architecture for networked systems must be developed. Traditional security solutions as practiced that impose static structure and partitioning are not viable. Covert channels, created under cover of reconfiguration must be prevented. These SoS solutions must be interoperable in a coalition environment. Significant effort is being expended on the development of system of system architectures that can support Multiple Independent Levels of Security (MILS). MILS is an enabling architecture that can dramatically reducing the size and complexity of security-critical code, thus allowing faster and more cost-effective development and evaluation. MILS is based on work initiated by John Rushby in the early 1980s, and has evolved in a cooperative effort among government (e.g. US Air Force Research Laboratory), education (University of Idaho) and commercial organizations (e.g. Greenhills, Objective Interface Systems, and the major aerospace contractors including Boeing, Lockheed Martin, and Raytheon). Further details on MILS, its implications and state of development can be found in [19] which provides an extensive tutorial and many references on the broad subject of MILS and its relationship to networked embedded systems.

Networked real-time embedded systems truly pose a multi-dimensional development challenge. We need to consider multiple system aspects including hard and soft real-time operation, timeliness, security, and safety in the design space as we start to build our system designs. Maturity of the potential solution is also quite important as we look to integrating system components. Maturity is typically referred to as Technology Readiness Level (TRL). TRL 1 is associated with basic technology research. TRL 6 represents a System/subsystem model or prototype demonstration in a relevant environment. TRL 8 and 9 represent maturity for a system that has been flight demonstrated or 'flight proven' through successful mission demonstration or operation respectively. Achieving the multiple aspects of design requires a holistic design approach with technology needs in the areas of: 1) Component models; 2) Process technologies and tools for correct by construction design; and 3) Product technologies including use of product line architectures [3]. Fig. 5 highlights the multi-dimensional aspect of this system design problem.

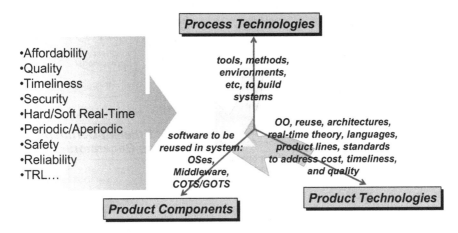

Fig. 5. Networked SoS Information Technology Challenges

2.2 Software Engineering Challenges

Creating component models/development environments for fielded "Legacy" systems is challenging. Rather than being able to select the component model first, we may have, instead, an existing infrastructure to create a component model and development environment for. In this case we must define the component model consistent with the legacy platform using abstractions appropriate for: Component-based development, Existing infrastructure, and Functional and non-functional requirements. We must generate the development environment using: Modeling tools, Code generators, Infrastructure adapters, and Testing/analysis tools. Finally analysis techniques may require data that does not currently exist such as timing and state transition data for legacy systems and components. This is frequently difficult to obtain and impractical to create directly.

One of the major challenges in software engineering is component / system integration. Large scale systems such as tactical fighters contain hundreds and thousands of components that must be integrated together to build an executable. DARPA in the Model Based Integration of Embedded Systems (MoBIES) program made initial progress and showed through benchmarked experiments that this approach can have huge savings in integration time and dramatic reductions in software errors [4]. Component integration remains a daunting problem. Fig. 6 shows a perspective of the integration challenge. We need an integrated environment that can provide multi-view modeling, analysis, and configuration of component based simulations to support design meeting multiple aspect constraints. Progress has been slowed by the lack of embedded system modeling and closed tool interfaces. Vanderbilt University has led in the development of an Open Tool Integration Framework (OTIF) and model based design technology that have great potential in achieving this goal [5].

Scalable technologies to design, analyze, verify and validate large networked SoS are needed. For design, multi-view modeling and analysis tools are needed to capture cross-cutting systematic concerns (deployment, composition, messaging, fault

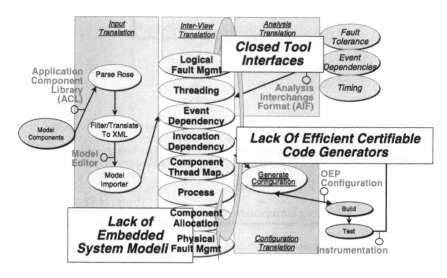

Fig. 6. Software Integration Challenges

tolerance, etc.) in native architectural terms.   Integrated dynamic design space exploration and analysis tools to address traffic analysis, system loading, operational latencies, path tracing, safety/security non-interference, etc. are also required. Generative technologies for correct-by-construction syntheses would address architectural abstractions, common pattern application, synthesized composition configuration, middleware integration, etc.

Underlying all the aforementioned system complexities and resulting embedded software challenges is the requirement to verify and validate (V&V), as well as certify the systems that will contain this software and operate in networked and SoS contexts, while providing the system capabilities demanded by our customers.

Federal Aviation Administration (FAA) certification for commercial aircraft is a costly and lengthy process. It involves review of testing artifacts as well as design processes. Certification technology has not advanced much since the publication of DO 178B - Software Considerations in Airborne Systems and Equipment Certification which is the standard for software development published by RTCA, Incorporated [23]. The standard was developed by RTCA and EUROCAE and first published in 1982 [24]. As systems have become more complex, the costs have certification have increased exponentially. In fact, there is some debate on whether the costs for certifying the next generation systems can be met by industry.

Although technology for developing componentized systems is beginning to be widely used, the certification community has not yet developed an approach that certifies components and then re-uses the certification over other systems. In the past, issues of FAA certification were not directly applicable to military systems. However, with the potential for unmanned air vehicles to travel in controlled National Airspace, the applicability of certification is becoming likely.

Fig. 7 highlights some of the challenges for V&V and certification. Critical areas are in the domain of mixed initiative operations in which a human interfaces with automata, adaptive and highly dynamic systems that change control capability in response to sensed environment, and mixed criticality systems in which different levels of safety or assurance exist in subsystems. There are some success stories emerging. Recent efforts are developing techniques in "proof carrying code" and certifiable protocols for human automata interactions that show great potential [6]. In addition, there is new research looking at tools for certifying component systems that may provide sufficient evidence to enable re-using certification on other systems. Whilst technology may be available in the future, a sea change in certification processes may also be needed to accrue the benefits.

- **V&V and Certification is expensive, and getting more expensive, for fielded systems**
- **Future advanced manned and un-manned systems may not fit naturally under current V&V and Certification regimes**
- **Need approaches for efficient V&V and Certification for emerging technologies for them to be deployable**
  - **Multi-entity Systems**
  - **Human interaction with Autonomy.**
  - **Fused Sensor Systems**
  - **Adaptive Systems that change with environmental stimulus**
  - **Mixed Criticality- Functions dependent on information of varying confidence**

Fig. 7. Verification, Validation and Certification Challenges

For V&V, flexible and reconfigurable SoS simulation and validation tools must be tailorable to the specific mission context. These must be composable in number and type of participants, topology, etc., and must integrate real and simulated / surrogate / synthesized elements. They must also provide completeness in varying topologies and operational context.

For Product technologies, we also need composable approaches to enable heterogeneous system variability while addressing changing resource availability. Product line architecture analysis must address product variability in heterogeneous security, criticality, timeliness and physical deployment concerns. Component models and patterns for uber-scale systems must enable software variability across and within systems while addressing cross-cutting aspects. For QoS and resource management, tools must address resource and behavioral adaptation at both the system and SoS levels.

3 Some Successes

Boeing has utilized various system and software engineering technologies, such as component-based designs and model-driven development, to address complexity challenges. For example, the Bold Stroke [7] effort started in the mid-1990s addressed software challenges with a product-line architecture featuring:

- Component-based design of complex Mission Management System on-board Operational Flight Programs (OFPs) facilitating re-use of components across manned strike fighter and trainer platforms, and eventually transitioning to complex unmanned strike fighter platforms,
- Isolation of application components by middleware [28] from underlying compute platforms, including underlying operating systems and compute hardware, facilitating (1) application development on desktop systems with seamless migration to embedded systems during the development process, and (2) less expensive system upgrades to more capable compute platforms during system evolution.

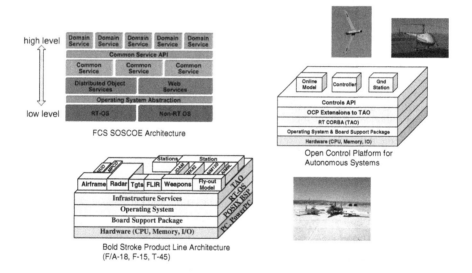

Fig. 8. Boeing Leverages Middleware Based Architectures to provide Hardware and Operating System Independence

Boeing has continued to build upon the Bold Stroke architecture to produce a family of middleware based architectures that have successfully provided hardware and operating system independence to entire families of manned and unmanned systems, Fig. 8. These architectures include the Open Control Platform, successfully used in DARPA's Software Enabled Control (SEC) Program and the System of Systems Common Operating Environment (SoSCOE) that is the software foundation of the Future Combat System (FCS) [25].

In the world of unmanned flight platforms, the concept of component-based designs and compute platform isolation was demonstrated numerous times with the Open Control Platform (OCP) middleware and tool suite as part of the DARPA Software-Enabled Control (SEC) program [8]. With the OCP tool suite, model-driven development of advanced Unmanned Aerial Vehicle (UAV) controllers with design tools such as MathWorks Simulink was supported. Development and testing of UAV controller software on desktop computers was enabled using OCP middleware and its compute platform isolation features. After this development and testing phase, the controller software was then delivered to the Boeing SEC team for final integration and testing on target on-board avionics hardware prior to live flight.

During the course of the SEC program, component-based UAV controller software from various research teams executing within the OCP was flight testing on a mix of relevant flight platforms. Paragraphs below describe some of the characteristics of the platforms.

- Large, fixed-wing platforms – J-UCAS X-45A flight test platform (T-33 flown in autonomous mode) and an F-15E strike fighter, flying numerous manned / unmanned collaborative war-fighting scenarios, communicating over a legacy Link 16 data-link at Edwards Air Force Base, [9].
- Small, fixed-wing platform – the Boeing ScanEagle low-cost, high-endurance reconnaissance UAV, flying complex autonomous maneuvers at the Boardman, Oregon flight range, [10]
- Large, rotary-wing platform – the Boeing Maverick UAV, currently the avionics and Command and Control test bed for the DARPA A160 Hummingbird UAV, in demonstrations of autonomous routing and automated landing features at the A160 flight range at Victorville, California, [11]
- Small, rotary-wing platform – a Yamaha RMAX, demonstrating multiple warfighting support capabilities at the McKenna Military Operations in Urbanized Terrain (MOUT) site at Fort Benning, Georgia [12].

As referenced in the above descriptions, Link 16 is a Time Division Multiple Access based secure, jam-resistant high-speed digital data link which operates over-the-air in the L band portion (969–1206 MHz) of the UHF spectrum. It is used by the United States and many NATO countries for communication between air, ground, and sea units. Link 16 limits the exchange of information to users within line-of-sight of one another. It uses the transmission characteristics and protocols, conventions, and fixed-length (or variable length) message formats defined by MIL-STD 6016C (formerly the JTIDS technical interface design plan). Link 16 is one of the digital services of the Multifunctional Information Distribution System (MIDS) in the Standardization Agreement STANAG 5516. Information is typically passed at a rate on the order of 100 kbits/second. Link 16 equipment is typically installed in ground, airborne, and sea-based air defense platforms and selected fighter aircraft. [14]

A recent demonstration at White Sands Missile Range (WSMR) provided a showcase for multi-entity UAV operations involving component-based embedded software for rerouting UAVs in response to changing battlespace conditions [26]. In the demonstration, Fig. 9, multiple ScanEagle UAVs were populated with

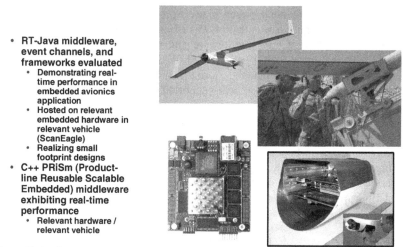

- **RT-Java middleware, event channels, and frameworks evaluated**
  - Demonstrating real-time performance in embedded avionics application
  - Hosted on relevant embedded hardware in relevant vehicle (ScanEagle)
  - Realizing small footprint designs
- **C++ PRiSm (Product-line Reusable Scalable Embedded) middleware exhibiting real-time performance**
  - Relevant hardware / relevant vehicle

Source: Boeing Public Release video for PCES demonstration

Fig. 9. Technical Progress and Tech Transition

embedded research software components executing on Boeing Product-line Reusable Scalable eMbedded (PRiSm) middleware platforms. The PRiSm-based software executed on a special Payload Processor board installed within the ScanEagle avionics, isolating the research software from the existing qualified flight control software. The research software autonomously re-routed the UAVs in response to higher-level commanders' request for effects in target areas. Target area effects that were requested and demonstrated included: looking for targets in a specified geographic area; performing maneuvers in a target area to support generation of weapon-quality aimpoints for a subsequent strike; positioning the vehicle in safe locations for live monitoring of an incoming weapon strike; and control of the vehicle supporting post-strike battle damage assessment of the target. The ScanEagle UAVs received requests for effects from a mission commander in an Air Operations Center (AOC) through a net-centric mix of terrestrial LANs (connecting the AOC to the ScanEagle Ground Control Stations (GCSs)) and Radio Frequency (RF) communications (connecting the GCSs to the UAVs).

In the WSMR ScanEagle demonstration, two variants of PRiSm middleware were implemented – C++ and Real Time Java (RT-Java). Both variants exhibited proper real-time performance and successfully routed the ScanEagle UAVs through a dynamic war fighting scenario that involved multiple pop-up targets. The use of RT-Java in the ScanEagle flight earned the demonstration team an international award for innovations in the use of Java.

4 Summary

The wide range of challenges facing embedded system designers in our industry is daunting. The demands of ever-increasing system complexity and the need to operate in a system of systems context stretch our ability to design, verify, validate, and certify these systems. A portfolio of research programs at Boeing is aimed at meeting these challenges. From the initial open systems architecture work of Bold Stroke to the further advances made possible by a string of DARPA programs, the concepts of object-oriented design, enabled by advances in middleware and component models, are providing important solutions to help us affordably compose these complex systems. Other work in system-of-systems interoperability and network quality of service are providing the base technology to allow us to effectively network these systems together. Finally, our work in verification, validation, and certification, under the leadership of the Air Force Research Laboratory, is helping ensure that the designs of these advanced platforms can be successfully and affordably certified and made available to our customers.

References

1. United States Government Accountability Office, Tactical Aircraft – Opportunity to Reduce Risks in the Joint Strike Fighter Program with Different Acquisition Strategy, GAO-05-271 (2005)
2. Corman, D.E., Gossett, J.: WSOA - Weapons System Open Architecture –An Innovative Technology Framework for Time Critical Target Operations. In: 6th International Command and Control Research and Technology Symposium, Command and Control Research Program (2001)
3. Sharp, D.C.: Reducing Avionics Software Cost Through Component Based Product Line Development. In: Software Technology Conference (1998)
4. Sharp, D.C.: Variable Aspects and Models for Reusable Component-based Avionics Systems. In: 2nd Workshop on Reflective and Adaptive Middleware, pp. 149–152 (2003)
5. Institute for Software Integrated Systems, Open Tool Integration Framework, www.isis.vanderbilt.edu/Projects/WOTIF/
6. Paunicka, J.L., Crum, V., Bortner, R., Homan, D.: Advanced UAV Flight Control and Certification Impacts. In: American Institute of Engineers UAV Payloads Conference, San Diego, CA (December 2006)
7. Sharp, D.C.: Distributed Real-Time Embedded Middleware for Avionics Systems. In: Systems and Software Technology Conference (April 2002)
8. Paunicka, J.L., Corman, D.E., Mendel, B.: The OCP-an open middleware solution for embedded systems. In: American Control Conference (June 2001)
9. Paunicka, J.L., Mettler, B., Schouwenaars, T., Valenti, M., Kuwata, J., How, J., Feron, E.: Autonomous UAV Guidance Build-Up: Flight Test Demonstration and Evaluation Plan. In: AIAA Guidance, Navigation and Control Conference, Austin, TX (August 2003)
10. Boeing/Insitu UAV Demonstrates Next-Generation Software, Autonomy Technology, http://www.boeing.com/phantom/news/2004/q1/nr_040218t.html
11. Boeing Team Demonstrates Advanced Autonomous Flight Control for UAVs, http://www.boeing.com/phantom/news/2005/q2/nr_050621a.html
12. Tech Successfully Flies Smarter Rotary Wing UAV, http://www.gatech.edu/newsroom/release.php?id=515
13. Loyall, J., Schantz, R., Corman, D.E., Paunicka, J.L., Fernandez, S.: A Distributed Real-time Embedded Application for Surveillance, Detection, and Tracking of Time Critical Targets. In: 11th IEEE Real-Time and Embedded Technology and Applications Symposium, San Francisco, CA (March 2005)

14. Wikipedia entry for Link 16 (September 24, 2007), http://en.wikipedia.org/wiki/Link_16
15. Corman, D., Gossett, J.: WSOA - Using Emerging Open System Architecture Standards to Enable Innovative Techniques for Time Critical Target Prosecution. In: IEEE AES 2002 (2002)
16. Mixed Initiative Control of Automa-teams (MICA) public released overview briefing(September 24, 2007), http://dtsn.darpa.mil/IXO/programs.asp?id=41
17. General Accountability Office Report, Testimony Before the Subcommittee on Airland, Committee on Armed Services, U.S. Senate March 16, 2005. Future Combat Systems Challenges and Prospects for Success (2005), http://www.gao.gov/new.items/d05442t.pdf
18. MILS Architecture: Multiple Independent Levels of Security - High-assurance security at an affordable cost, Military Embedded Systems (September 24, 2007), http://www.mil-embedded.com/articles/white_papers/jacob/
19. Van Fleet, W.M., et al.: MILS:Architecture for High-Assurance Embedded Computing. Software Technology Support Center Cross Talk Magazine (August 2005), http://www.stsc.hill.af.mil/crosstalk/2005/08/0508Vanfleet_etal
20. Combs, V.T., Hillman, R.G., Muccio, M.T., McKeel, R.W.: Joint Battlespace Infosphere: Information Management Within a C2 Enterprise, Defense Technical Information Center Accession Number ADA463694 (June 2005)
21. Martens, E.J., Corman, D.E.: Live-flight demonstration of agent technology for connecting the tactical edge to the global information grid, Defense Transformation and Net-Centric Systems. In: Suresh, R. (ed.) Proceedings of the SPIE, vol. 6578 (May 2007)
22. Technology and Acquisition Systems Security and Program Protection, Air Force Policy Directive 63-17 (November 2001), www.e-publishing.af.mil/shared/media/epubs/AFPD63-17.pdf
23. RTCA/DO-178B, Software Considerations in Airborne Systems and Equipment Certification (December 1, 1992)
24. RTCA/DO-178, Software Considerations in Airborne Systems and Equipment Certification, RTCA, Inc. (September 13, 1982)
25. Sharp, D.: Boeing, Future Combat Systems, and the OMG. OMG Technical Meeting, St. Louis, Missouri (April 2004)
26. Wilson, J.R.: The Evolution of UAV Avionics. Military and Aerospace Electronics (September 2005)
27. Gansler, J.S.: Implementing Anti-Tamper. Under Secretary of Defense Memorandum (January 2001), http://www.at.dod.mil/Docs/gansler_2001.pdf
28. Sharp, D.: Distributed Real-Time Embedded Middleware for Avionics Systems. In: Software Technology Conference, Salt Lake City, Utah (April-May 2002)

Deep Random Search for Efficient
Model Checking of Timed Automata

R. Grosu[1], X. Huang[1], S.A. Smolka[1], W. Tan[1], and S. Tripakis[2]

[1] Dept. of CS, Stony Brook Univ., Stony Brook, NY 11794, USA
{grosu,xhuang,sas,wktan}@cs.sunysb.edu
[2] Verimag, Centre Equation, 38610 Gieres, France
tripakis@imag.fr

Abstract. We present DRS (*Deep Random Search*), a new Las Vegas algorithm for model checking safety properties of timed automata. DRS explores the state space of the simulation graph of a timed automaton by performing random walks up to a prescribed depth. Nodes along these walks are then used to construct a random fringe, which is the starting point of additional deep random walks. The DRS algorithm is complete, and optimal to within a specified depth increment. Experimental results show that it is able to find extremely deep counter-examples for a number of benchmarks, outperforming Open-Kronos and UPPAAL in the process.

1 Introduction

The goal of this paper is to demonstrate the effectiveness of random search in the model checking of timed automata (TA). To this end, we present the *Deep Random Search* (DRS) algorithm for checking safety properties of TA. DRS is an iterative-deepening, deep-random-walk, random-fringe-backtracking Las-Vegas algorithm. By "deep random walk" we mean that in any state of a random walk, DRS always chooses a random *non-visited* child, as long as such a state exists. By "random fringe backtracking" we mean that the algorithm does not limit backtracking to predecessors; rather it randomly selects a node from the fringe as the starting point for a deep random walk. This strategy removes much of the bias towards the initial state of the search space. We now discuss the algorithm in more detail, highlighting its main features.

- The DRS algorithm operates on *simulation graphs*, an efficient, symbolic representation of timed automata that can be generated on-the-fly [5,13]. A node of a simulation graph is a symbolic state comprising a finite set of regions all having the same discrete state. Although, in the worst case, a simulation graph can be exponentially large in the size of the underlying TA, in practice, it is orders of magnitude smaller than the region graph.
- DRS is a Las Vegas algorithm, i.e. a randomized algorithm that always produces the correct answer but whose running time is a random variable. The quintessential Las Vegas algorithm is randomized quick sort, which chooses its pivot element randomly and consequently runs in expected time

F. Kordon and O. Sokolsky (Eds.): Monterey Workshop 2006, LNCS 4888, pp. 111–124, 2007.

$O(n \log n)$ for *all* input of length n. As explained below, DRS uses iterative deepening to perform a *complete*, albeit random, search of the state space under investigation, thereby qualifying it for its Las Vegas status.

- DRS performs *deep random search* by taking random walks that are as *deep as possible*: they reach a leaf node, a prescribed *cutoff depth*, or a node whose children were already visited (a *closed* node). A node with at least two unvisited children that is encountered along such a walk it is added to the *fringe*. A closed node is deleted from the fringe.
- Instead of limiting backtracking to predecessors, DRS employs *random fringe backtracking*. That is, when a deep random walk terminates, a node is picked *at random* from the fringe to commence a new deep random walk. This process continues until the fringe is empty, thereby ensuring completeness up to the cutoff value. In contrast, most model-checking algorithms based on a Monte Carlo search strategy, such as [15,8,19,11,16,7], commence a new random walk from the initial state of the search space. A bias towards the initial state of the search space can therefore be seen with these techniques. Random fringe backtracking is, in contrast, designed to eliminate this bias.
- DRS allows the user to initialize the fringe by taking *walks* initial deep random walks, where *walks* ranges between 1 and the number of children of the initial state. Parameter *walks*, in combination with the cutoff value, gives the user control over both the breadth and depth of the random search performed by DRS. Should the user have a priori knowledge about the "shape" (density and length) of the execution space and potential counter-examples, then these parameters can be used to fine-tune DRS's performance accordingly.
- Iterative deepening is realized by repeating the deep-random-search process with a new cutoff value equal to that of the old cutoff plus a prescribed *increment*. For an increment of one, DRS is *optimal* [17] in the sense that it always finds the shortest counter-example, should one exist. Otherwise, it is optimal up to the value of the increment.

Our experimental results show that for all benchmarks having a counter-example, DRS consistently outperforms the Open-Kronos [5] and UPPAAL [13] model checkers. Otherwise, its performance is consistent with that of Open-Kronos. The benchmarks were chosen to exhibit a wide range of counter-examples, with depth from 6 to 13,376. Open-Kronos performs traditional depth-first on simulation graphs. UPPAAL uses Difference Bounded Matrices, Minimal Constraint Representation and Clock Difference Diagrams to symbolically represent the state space, and allows the user to choose between breadth-first and depth-first search.

In related work, a number of researchers have investigated the use of random search (i.e. random walk) in model checking and reported on its benefits, including [15,8,19,11,16]. To the best of our knowledge, DRS is the first *complete* Las Vegas algorithm to be proposed for the problem.[1]

---

[1] Randomized SAT solvers for bounded model checking [3] and the algorithm of [11] are heuristics-based guided search algorithms in which randomization plays a secondary role; e.g., to break ties among alternatives with the same cost. In contrast, randomization is the primary algorithmic technique utilized by DRS.

The rest of the paper is organized as follows. Sections 2 and 3 review the theory of timed automata and simulation graphs. Section 4 presents our DRS algorithm, while Section 5 discusses our experimental results. Section 6 offers our concluding remarks.

2   Timed Büchi Automata

In this section we define Timed Büchi automata, a real-time extension of classical Büchi automata that will serve as our formal model of real-time systems. We begin with some preliminary definitions. Let $\mathbb{N}$ denote the natural numbers, $\mathbb{R}^+$ the non-negative real numbers, and let $\mathcal{X}$ be a finite set of variables taking values in $\mathbb{R}^+$. In our definition of a Timed Büchi automaton to follow, $\mathcal{X}$ will be a finite set of *clock* variables. An $\mathcal{X}$-*valuation* is a function $\mathbf{v} : \mathcal{X} \to \mathbb{R}^+$ that assigns to each variable in $\mathcal{X}$ a value in $\mathbb{R}^+$. $\mathbf{0}$ denotes the valuation assigning 0 to all variables in $\mathcal{X}$. Given a valuation $\mathbf{v}$ and $\delta \in \mathbb{R}^+$, $\mathbf{v} + \delta$ is defined to be the valuation $\mathbf{v}'$ such that $\mathbf{v}'(x) = \mathbf{v}(x) + \delta$ for all $x \in \mathcal{X}$. Given a valuation $\mathbf{v}$ and $X \subseteq \mathcal{X}$, $\mathbf{v}[X := 0]$ is defined to be the valuation $\mathbf{v}'$ such that $\mathbf{v}'(x) = 0$ if $x \in X$ and $\mathbf{v}'(x) = \mathbf{v}(x)$ otherwise.

An *atomic constraint* on $\mathcal{X}$ is a constraint of the form $x \# c$, where $x \in \mathcal{X}$, $c \in \mathbb{N}$ and $\# \in \{<, \leq, \geq, >\}$. A valuation $\mathbf{v}$ *satisfies* an atomic constraint α, denoted $\mathbf{v} \models \alpha$, if substituting the values of the clocks in the constraint yields a valid inequality. For example, $\mathbf{v} \models x \leq 5$ iff $\mathbf{v}(x) \leq 5$. A conjunction of atomic constraints defines a set of $\mathcal{X}$-valuations, called an $\mathcal{X}$-*zone*. For example, $x \leq 5 \wedge y > 3$ defines the set of all valuations $\mathbf{v}$ such that $\mathbf{v}(x) \leq 5 \wedge \mathbf{v}(y) > 3$.[2]

Definition 1 (Timed Büchi Automaton [1]). *A* timed Büchi automaton *(TBA) is a six-tuple* $T = (\mathcal{X}, Q, q_0, E, \mathsf{invar}, F)$, *where:*

- $\mathcal{X}$ *is a finite set of* clocks.
- Q *is a finite set of* discrete states, $q_0 \in Q$ *being the* initial *discrete state.*
- $F \subseteq Q$ *is a finite set of* accepting states.
- E *is a finite set of* edges *of the form* $e = (q, \zeta, X, q')$, *where* $q, q' \in Q$ *are the* source *and* target *discrete states,* ζ *is an* $\mathcal{X}$-zone, *called the* guard *of* e, *and* $X \subseteq \mathcal{X}$ *is a set of clocks to be* reset *upon taking the edge.*
- invar, *the* invariant *of* q, *is a function that associates an* $\mathcal{X}$-zone *with each discrete state* q.

Given an edge $e = (q, \zeta, X, q')$, we write $\mathsf{source}(e)$, $\mathsf{target}(e)$, $\mathsf{guard}(e)$ and $\mathsf{reset}(e)$ for q, q', ζ and X, respectively. Given a discrete state q, we write $\mathsf{in}(q)$ (resp. $\mathsf{out}(q)$) for the set of edges of the form $(\_, \_, \_, q)$ (resp. $(q, \_, \_, \_)$). We assume that for each $e \in \mathsf{out}(q)$, $\mathsf{guard}(e) \subseteq \mathsf{invar}(q)$.

---

[2] Zones are particularly interesting since they can be represented using $O(n^2)$ space-efficient data-structures such as *difference-bound matrices* [6], where n is the number of clocks. Standard operations on these data structures are also time-efficient; e.g., intersection in $O(n^2)$, test for emptiness in $O(n^3)$.

A *state of A* is a pair $s = (q, \mathbf{v})$, where $q \in Q$ and $\mathbf{v} \in \mathsf{invar}(q)$. We write discrete$(s)$ to denote q. The *initial state* of A is $s_0 = (q_0, \mathbf{0})$.

An edge $e = (q_1, \zeta, X, q_2)$ can be seen as a (partial) function on states. Given a state $s = (q_1, \mathbf{v})$ such that $\mathbf{v} \in \zeta$ and $\mathbf{v}[X := 0] \in \mathsf{invar}(q_2)$, $e(s)$ is defined to be the state $s' = (q_2, \mathbf{v}[X := 0])$. Whenever $e(s)$ is defined, we say that a *discrete transition* can be taken from s to s'.

A real number $\delta \in \mathbb{R}^+$ can also be seen as a (partial) function on states. Given a state $s = (q, \mathbf{v})$, if $\mathbf{v} + \delta \in \mathsf{invar}(q)$ then $\delta(s)$ is defined to be the state $s' = (q, \mathbf{v} + \delta)$; otherwise $\delta(s)$ is undefined. Whenever $\delta(s)$ is defined, we say that a *time transition* can be taken from s to s'.

An infinite sequence of pairs $(\delta_0, e_0), (\delta_1, e_1), ...$, where for all $i = 0, 1, ...$, $\delta_i \in \mathbb{R}^+$ and $e_i \in E$, defines a *run of A starting at state s*, if s is a state of A and the sequence of states $s_0 = s$, $s_{i+1} = e_i(\delta_i(s_i))$ is defined for all $i \geq 0$. The run is called *accepting* if there exists an infinite set of indices $J \subseteq \mathbb{N}$, such that for all $i \in J$, discrete$(s_i) \in F$. The run is called *zeno* if the sequence $\delta_0, \delta_0 + \delta_1, \delta_0 + \delta_1 + \delta_2, ...$ *converges*, that is, if $\exists \delta \in \mathbb{R}^+, \forall k \in \mathbb{N}, \Sigma_{i=0,...,k}\delta_i < \delta$. Otherwise, the run is called *non-zeno*.

Example 1. Consider the two TBA of Figure 1. Circles represent discrete states, double circles represent accepting states, and arrows represent edges. Labels a, b, c refer to edges. A run of A_1 starting at state $(q_0, \mathbf{0})$ is $(0.5, a)$, $(0.25, a)$, $(0.125, a)$, ...; this run is zeno. In fact, any run of A_1 taking a-transitions forever is zeno. On the other hand, the run $(0, b), (1, c), (1, c), \cdots$ of A_1 is non-zeno. Finally, every accepting run of A_2 is non-zeno.

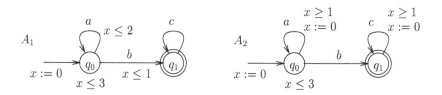

Fig. 1. A TBA with zeno runs (left) and a strongly non-zeno TBA (right)

When drawing a TBA, we typically omit "rewriting" into the guards those constraints that are already enforced by an invariant. So, for example, the guard on the a-transition of TBA A_2 of Figure 1 should have been $1 \leq x \leq 3$. Since, however, the atomic constraint $x \leq 3$ is already enforced by q_0's invariant, it can be omitted in the figure. This is done for notational simplificity.

Example 2. As a more practical example, consider the TBA of Figure 2 representing the well-known Fischer real-time mutual exclusion protocol. The automaton encodes the protocol each process executes in order to gain entry into its critical section. The idea behind the protocol is as follows. A process, having process id `pid`, has a local clock `x` and access to a global variable `id`. The timing constraints on `x` are such that all processes can change the global variable to their own process id, then read the global variable later and if the shared variable is still equal to its own id, enter the critical section. Note that although the Fischer automaton is a TBA, it does not have any final states. To introduce liveness into the model, once could encode a liveness property as an auxiliary "monitor" TBA, or simply a Büchi automaton. Then the composition of the Fischer automaton and the monitor automaton gives the global timed Büchi automaton. This is the approach taken, for example, in [18]. Note that the Fischer mutual exclusion protocol is one of the benchmarks we consider in Section 5.

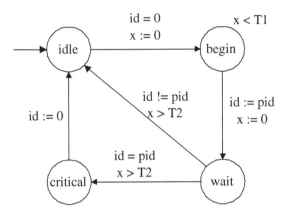

Fig. 2. A TBA for the Fischer real-time mutual exclusion protocol

Definition 2 (Language and emptiness problem for TBA). *The* language *of A, denoted $Lang(A)$, is defined to be the set of all non-zeno accepting runs of A starting at the initial state s_0. The* emptiness problem *for A is to check whether $Lang(A) = \emptyset$.*

The emptiness problem for TBA is known to be PSPACE-complete [1]. More precisely, the worst-case complexity of the problem is linear in the number of discrete states of the automaton, exponential in the number of clocks, and exponential in the encoding of the constants appearing in guards or invariants. This worst-case complexity is inherent to the problem: as shown in [4], both the number of clocks and the magnitude of the constants render PSPACE-hardness independently of each other.

Definition 3 (Strong non-zenoness). *A TBA A is called* strongly non-zeno *if all accepting runs starting at the initial state of A are non-zeno.*

A *structural loop* of a TBA A is a sequence of distinct edges $e_1 \cdots e_m$ such that $\mathsf{target}(e_i) = \mathsf{source}(e_{i+1})$, for all $i = 1, ..., m$ (the addition $i + 1$ is modulo m). We say that the structural loop is *accepting* if there exists an index $1 \le i \le m$ such that $\mathsf{target}(e_i)$ is an accepting state. We say that the structural loop *spends time* if there exists a clock x of A and indices $0 \le i, j \le m$ such that:

1. x is reset in step i, that is, $x \in \mathsf{reset}(e_i)$, and
2. x is bounded from below in step j, that is, $(x < 1) \cap \mathsf{guard}(e_j) = \emptyset$.

Definition 4 (Structural non-zenoness). *We say that a TBA A is structurally non-zeno if every accepting structural loop of A spends time.*

For example, in Figure 1, automaton A_1 is not structurally non-zeno, while automaton A_2 is. A_2 would not be structurally non-zeno if any of the guards $x \geq 1$ were missing.

Lemma 1 ([18]). *If A is structurally non-zeno then A is strongly non-zeno.*

Theorem 1 ([18]). *Any TBA A can be transformed into a strongly non-zeno TBA A', such that: (1) A' has one clock more than A and (2) $Lang(A) = \emptyset$ iff $Lang(A') = \emptyset$.*

3   Simulation Graphs

Simulation graphs were introduced in [5] as a technique for checking reachability in timed automata. In [18,2], it is shown how simulation graphs can also be used to check TBA emptiness. We summarize these results in this section.

Consider a TBA $A = (\mathcal{X}, Q, q_0, E, \mathsf{invar}, F)$. A *symbolic state* S of A is a finite set of *regions* [1] $r_i = (q, \zeta_i)$, $1 \leq i \leq k$, all associated with the same discrete state $q \in Q$. We also denote S as (q, ζ), where $\zeta = \cup_i \zeta_i$.[3] Given an edge $e \in E$, let $e(S)$ be the set of all regions r' for which there exists $r \in S$ such that r can reach r' by a transition labeled e in the region graph. Similarly, let $\epsilon(S)$ be the set of all regions r' for which there exists $r \in S$ such that r can reach r' by a (possible empty) sequence of time-passing transitions in the region graph (thus, $S \subseteq \epsilon(S)$). Then, we define $\mathsf{post}(S, e) = \epsilon(e(S))$.

Definition 5 (Simulation graph). *The simulation graph of a TBA A, denoted $SG(A)$, is the graph whose set of nodes $\mathcal{S}$ is the least set of non-empty symbolic states of A, such that:*

1. $\epsilon((q_0, \mathbf{0})) \in \mathcal{S}$ is the initial node of $SG(A)$, and
2. if $e \in E$, $S \in \mathcal{S}$ and $S' = \mathsf{post}(S, e)$ is non-empty, then $S' \in \mathcal{S}$.

$SG(A)$ has an edge $S \xrightarrow{e} S'$ iff $S, S' \in \mathcal{S}$ and $S' = \mathsf{post}(S, e)$.

An example of a TBA and its simulation graph is given in Figure 3. The simulation graph was automatically generated using the KRONOS [5] tool. The intuition behind the three nodes of the simulation graph is as follows. The initial node captures all regions associated with initial state q_0 of the TBA by letting time pass until the a-transition occurs. The constraints in this node reflect that fact that all clocks of a TBA are synchronized, and therefore proceed at the same

---

[3] A union of regions is generally not convex. In practice, tools such as Kronos work with symbolic states that can be represented by zones; i.e., such that $\cup_i \zeta_i$ is convex.

constant rate. They are also reflective of the fact that, because of q_0's invariant, x cannot advance past 7, at which time the a-transition is taken. The node of simulation graph associated with state q_1 is indicative of the fact that y was reset by the a-transition but not x, and that the a-transition is taken at time 7. The remaining node indicates that the b-transition resets x but not y, and that when it does occur, y has not advanced past 3. It also indicates that, as in the initial node, x cannot advance past 7 while the TBA resides in q_0.

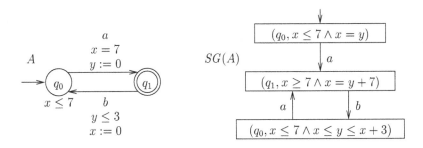

Fig. 3. A TBA and its simulation graph

A node $(q, \zeta) \in \mathcal{S}$ is *accepting* if $q \in F$. Let $\mathcal{F}$ and Δ be the set of accepting nodes and the set of edges of $SG(A)$, respectively. The simulation graph $SG(A) = (E, \mathcal{S}, \mathcal{S}_0, \Delta, \mathcal{F})$ defines a discrete Büchi automaton (BA) over the input alphabet E and symbolic states $\mathcal{S}$.

A sequence $\sigma = S_0 \overset{e_0}{\to} S_1 \overset{e_1}{\to}, ...,$ where $S_0 \in \mathcal{S}_0$ and for all $i \geq 0$, $S_i \overset{e_i}{\to} S_{i+1} \in \Delta$ is called an *infinite run* of $SG(A)$ if the sequence is infinite and a *finite run* otherwise. An infinite run is called *accepting* if there exists an infinite set of indices $J \subseteq \mathbb{N}$, such that for all $i \in J$, $S_i \in \mathcal{F}$. We say that σ is ultimately periodic if there exist $i \geq 0$, $l \geq 1$ such that for all $j \geq 0$, $S_{i+j} = S_{i+j \bmod l}$. This means that σ consists of a finite prefix $S_0 \overset{e_0}{\to} \cdots S_{i-1} \overset{e_{i-1}}{\to}$, followed by the "infinite unfolding" of a *cycle* $S_i \overset{e_i}{\to} \cdots S_{i+l-1} \overset{e_{i+l-1}}{\to} S_i$. The cycle is called *simple* if for all $0 \leq j \neq k < l$, $S_{i+j} \neq S_{i+k}$, that is, the cycle does not visit the same node twice. In the following, we refer to such a reachable simple cycle as a *lasso* and say that the lasso is accepting if its simple cycle contains an accepting node.

Theorem 2 ([18]). *Let A be a strongly non-zeno TBA. $Lang(A) \neq \emptyset$ iff there is an accepting lasso in the simulation graph of A.*

4   The Deep Random Search Algorithm

Let A be a strongly non-zeno TBA and let $S = SG(A)$ be A's simulation graph; as shown in Section 3, S exists and there is an efficient procedure for generating it from A. Moreover, S is a Büchi automaton (BA). Now let φ be a real-time property expressed in a logic for timed automata, e.g., TECTL$_\exists^*$ [2]. Since the formulas of this logic are built up from timed automata, we can construct, as shown in [2], a corresponding BA $T = SG(A_{\neg\varphi})$, the simulation graph of the strongly non-zenoTBA $A_{\neg\varphi}$. The TECTL$^*_\exists$model-checking problem $A \models \varphi$ is then naturally defined in terms of the TBA emptiness problem for $S \times T$.

If φ is a *safety property*, then T has an associated deterministic finite automaton $\mathrm{pref}(T)$ that recognizes all finite trajectories violating the property [12]. As a consequence, the model-checking problem for safety properties can be reduced to a reachability (of accepting states) problem on the product automaton $B = \mathrm{fin}(S) \times \mathrm{pref}(T)$, where $\mathrm{fin}(S)$ is the finite automaton recognizing all finite trajectories of S.

Our model checker for timed automata applies the deep-random-search (DRS) algorithm described below to the finite automaton B. As discussed in Section 1, DRS is an iterative-deepening, deep-random-walk, random-fringe-backtracking Las-Vegas algorithm. By "deep random walk" we mean that in any state of a random walk, DRS always chooses a random non-visited child (immediate successor) state, as long as such a state exists. By "random fringe backtracking" we mean that the algorithm does not limit backtracking to predecessors; rather it randomly selects a node from the fringe as the starting point for a deep random walk. This strategy removes much of the bias towards the initial state of the search space. We assume that B is given as the triple (initState, Next-Child, Acc) where initState is the initial state, Next-Child is an iterator function for the immediate successors of a state of B, and Acc is a predicate defining the accepting states of B.

To fine tune the breath and the depth of the search, DRS inputs three additional parameters: walks, cutoff and increment. The first of these is the number of initial deep random walks taken by the algorithm from the root, which is always constrained to be greater than one and less then the number of children of initState. While not affecting completeness, this parameter determines the initial fringe, and therefore influences the way the computation tree grows. The second parameter bounds the depth of the search; thus, it affects completeness. To obtain a complete algorithm, cutoff has to be set to infinity. The third parameter is the iterative-deepening increment. While not affecting completeness, this parameter may affect optimality. Setting increment to one ensures the algorithm is optimal. Note, however, that (theoretical) optimality may lead to poor performance for deep counter-examples, as the search has to explore all the states in the tree above the counter-example.

The pseudo-code for DRS is shown in Figure 4. It uses the following three global variables: generated, fringe and done. The first of these is the set of so-far-generated states and is used to ensure that no state is visited more than once. The second variable is the set of generated states with unexplored successors, together with their depth. We call a state together with its depth a *node*. The third variable is a flag which is true when no random walk has been cutoff and therefore the entire search space has been explored.

Procedure DRS has an iterative-deepening for-loop. In each iteration, it initializes the global variables, it increments the cutoff depth and then calls procedure Bounded-DRS. This procedure returns only if no counter-example was found.

```
State initState; /* Initial state of the search space */
State Next-Child(State); /* Iterator function for immediate successors */
Bool Acc(State); /* Predicate define accepting states */
Node Set fringe = empty; /* Generated states with unexplored successors */
State Set generated = empty; /* Set of generated states */
Bool done = false; /* True when search space explored */

void DRS(Int increment) {
  /* Deep Random Search: iterative-deepening for-loop. In each iteration, */
  /* initialize global variables, increment cutoff depth, call Bounded-DRS */
  for (Int co = increment; (!done && co ≤ cutoff); co += increment); {
    done = true; generated = empty; fringe = empty;
    Bounded-DRS(co); }
  exit ("no counter-example"); }

void Bounded-DRS(Int cutoff) {
  /* Perform complete search up to cutoff depth. Initialize fringe by */
  /* taking no. deep walks specified by param walks. Then repeatedly */
  /* take deep walks from random node in fringe by calling Random-Walk */
  if (Acc(initState)) exit ("counter-example", initState);
  Insert(generated, initState);
  Node Set children = Nonaccepting-Interior-Children((initState,1));
  for (Int i = 1; (children != empty && i ≤ walks); i++) {
    Node node = Random-Remove(children);
    Insert(generated, node.state); Insert(fringe, node);
    Random-Walk(node, cutoff); }
  while (fringe != empty) {
    node = Random(fringe);
    Random-Walk(node, cutoff); }
  return;}

void Random-Walk(Node node, Int cutoff) {
  /* Perform random walk in search of accept state up to cutoff depth. */
  /* Visited states added to generated and fringe. Node removed from */
  /* from fringe when all its children visited. */
  Node next = node;
  while (next.depth < cutoff) {
    Node Set children = Nonaccepting-Interior-Children(next) ;
    if (|children| ≤ 1) {Remove(fringe, next); if (|children| == 0) return;}
    next = Random(children);
    Insert(generated, next.state); Insert(fringe, next); }
  Remove(fringe, next); done = false; return;}

Node Set Nonaccepting-Interior-Children(Node nd) {
  /* construct set of interesting children of current node; i.e. those */
  /* nodes not previously generated, non-accepting, non-leaf. */
  Node Set children = empty;
  for (State nx = Next-Child(nd.state); nx != Null; nx = Next-Child(nd.state)){
    if (! In(generated, nx)) {
      if ( Acc(nx) ) exit ("counter-example", nx);
      if (! Leaf(nx) ) Insert(children, (nx, nd.depth+1));} } }
  return children;}
```

Fig. 4. DRS model-checking algorithm

Moreover, if no random walk was cut off, upon return from `Bounded-DRS`, the flag `done` is still true, signaling that the entire state space of B has been explored without finding a counter-example.

Procedure `Bounded-DRS` performs a complete search of the transition graph of B up to the cutoff depth. The procedure first checks whether the initial state is accepting in which case it exits and signals that it has found a counter-example. Otherwise, it initializes the fringe by taking the number of deep walks specified by the parameter `walks`. Each such walk starts from a different child of the initial state. As long as the fringe is not empty, the procedure then repeatedly starts deep random walks from a random node in the fringe and up to the cutoff depth, by calling `Random-Walk`.

Procedure `Random-Walk` traverses a deep random path in the computation tree of B. For each node along the path, it first obtains the set of all the non-accepting, non-generated, interior children of the node. If this set is empty, or if it contains only one node, the current node can be safely removed from the fringe, as all its successors have been (or are in the process of being) explored. Moreover, if the set is empty, the walk cannot be continued and the procedure returns. Otherwise, it randomly picks one of the children, inserts it in the generated set and in the fringe and continues from this node. The procedure is guaranteed to stop when the cutoff value is reached. In this case, the cutoff node is removed from the fringe and `done` is set to false.

Procedure `Nonaccepting-Interior-Children` uses the iterator `Next-Child` of B to construct the set of interesting children of the current node. A child state of the current node's state is inserted (together with its depth) in this set only if the state was not previously generated, is non-accepting, and has at least one enabled successor (it is not a leaf).

Theorem 3 (Correctness & completeness). *Given a timed automaton A and safety property φ, DRS-MC returns a counter-example if and only if $A \not\models \varphi$. Proof.* The proof follows from Theorems 1, 2 and the fact that the DRS model-checking algorithm is complete.

Theorem 4 (Complexity). *Let $B = \operatorname{fin}(S) \times \operatorname{pref}(T)$ be the finite automaton discussed above. Then DRS uses $O(|B|)$ time and space, where $|B|$ is the number of states in B.*

Theorem 5 (Optimality). *Let d be the smallest depth of an accepting state of B. Then the depth of a counter-example returned by DRS is never greater than $d + $ `increment`.*

Theorem 5 is an "optimality up to `increment`" result. Assuming that DRS finds a counter-example during iteration $k + 1$, $k \geq 1$, we have that $k \cdot $ `increment` $< d \leq (k + 1) \cdot $ `increment`, and the result follows.

5   Experimental Results

We have implemented the DRS model-checking algorithm as an extension to the Open-Kronos model checker for timed automata [18]. Open-Kronos takes as input a system of extended timed automata and a boolean expression defining the accepting states of the automata. The input is translated into a C program which is compiled and linked to the Profounder, a tool that performs on-the-fly generation of the simulation graph of the input TA model and applies standard depth-first search for reachability analysis.

To assess the performance and scalability of DRS, we compared its performance to Open-Kronos and UPPAAL (3.4.11) on the following real-time model-checking benchmarks: the *Fischer Real-Time Mutual-Exclusion Protocol*, the *Philips Audio Protocol*, and the *Bang & Olufsen Audio/Video Protocol*. All reported results (Tables 1-4) were obtained on a PC equipped with an Athlon 2600+ MHz processor and 1GB RAM running Linux 2.6.5 (Fedora Core 2).

In the tables, the meaning of the column headings is the following: proc is the number of processes; sender is the number of senders (Tables 3 and 4); time is given in seconds; states is the number of visited states—for DRS, this is the size of the set *generated*; depth is the depth of the accepting state found by the model checker; and oom means the model checker ran out of memory. The statistics provided for DRS are averages obtained over a representative number of runs of the algorithm. Because UPPAAL does not provide the number of visited states, path depth, etc., only its execution time is given here.

The Fischer protocol uses timing constraints and a shared variable to ensure mutual exclusion among processes competing for access to a critical section [14]. Table 1 contains the results for checking mutual exclusion (a safety property) on a buggy version of the protocol. As the results indicate, DRS consistently outperforms

Table 1. Mutual exclusion for Fischer protocol (buggy version)

	Open-Kronos			DRS			UPPAAL
proc	time	states	depth	time	states	depth	time
2	0.038	63	44	0.003	20	6	0.021
4	2.968	1227	1166	0.006	67	28	0.041
8	13.20	35409	2048	0.082	216	211	1.280
12	204	332253	2048	0.512	386	374	18.61
16	>12hrs	?	?	0.906	238	222	223 (oom)

Table 2. Mutual exclusion for Fischer protocol (correct version)

	Open-Kronos		DRS	UPPAAL
proc	time	states	time	time
2	0.004	203	0.011	0.02
3	0.386	24949	0.513	0.03
4	943	3842501	1388	0.14
5	4hrs	oom	oom	2.01
6	4hrs	oom	oom	124
7	4hrs	oom	oom	>5hrs

Table 3. Results for the Phillips audio protocol

sender	Open-Kronos			DRS			UPPAAL
	time	states	depth	time	states	depth	time
1	0.004	72	71	0.003	16	12	0.026
4	3.259	46263	2048	0.007	30	26	0.041
8	422.2	1026446	2048	0.041	93	26	0.158
12	>12hrs	?	?	0.736	375	42	0.802
24	>12hrs	?	?	0.020	41	17	39.095
28	>12hrs	?	?	0.033	50	22	107 (oom)

Table 4. Results for the B&O audio/video protocol

sender	Open-Kronos			DRS			UPPAAL
	time	states	depth	time	states	depth	time
2	0.226	1285	1284	0.034	1659	1657	0.174
3	35.161	1135817	1997	10.76	166113	2318	1.050
4	53.532	1130669	1608	50.554	617760	2972	10.1
5	1200	oom	-	10 min	6769520	4734	2 min
6	1200	oom	-	37 min	30316978	13376	12 min (oom)

Open-Kronos and UPPAAL, thereby illustrating the power of deep random search in finding counter-examples. Table 2 contains the mutual-exclusion results for the correct version of the protocol. In this case, DRS, like Open-Kronos, must perform a complete search of the state space and the performance of the two model checkers is similar. In particular, the number of states visited is essentially the same for both model checkers, and therefore given only once in Table 2. UPPAAL's performance, on the other hand, is superior to that of Open-Kronos and DRS, although it too struggles when the number of processes reaches 7.

The purpose of the Phillips audio protocol is to exchange control information between audio components using the Manchester encoding [10]. The correctness of the encoding relies on timing delays between signals. The protocol was designed to satisfy the following safety property: communication between components should be reliable, with a tolerance of ±5% on the timing. However, the protocol is faulty and our results are given in Table 3 for a varying number of sender components. For this benchmark, DRS consistently outperforms both Open-Kronos and UPPAAL.

The Bang & Olufsen audio/video protocol was designed to transmit messages between audio/video components over a single bus. Its behavior is highly timing dependent. The protocol is intended to satisfy the following safety property: whenever a frame has been sent, the transmitted frame must be intact, and other senders must not have discovered a collision [9]. The results of Table 4 show once again that deep random search is superior to depth-first search (Open-Kronos) in finding deep counter-examples. DRS's performance is similar to that of UPPAAL on this benchmark. For 6 senders, the results reported for DRS are those for one out of 20 executions of the model checker; the other 19 ran out of memory.

6   Conclusions

We have presented the DRS deep-random-search algorithm for model checking timed automata. DRS performs random walks up to a prescribed depth within the TA's simulation graph. Nodes along these walks are then used to construct a random fringe, which is the starting point of additional deep random walks. DRS is complete, and optimal to within a specified depth increment. Our experimental results show that it is able to find extremely deep counter-examples while consistently outperforming the Open-Kronos and UPPAAL model checkers. Our DRS algorithm is not restricted to timed automata; it may be beneficially applied to the model checking of safety properties of any concurrent system.

A version of DRS that is more in line with classic depth-first or breadth-first search, would put all the non-accepting, non-generated interior children (except for the one randomly selected) in the fringe and not the node itself. Intuitively, this version should perform less work, as it explores the children of a node only once. We have implemented this version too, but found that it performed worse in terms of finding counter-examples. The reason for the performance degradation may be the fact that more nodes are inserted in the fringe with each deep random walk and therefore the chance of selecting the right deep candidate node may decrease, at least for the examples that we have tested.

The expected time complexity of DRS is related to the random variable X, the number of states visited before an accepting state is found. Getting a closed-form expression for the mean and variance of X is difficult due to the intricate interdependence between the random walks taken by the algorithm. This is a subject for future work. Experimental results for a guided-search algorithm, where randomization is used to select a successor among the first n elements in a priority queue, showed that X follows a normal distribution [11]. Increasing n was shown to increase both the variance and the mean of X. Randomization improved the search performance because the probability of observing a small value of X increased logarithmically with the variance, provided the mean remained unchanged.

We also plan to investigate how to extend the deep-random-search technique to liveness properties. The main issue here is deciding when a deep random walk has formed a lasso. It is not enough to terminate such a walk when a previously visited state is re-encountered; rather one must correctly distinguish cross-edges from back-edges in the simulation graph. This would probably require storing parent edges, which are also useful in determining the path from the initial state to the accepting state.

Acknowledgments. We thank the anonymous reviewers for their valuable comments.

References

1. Alur, R., Dill, D.: A theory of timed automata. Theoretical Computer Science 126, 183–235 (1994)
2. Bouajjani, A., Tripakis, S., Yovine, S.: On-the-fly symbolic model checking for real-time systems. In: RTSS 1997. 18th IEEE Real-Time Systems Symposium, San Francisco, CA, pp. 25–34. IEEE, Los Alamitos (1997)
3. Clarke, E., Biere, A., Raimi, R., Zhu, Y.: Bounded model checking using satisfiability solving. Formal Methods in System Design 19(1), 7–34 (2001)
4. Courcoubetis, C., Yannakakis, M.: Minimum and maximum delay problems in real-time systems. In: Larsen, K.G., Skou, A. (eds.) CAV 1991. LNCS, vol. 575, Springer, Heidelberg (1992)
5. Daws, C., Olivero, A., Tripakis, S., Yovine, S.: The tool Kronos. In: Alur, R., Sontag, E.D., Henzinger, T.A. (eds.) Hybrid Systems III, Verification and Control. LNCS, vol. 1066, pp. 208–219. Springer, Heidelberg (1996)
6. Dill, D.L.: Timing assumptions and verification of finite-state concurrent systems. In: Sifakis, J. (ed.) Automatic Verification Methods for Finite State Systems. LNCS, vol. 407, pp. 197–212. Springer, Heidelberg (1990)
7. Grosu, R., Smolka, S.A.: Monte carlo model checking. In: Halbwachs, N., Zuck, L.D. (eds.) TACAS 2005. LNCS, vol. 3440, pp. 271–286. Springer, Heidelberg (2005)
8. Haslum, P.: Model checking by random walk. In: Proc. of 1999 ECSEL Workshop (1999)
9. Havelund, K., Skou, A., Larsen, K.G., Lund, K.: Automated analysis of an audio control protocol. In: Proc. of 18th IEEE Real-Time Systems Symposium, San Francisco, California, USA, pp. 2–13 (December 1997)
10. Ho, P.-H., Wong-Toi, H.: Automated analysis of an audio control protocol. In: Wolper, P. (ed.) CAV 1995. LNCS, vol. 939, pp. 381–394. Springer, Heidelberg (1995)
11. Jones, M., Mercer, E.: Explicit state model checking with Hopper. In: Graf, S., Mounier, L. (eds.) Model Checking Software. LNCS, vol. 2989, Springer, Heidelberg (2004)
12. Kupferman, O., Vardi, M.Y.: Model checking of safety properties. Formal Methods in System Design 19(3), 291–314 (2001)
13. Larsen, K., Petterson, P., Yi, W.: Uppaal in a nutshell. Software Tools for Technology Transfer 1(1/2) (October 1997)
14. Larsen, K.G., Pettersson, P., Yi, W.: Model checking for real-time systems. In: Reichel, H. (ed.) FCT 1995. LNCS, vol. 965, pp. 62–88. Springer, Heidelberg (1995)
15. Mihail, M., Papadimitriou, C.H.: On the random walk method for protocol testing. In: Dill, D.L. (ed.) CAV 1994. LNCS, vol. 818, pp. 132–141. Springer, Heidelberg (1994)
16. Pelánek, R., Hanžl, T., Černá, I., Brim, L.: Enhancing random walk state space exploration. In: FMICS 2005. Proceedings of the 10th international workshop on Formal methods for industrial critical systems, pp. 98–105. ACM Press, New York (2005)
17. Russell, S.J., Norvig, P.: Artificial Intelligence: A Modern Approach, 2nd edn. Prentice-Hall, Englewood Cliffs (2002)
18. Tripakis, S., Yovine, S., Bouajjani, A.: Checking timed Büchi automata emptiness efficiently. Formal Methods in System Design 26(3), 267–292 (2005)
19. Tronci, E.G., Penna, D., Intrigila, B., Venturini, M.: A probabilistic approach to automatic verification of concurrent systems. In: APSEC. Proc. of 8th IEEE Asia-Pacific Software Engineering Conference (2001)

OASiS: A Service-Oriented Architecture for Ambient-Aware Sensor Networks*

Xenofon Koutsoukos, Manish Kushwaha, Isaac Amundson,
Sandeep Neema, and Janos Sztipanovits

Institute for Software Integrated Systems
Department of Electrical Engineering and Computer Science
Vanderbilt University
Nashville, Tennessee 37235, USA
{xenofon.koutsoukos,manish.kushwaha,isaac.amundson
sandeep.neema,janos.sztipanovits}@vanderbilt.edu

Abstract. Heterogeneous sensor networks are comprised of ensembles of small, smart, and cheap sensing and computing devices that permeate the environment, as well as resource intensive sensors such as satellite imaging systems, meteorological stations, and security cameras. Emergency response, homeland security, and many other applications have a very real need to interconnect these diverse networks and access information in real-time. Web service technologies provide well-developed mechanisms for exchanging data between heterogeneous computing devices, but they cannot be used in resource-constrained wireless sensor networks. This paper presents OASiS, a lightweight service-oriented architecture for sensor networks, which provides dynamic service discovery and can be used to develop ambient-aware applications that adapt to changes in the network and the environment. An important advantage of OASiS is that it allows seamless integration with Web services. We have developed a middleware implementation that supports OASiS, and a simple tracking application to illustrate the approach. Our results demonstrate the feasibility of a service-oriented architecture for wireless sensor networks.

1 Introduction

Wireless sensor networks (WSNs) consist of small, inexpensive computing devices which interact with the environment and communicate with each other to identify spatial and temporal patterns of physical phenomena [1]. A sensor web is a heterogeneous collection of such networks, and can also include resource-intensive sensing platforms such as satellite imaging systems, meteorological stations, and security cameras. Such heterogeneous sensor networks can greatly benefit applications ranging from emergency response to homeland security [2], [3], [4].

---

* This work is partially supported by ARO MURI W911NF-06-1-0076, Microsoft External Research, and by NSF Grant CCR-0225610.

F. Kordon and O. Sokolsky (Eds.): Monterey Workshop 2006, LNCS 4888, pp. 125–149, 2007.

At present, users wishing to deploy WSN applications must be adept at low-level sensor network programming, as well as implementing the necessary domain-specific functionality. These applications must be able to run on large networks with nodes that have varying capabilities, are manufactured and operated by different vendors, and are accessed by multiple clients exercising different functionalities. A *service-oriented architecture* (SOA) offers flexibility in the design of WSN applications since it provides accepted standards for representing and packaging data, describing the functionality of services, and facilitating the search for available services which can be invoked to meet application requirements [5]. SOA deployment has already proved successful on the World Wide Web, however Web service technologies have been developed assuming standard Internet protocols and are not realizable in resource-constrained sensor networks.

This paper presents OASiS, an Object-centric, Ambient-aware, Service-oriented Sensornet programming model and middleware implementation for WSN applications. In the *object-centric* paradigm, the application programmer is presented with a layer of abstraction in which the phenomenon monitored by the sensor network is represented by a unique logical object which drives the application [6]. The model is *ambient-aware*, which enables the application to adapt to network failures and environmental changes by employing a dynamic service discovery protocol. OASiS is a *lightweight* framework which avoids the use of bulky XML-based messages found in Web service standards, however, it still provides a simple mechanism for Web service integration.

We have implemented a suite of middleware services for the Mica2 mote hardware platform [17] running TinyOS [18] to support OASiS. Key characteristics of our approach that can benefit the design of sensor network applications are:

- Dynamic service discovery and configuration for reacting to changes in the network due to failures and unreliable communication links.
- Application reconfiguration for reacting to changes in the behavior of the monitored phenomenon.
- Service deployment onto heterogeneous platforms using well-defined interfaces enabling a seamless integration.
- Real-world integration by incorporating spatial service constraints that are necessary to monitor physical phenomena.
- Data aggregation by using services which accept input from multiple sensor nodes.

The OASiS programming model can be used to build a wide variety of dataflow applications such as target tracking, fire detection and monitoring, and distributed gesture recognition. To demonstrate the feasibility and utility of OASiS, we have developed a simplified indoor tracking experiment, which monitors a heat source as it travels through the sensor network region. The application is comprised of services provided by several resource-constrained sensor nodes, but it also invokes a Web service provided by a remote server. By providing access to the Web service, we incorporate functionality into our WSN application that would otherwise be unattainable.

This paper is organized as follows. Section 2 overviews our programming model and Section 3 describes dynamic service configuration. Our middleware implementation is presented in Section 4. Section 5 presents a case study followed by a scalability analysis in Section 6. In Section 7, we compare our research to similar work that has recently appeared in the literature. Section 8 concludes.

2   The OASiS Programming Model

This section presents the OASiS programming model. To illustrate the model, we use an environmental monitoring example in which a network of chemical sensor nodes is deployed for detecting and tracking chemical clouds. Upon detection, the sensor network begins estimating the speed and heading of the cloud, and continues to do so until the cloud leaves the sensing region. This tracking data is forwarded to a base station, which alerts local emergency management officials.

2.1   The Object-Centric Paradigm

The entity that drives an *object-centric* application is the *physical phenomenon* under observation. In OASiS, the physical phenomenon is represented by a *logical object*, which is comprised of a finite state machine (FSM), a service graph for each FSM mode, and a set of state variables. Figure 1 illustrates this representation in the context of the chemical cloud example. The estimated position of the chemical cloud is maintained by the logical object using the state variables (e.g. the mean and variance of the center of the chemical cloud). Each FSM mode represents a specific behavior of the chemical cloud, (e.g. stationary or moving), and contains a service graph that represents a dataflow algorithm. The algorithm is executed periodically, and its output is used to update the state. When the behavior of the physical phenomenon changes, the logical object transitions to a new mode containing a different service graph.

The logical object is instantiated upon detection of a physical phenomenon of interest. This is achieved by comparing sensor data with an *object context*, which defines the detection conditions for the physical phenomenon. This comparison is made periodically at a frequency specified by a refresh rate. Because multiple nodes may detect the same physical phenomenon at roughly the same time, a mechanism is required to ensure that only one logical object is instantiated. To provide this guarantee, OASiS employs an object-owner election algorithm similar to that of [6], which is executed by each candidate node.

After object instantiation completes, exactly one node, referred to as the *object node*, is elected owner of the logical object. The logical object initiates in the default mode of the FSM and starts the process of dynamic service configuration (described below), after which the application begins execution. The object maintenance protocol evaluates the mode transition conditions every time the object state is updated. If a mode transition condition evaluates *true*, the protocol makes the transition to the new mode. The mode transition involves resetting any logical object state variables, if applicable, and configuring the new

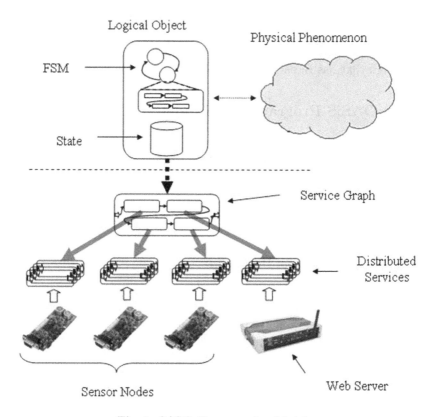

Fig. 1. OASiS: Programming Model

service graph corresponding to the new logical object mode. Because OASiS is a programming model for resource constrained WSNs, the FSM is intended to contain only a small number of modes representing a few broad behaviors of the physical phenomenon. We also assume the frequency of mode transitions will be much slower than the sampling rate required for tracking the phenomenon.

The logical object has a migration condition, which if evaluates *true*, invokes the object migration protocol. The selection policy for the migration destination is tied to the condition that triggers the migration protocol. In the above example, an increase in the variance of the location estimate can serve as a migration condition, and the owner selection policy will choose the node that is currently closest to the chemical cloud. Another migration condition could be a low power reading on the object-node, in which case the selection policy chooses a nearby node with a sufficient power reserve. The migration process consists of running the owner election algorithm to select the migration destination based on the selection policy and transferring the object state to the new object node. In this way the logical object follows the physical phenomenon through the sensing region. When the sensor network is no longer able to detect the physical phenomenon, the logical object must be destroyed. This is a simple matter of resetting the logical object state to *null*. After an object has been destroyed, the sensor network begins searching for a new physical phenomenon.

The goal of an object-centric programming model is to provide abstractions focusing on the physical phenomena being monitored, thus bypassing the complex issues of network topology and distributed computation inherent to sensor network application programming. This effectively transfers ownership of common tasks such as sensing, computation, and communication from the individual nodes to the object itself. In addition, object-centric programming in OASiS facilitates dynamic service discovery and configuration by considering only a single neighborhood in the network and solving a localized constraint satisfaction problem. Details are discussed in Section 3.

2.2   Services in Sensor Networks

In OASiS, each mode in the logical object FSM contains a *service graph* whose constituent services provide the functionality necessary to update the state. Specifically, a service graph contains a set of services, a set of bindings, and a set of constraints, where a binding is a connection between two services, and a constraint is a restrictive attribute relating one or more services. We assume that the service graph is known a priori for each mode. Note that the service graph is simply a specification of an application and not the actual implementation. The implementation is provided by the services themselves, which may or may not be provided by the object node. *Services* are resources capable of performing tasks that form a coherent functionality from the point of view of provider entities and requester entities [7]. They are the basic unit of functionality in OASiS, and have well-defined interfaces which allow them to be described, published, discovered, and invoked over the network. Each service can have zero or more *input ports* and zero or one *output port*. Services are modular and autonomous, and are accessible by any authorized client application. For these reasons, services are typically stateless.

Figure 2 depicts the service graph for tracking a moving chemical cloud. Our localization algorithm requires chemical concentration measurements from sensor nodes surrounding the center of the cloud, and the current wind velocity in the region. Therefore, the service graph consists of Chemical Sensor services and one Wind Velocity service whose outputs are connected to the inputs of a Localization service. The Localization service uses a Kalman filter [8], and therefore requires current state variables obtained via an input port connected directly to the object. Similarly, the Localization service passes the updated coordinates of the chemical cloud back to the logical object. The Localization service is also connected to a Notification service, which informs the emergency management agency of the cloud's current position.

Because services can be publicly accessible, an attempted invocation might be blocked due to mutual exclusion if the service is currently executing some shared resource. Our programming model accounts for this with a globally asynchronous, locally synchronous (GALS) model of computation [9]. GALS

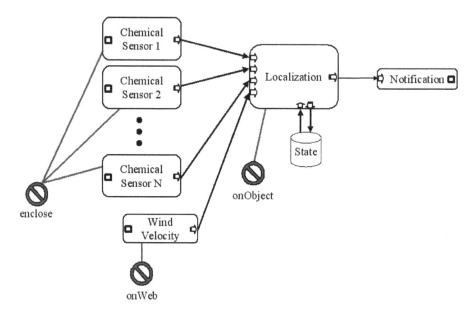

Fig. 2. Service Graph for Chemical Cloud Tracking Application

guarantees that communication between services will occur asynchronously (i.e. non-blocking), while intra-service communication such as method calls will exhibit synchronous (blocking) behavior. In this manner, a service never has to wait for its output to be consumed before processing data arriving on an input port. As such, GALS is an important and desirable paradigm for service-oriented applications for sensor networks.

Application services can run on the resource-constrained nodes of the sensor network or they may be executed on more powerful sensor nodes in a high-bandwidth network. In our work, these resource-intensive services are implemented as *Web services*. We elect to use Web services due to their well-defined and documented standards. By taking advantage of Web services, applications have access to a wide range of functionality which would otherwise be unattainable. For example, our Localization service requires the wind velocity in the region. One option for obtaining the wind velocity is to equip a subset of sensor nodes with anemometers, however this approach can be cost-prohibitive and difficult to implement. Instead, we rely on an Internet-based *Wind Velocity* service, for example, one provided by the U.S. National Weather Service. The service interface definition is provided in a *Web Service Definition Language* (WSDL) file available on the host server. This provides us with the information necessary to access the Web service, including input and output parameters and their data types.

The modular and autonomous properties of services facilitate application programming and provide an efficient mechanism for application reconfiguration during runtime. Because services provide an interface describing their functionality in terms of inputs and outputs, the programmer does not have to be concerned with their physical placement, hardware platform, or implementation language. Furthermore, services allow new functionality to be easily inserted into the network without having to redeploy the underlying WSN application.

2.3   Service Constraints

It is often undesirable for multiple services in an application to be running concurrently on the same node. Conversely, there arise situations in which two services must be running on the same node. Many localization algorithms require sensing services to be situated in a precise spatial configuration. Other sensor node properties such as power level and physical position may also be important when deciding where to run a service. The ability to specify these types of constraints is a necessary aspect of composing service graphs at run-time.

Typical constraints associated with a service graph can be categorized as either *property* or *resource-allocation* constraints. Property constraints specify a relation between the properties of services (or the nodes providing the services) and some constant value. The ENCLOSE property constraint, for example, specifies that nodes providing services a, b, and c must surround the physical phenomenon of interest. The ENCLOSE constraint is very important for tracking spatial phenomena and is discussed in more detail in Section 3. Resource-allocation constraints define a relationship between the nodes that provide the services. For example, a resource-allocation constraint can specify that services a, b, and c must run on different nodes (or must all run on the same node).

Constraints can further be categorized as being either *atomic* or *compositional* based on their cardinality, or *arity*. Hence, a constraint involving a single service is an atomic (*unary*) constraint, while constraints involving two (*binary*) or more (*n-ary*) services are compositional constraints.

In the following, we formally define the constraints considered in our framework. A method for determining a service configuration which satisfies such constraints is presented in Section 3.

(1) *Atomic property constraint:*

$$\textbf{service}.provider.p \ \textbf{op} \ K$$

where p is a property of the node providing **service**, **op** is a relational operator (**op** $\in \{>, \geq, <, \leq, ==, \neq\}$), and K is some constant value. For example, the constraint that service a must be provided by a node at least one meter above the ground is written as $a.provider.\text{z} \geq 1$.

(2) *Compositional property constraint:*

$$F(provider.p) \ \textbf{op} \ K \ \textbf{over} \ S$$

where p and **op** are defined above, and F is a composition function on property p for all services in the set S. For example, to specify that the average power level of nodes providing services a, b, and c must be greater than or equal to 85% is written as **average**$(provider.\text{POWER}) \geq 85$ **over** $\{a, b, c\}$.

(3) *Atomic resource-allocation constraint:*

$$\textbf{service}.\textit{provider}.\textit{type} \textbf{ op } \text{TYPE\_SET}$$

where $\textbf{op} \in \{==, \neq, \in, \notin\}$. For example, $a.\textit{provider}.\text{ID} \notin \{NODE_1, NODE_2, NODE_3\}$ is used to ensure that service a does not run on a set of nodes with particular IDs.

(4) *Compositional resource-allocation constraint:*

$$F(\textit{provider}.\textit{type}) \textbf{ over } \mathcal{S}$$

where $F \in \{\textbf{allSame}, \textbf{allDifferent}\}$. For example, the constraint that services a and b must run on the same node, and c must run on a different node can be written as $allSame(\textit{provider}.\text{ID}) \textbf{ over } \{a, b\} \&\& allDifferent(\textit{provider}.\text{ID}) \textbf{ over } \{a, c\}$. Similarly, more complex compositional resource-allocation constraints can be specified by using combinations of *allSame* and *allDifferent*.

2.4 Service Discovery and Composition

There are three types of events that will trigger service discovery and composition: object instantiation, mode transition, and migration. Object instantiation and mode transition are similar in that the logical object enters a new (possibly default) mode containing a service graph. For migration, the mode may not change, but the logical object is transferred to a new provider, which must parse the service graph in the current mode in order to execute it.

Before an object can start executing the service graph, a *Service Discovery Protocol* (SDP) is invoked to determine which nodes in the network provide which services. Our model employs passive service discovery, in which a provider advertises a service only when a request for that service has been received [10]. The SDP is provided as a service by each node and maintains a local *service repository* (SR) which catalogs application services running both locally and remotely. Should an entry become stale due to communication failure or node dropout, for example, or a new service request arrives for a service that is not present in the SR, the SDP locates a new provider for that service. The service discovery algorithm receives as input a service ID, which if not present in the service repository, will prompt the SDP to broadcast a service request to other nodes in the network, up to a specified number of hops. The outgoing *service discovery message* contains the ID of the requested service and the node ID of the sender. Nodes providing the requested service will send a *service discovery reply message*, which includes information such as physical location and remaining power level. The SDP caches the provider node information in the SR, and forwards the message to the *Composer*.

The objective of the Composer is to instantiate the configuration that satisfies the constraints specified in the service graph. These services are then *bound* together and eventually invoked. The ID of each service in the service graph is passed to the SDP. Because several instances of the same service could be residing on multiple nodes across the network, the Composer can expect multiple replies.

As replies arrive, the Composer checks to see that any atomic service graph constraints are satisfied, and if so, the node information is stored. Compositional constraint satisfaction commences after all replies have been received. Finally, the connections between the services in the service graph are examined, and a *service binding message* is created for each. The binding message contains the service and node IDs of the connection source, as well as the service and node IDs of the connection destination. The message is sent to the connection source node so that it may properly direct the output of its service to the input of the service specified by the connection destination. The Composer will not reuse bindings in the event a mode had been entered previously, because service graph constraints may no longer be valid.

Dynamic network behavior in WSNs can cause problems during application execution such as service unavailability and violation of constraints. Querying a centralized service repository each time a new service instance is needed can be expensive, especially when the repository is located multiple transmission hops away. The passive service discovery approach was found to be the most energy efficient for mobile ad hoc networks with limited power resources [10]. Requests are flooded a limited number of hops throughout the network, and all providers of the requested service respond with a message that follows a direct path back to the object node. The Composer is then provided with a list containing only those services requested.

Service discovery over *multiple hops* is achieved using a protocol similar to DSR [11]. There are three types of messages that require routing information: (i) service discovery reply messages, (ii) service binding messages, and (iii) service access messages. Service discovery request messages are flooded throughout the network, and therefore do not require any routing information. Routing information is maintained in a *next-hop table*, which stores the node ID of a known service provider, along with the ID of the next node along the multi-hop path to that provider. As a service discovery message travels from the object node to the service provider nodes, each intermediate node along the path records the ID of the preceding node. This gives the service provider a direct path back to the object node for service discovery reply messages.

A service discovery request message will flood the network up to a maximum number of hops, specified a priori by the domain-service or application developer. At each intermediate node, a *hop-number* counter in the message header is incremented, and the message will not be forwarded once the counter reaches the maximum number allowed. Note that this maximum is the largest number of hops from the object node to a service provider. This implies that service-to-service communication could possibly travel twice as many hops, if each service provider were the maximum number of hops from the object node on opposite sides. Rather than expending energy by sending out numerous path-probing message transmissions, the shortest path between two service providers is estimated by using the knowledge of the physical location of the service provider and the maximum physical distance a message can be transmitted. This method does not guarantee that the shortest path selected will be a feasible one, in which case another path should be selected.

3   Dynamic Service Configuration

This section describes dynamic service configuration that is required for reacting to changes in the network or in the behavior of the physical phenomenon.

3.1   Constraint Satisfaction

Service graph instantiation can be modeled as a constraint satisfaction problem [12], where services in the *abstract* service graph are the constraint variables, and the nodes that provide a particular service constitute the domain.

A finite CSP $\mathcal{P} = (X, \mathcal{D}, \mathcal{C})$ is defined as a set of n *variables* $X = \{x_1, ..., x_n\}$, a set of finite *domains* $\mathcal{D} = \{D_1, ..., D_n\}$ where D_i is the set of possible *values* for variable i, and a set of *constraints* between variables $\mathcal{C} = \{C_1, ..., C_m\}$. A constraint C_i is defined on a set of variables $(x_{i_1}, ..., x_{i_j})$ by a subset of the Cartesian product $D_{i_1} \times ... \times D_{i_j}$. A solution is an assignment of values to all variables which satisfy all the constraints. The design space for a constraint satisfaction problem is the set of all possible tuples of constraint variables. Formally, $\mathcal{D} = \{(v_1, v_2, ..., v_n) | v_1 \in D_1, v_2 \in D_2, ..., v_n \in D_n\}$

Constraint satisfaction prunes the design space as much as possible for all different types of constraints until a feasible solution is found. The specific pruning method depends on the constraint under consideration, specifically the constraint property, constraint operator, and composition function.

1) Atomic Constraint Satisfaction: Atomic constraints are straightforward to satisfy. Because each atomic constraint is defined on a single variable, pruning the domain of that variable will leave the domain *consistent*, and hence satisfy the constraint.

2) Compositional Constraint Satisfaction

a) Compositional Property Constraints: The compositional property constraints are defined in Section 2, and involve the use of a composition function. OASiS includes several composition functions for aggregation, such as SUM, AVERAGE, and MEDIAN. In addition, we have defined a composition function called ENCLOSE for specifying the spatial configuration of sensor nodes. Many tracking applications employ localization algorithms which require measurement data to come from multiple sensors surrounding the physical phenomenon. The quality of the localization estimate often depends on how well the spatial configuration of these sensors is described. In the chemical cloud tracking example, three chemical concentration sensors are required, and they must be positioned such that they enclose the cloud. The constraint ENCLOSE(L) *over* $\mathcal{S} = \{s_1, s_2, s_3\}$, specifies that the location L must be enclosed by the sensor nodes which provide services s_1, s_2, and s_3. For example, ENCLOSE(s_4.location) *over* $\mathcal{S} = \{s_1, s_2, s_3\}$ specifies that the location of the node providing service s_4 must be enclosed by sensor nodes that provide services s_1, s_2, and s_3.

In general, higher-level, complex constraints are more difficult and demanding to satisfy. However, such constraints can be transformed into lower-level, simple constraints that provide the desired result, while minimizing the power and resources expended in satisfying it. We model the ENCLOSE constraint based on the AM_I_SURROUNDED query described in [13]. The two-dimensional definition of ENCLOSE is as follows: L is surrounded by $\{s_1, s_2, s_3\}$ if there is no line in the plane that can separate L from all of $\{s_1, s_2, s_3\}$. For this definition, the constraint can be reduced to ENCLOSE(L) *over* $\{s_1, s_2, s_3\}$ $\Rightarrow$ CCW(L, s_1, s_2) & CCW(L, s_2, s_3) & CCW(L, s_3, s_1), where CCW(a, b, c) specifies that locations a, b, and c form a counter-clockwise-oriented triangle in 2-D. The geometric constraint CCW(L, s_3, s_1) is easy to check by simple computation [13].

The definition of ENCLOSE varies for different sensor domains. For example, one domain can define an *enclosed* region to be the overlap of member sensing ranges. Consider another example of camera sensors with orientation and limited field-of-view. The enclosed region in this case is the intersection of fields of view recorded by all member cameras. Figure 3 illustrates different enclosed regions.

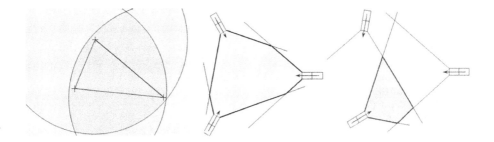

Fig. 3. Various definitions of ENCLOSE

b) Compositional Resource-Allocation Constraints: There are two types of composition functions for compositional resource-allocation constraints, *allSame* and *allDifferent*. Satisfying the *allSame* constraint is straightforward; the design space is the intersection of domains of all the participating constraint variables. To satisfy the allDifferent compositional constraint, a value is picked from the domain for each constraint variable. If the current set of values satisfy the constraint, a valid solution has been found. Otherwise, a backtracking algorithm [14] is used. The backtracking algorithm performs a depth-first search on the design space. Each leaf vertex represents a possible solution, assigning all constraint variables to a value. Non-leaf vertices are decision-points for constraint variables, where each path from the vertex assigns a value to the constraint variable. At the end of the backtracking step, either a solution has been found or the entire design space has been searched without finding any valid solution.

Algorithm 1 outlines the process of compositional constraint satisfaction. Lines 1-3 solve for constraints such as allSame as described above. The resulting pruned set is an exact set of solutions with respect to that constraint. In general, the pruned design space is an over-approximation that needs to be searched for a valid solution. Lines 4-14 solve for other compositional constraints by exploring the design space and backtracking. Although solving CSPs can be computationally expensive, by limiting the scope of the service discovery protocol in a neighborhood of the object node and by keeping the constraint specification syntax simple, the problem can be solved on resource-constrained sensor nodes. The constraint specification syntax still permits the user to accurately specify desired application behavior. OASiS implicitly assumes constraint satisfaction will terminate with a valid configuration. This assumption holds when services are redundantly distributed throughout the sensor network, and is reasonable for WSNs because redundancy is one of their main characteristics. Note that OASiS does not attempt to find an optimal configuration, because this can be too computationally expensive. Instead, the first feasible configuration that satisfies all the constraints is selected. If a better solution is desired, it must be specified in the form of additional constraints on the service graph.

Algorithm 1. Compositional Constraint Satisfaction

1: **for all** $C_i \in \mathcal{C}$ **do**
2:     $\tilde{\mathcal{D}} = \text{prune\_design\_space}(C_i, \mathcal{D})$
3: **end for**
4: $okay = \text{FALSE}$
5: **while** !$okay$ **do**
6:     $sol = \{(v_{index_1}, v_{index_1}, ..., v_{index_1}) | \forall i \ v_{index_i} \in \tilde{D}_i\}$
7:     $okay = \text{TRUE}$
8:     **for all** $C_j \in \mathcal{C}$ **do**
9:         **if** !satisfy(C_j, sol) **then**
10:             $okay = \text{FALSE}$
11:             $backtrack()$
12:         **end if**
13:     **end for**
14: **end while**

---

4   The OASiS Middleware

We have developed a suite of middleware services which support the features of our programming model. The middleware provides a layer of network abstraction, shielding the application developer from the low-level complexities of sensor network operation such as resource management and communication. It gracefully handles the decomposition of desired application behavior to produce node-level executable code for an object-centric, service-oriented WSN application.

4.1   Middleware Services

The middleware services include a *Node Manager*, *Object Manager*, and *Dynamic Service Configurator*. Figure 4 illustrates the relationship between the middle-

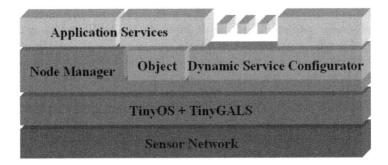

Fig. 4. Middleware

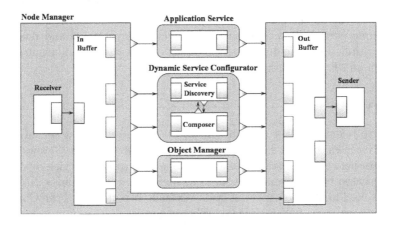

Fig. 5. Middleware architecture

ware and the sensor network, while Figure 5 illustrates the relationship between the application and middleware services at the sensor node level.

The Node Manager is responsible for message routing between services, both local and remote. This includes maintaining the multi-hop routing table and forwarding messages appropriately. The first eight bytes of any message handled by the Node Manager consist of a control structure which contains source and destination node IDs (2 bytes each), source and destination service IDs (1 byte each), message type (1 byte), and hop number (1 byte). The Node Manager examines the control structure and determines the appropriate destination for the message. For efficiency, it has *short circuit* functionality that allows it to catch outgoing messages bound for local services and reroute them directly.

Three key types of messages are handled by the Node Manager. *Service discovery messages* come from neighboring nodes inquiring if a specific service is available. The Node Manager passes these messages to the local Service Discovery Protocol. An incoming *service binding message* indicates that a local service has been registered for use by an object, and includes information on where to send its output data when complete. A *service access message* is a request to run a local service, and may also contain input data. The Node Manager invokes the specified service and passes in the data.

The Dynamic Service Configurator contains the SDP and Composer, and functions as described in Section 2. Dynamic service configuration is a relatively energy-intensive operation, due to the number of message transmissions involved in service discovery and composition. A node performing these operations will transmit $2S$ messages, where S is the number of services in the service graph. Nodes responding to service discovery requests transmit at most S replies, one for each service they provide. However, these transmissions only occur during configuration, and not during service graph execution, thus power consumption is kept to a minimum.

The Object Manager is responsible for 1) parsing the object-code byte string, 2) detecting the object context and evaluating the object creation condition at each sample period, 3) invoking the object creation protocol and owner election algorithm, and 4) maintaining the object state variables and evaluating the migration and FSM mode transition conditions.

4.2 WWW Gateway

In order to take advantage of high-bandwidth Web services, the sensor network must have access to at least one World Wide Web *Gateway*. The Gateway resides on a sensor network base station and provides access to Web services by translating node-based byte sequence messages to the comparatively bulky XML-based messages used in Web service standards. As such, it is the job of the Gateway to speak the language of Web services. When a service discovery message arrives, the Gateway must locate this service on the Internet. This is accomplished by using the *Universal Description, Discovery and Integration* (UDDI) protocol, a Web service standard used for locating and accessing services [15]. Given the proper keys, a UDDI inquiry returns the access point for a specific service as an URL string. Service access is achieved by means of XML-based *SOAP* messages [16]. If the service returns a value, it is also enclosed in a SOAP message. The Gateway composes and parses these XML messages and marshals the data appropriately when translating between the sensor network and the World Wide Web.

The role of the Gateway is transparent to the rest of the network. It appears simply as another node, running identical middleware services and providing a set of application services. That the available application services happen to be remotely located is of no interest to the object node making the request. Similarly, other application services inputting data from, or outputting data to a Web service believe the Web service is being provided by the Gateway node. Note also that communication between the sensornet and Internet is bidirectional. Not only can OASiS WSN applications access Web services, but OASiS services can be accessed from the World Wide Web. This permits users who have no experience with wireless sensor networks to retrieve sensor data or run sensor network applications from a website with access to the OASiS Gateway.

To return to our tracking example, while the application is running on the sensor network, the Gateway receives a service discovery message for the Wind-Velocity service. It receives this message because one of the nodes in the sensor network is attempting to bind a service graph requiring this service. If the Gateway does not already have the WindVelocity service in its cache of recently accessed services, it makes a UDDI inquiry to a registry at a known location, which returns the WindVelocity accesspoint URL, if available. The Gateway stores this information, then responds to the SDP of the requesting node that the WindVelocity service is available.

The Gateway may then receive a service binding message, indicating that the WindVelocity service may be accessed in the near future. The message contains the IDs of the node and service to send the wind velocity data to. This information is cached for rapid future access. When the Gateway receives a service access message from the sensor network, it packages the input data into a SOAP message and invokes the WindVelocity service. The reply is parsed using an XML parser and forwarded to the next service specified in the *service binding repository*.

4.3   Implementation

Our middleware[1] is implemented on the Mica2 mote hardware platform [17] running TinyOS [18]. Our main objective in developing the middleware was to minimize resource requirements while maintaining a robust component-based architecture. The code was developed using galsC [19], a GALS-enabled extension of nesC [20], the de facto programming language for the motes. The Gateway application was developed in Java. Our Web service implementation was realized using a suite of Apache services [21], including the Tomcat 5.5 web server, Axis 1.4 SOAP implementation, and jUDDI 0.9rc4, a Java-based UDDI implementation. MySQL 5.0 was used for the UDDI repository.

Table 1 lists each middleware service, with its code size and memory requirements. These memory sizes are suitable for executing applications on the motes, which have approximately 64 KB of programming memory and 4 KB of RAM. It should be noted that these components can be optimized to further reduce memory size, however there is a trade-off between an application's compactness and its robustness.

5   Case Study

We demonstrate the features of the OASiS programming model and middleware by developing a simplified indoor experiment which tracks a heat source.

---

[1] The source code for OASiS can be found on our project website at
   http://www.isis.vanderbilt.edu/Projects/OASiS/.

Table 1. Implementation Memory Requirements

Service	Program memory (bytes)	Required RAM (bytes)
Node Manager	8500	367
Dynamic Service Configurator	11894	822
Object Manager	3560	151
TinyGALS queues & ports	702	1013
Total	24656	2353

5.1   Experimental Setup

Our experimental setup is shown in Figure 6. Five sensor nodes equipped with thermistors are placed in a region, each providing a set of pre-loaded services, and a heat source passes through the region. A sixth node is connected to a Web server that provides a Velocity service. For this simple indoor experiment, the velocity provided by the Web service is set to a constant 5 m/s which is approximately the velocity of heat source. Table 2 summarizes the sensor node attributes. The Localization service, implemented using an extended Kalman filter, estimates the position of the heat source from the sensor data. This estimate is then sent to the Notification service. The application is represented by a service graph as in Figure 2 with three temperature services that must reside on different nodes in a spatial configuration that encloses the heat source.

Table 2. Experimental Setup

Node ID	Position	Preloaded Services
101	[400 800]	TEMPERATURE, NOTIFICATION
109	[700 400]	TEMPERATURE, notification
113	[0 500]	TEMPERATURE, notification, LOCALIZATION
143	[200 0]	TEMPERATURE, notification
169	[800 1000]	TEMPERATURE, notification
BASE STATION	N/A	VELOCITY ESTIMATION

5.2   Performance Evaluation

The feasibility and effectiveness of OASiS was evaluated by performing a set of experiments using the simple tracking application.

Experiment 1: Object creation and application execution. The number of message transmissions for object creation and application configuration is summarized in Table 3. The delay for object creation and application configuration is 2000 and 3000 ms, respectively, and depends on pre-defined timeout values; an *owner-election timeout* for object creation and a *service-configuration timeout* for service graph configuration.

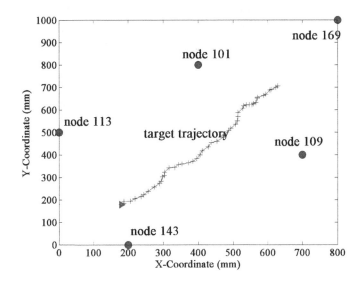

Fig. 6. Experimental setup

Table 3. Experiment 1 results

	number of messages	description
object creation	5	owner-election
service graph configuration	15	service request (3) service information (9) service binding (3)

Experiment 2: Service disruption / Object migration. Once the physical object goes beyond the enclosure of nodes 109, 113, and 143, the variance in the location estimate starts to grow, which triggers object migration. As part of the migration protocol, node 143 begins a new owner election procedure by broadcasting a migration message. Nodes reply with their most recently sampled temperature values. The current owner elects the node with the highest temperature value as the migration destination, sends the object to it, and *unbinds* all previously bound services. In our experiment, node 143 sends the object to node 109. The number of messages communicated for object migration and service graph unbinding are summarized in Table 4. The delay for object migration is approximately 2000 ms. This experiment indicates that OASiS incurs an overhead on the number of messages required and the time delay for object creation, maintenance, migration and service graph maintenance. Table 4 indicates that the number of messages communicated is reasonably small.

Experiment 3: Tracking. Tracking performance was evaluated by comparing the actual heat source trajectory with the estimated trajectory. The tracking

Table 4. Experiment 2 results

	number of messages	description
object migration	8	migration (5) object-migration (1) object-migration ack (1) object-migration notification (1)
service graph unbinding	3	*un*-binding

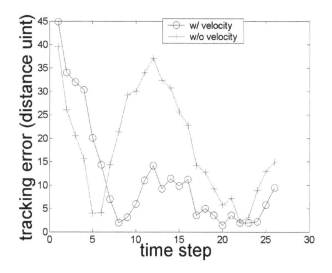

Fig. 7. Tracking results

accuracies for cases with and without estimated velocity data $(u_x = u_y = 0)$ was also measured, and is summarized in Figure 7.

In all experiments, message transmissions were kept to a minimum due to the passive service discovery protocol. The service message size for this application requires only one transmission per message. Service discovery and binding required a total of 14 transmissions, while a complete execution of the service graph required only six transmissions.

Response times for various operations were also obtained, and are displayed in Table 5. The service discovery response time is provided with and without the Web service. Additionally, Web service access is not included in the service graph execution time, but instead is provided separately to illustrate the overhead imposed on the system by adding Web service capability. It should be noted that our Web service implementation is not optimized for speed; however, the current service discovery and constraint satisfaction latency is quite acceptable for performing dynamic service configuration.

Table 5. Operation Response Times

Operation	Response Time (ms)	Standard Deviation
Service discovery	4092	113
Service discovery w/o Web service	1400	0.01
Constraint satisfaction	15	0
Service graph execution w/o Web service	81	13
Web service access	502	65
Localization service access	11	0

6   Scalability

To measure the effectiveness of our multi-hop service discovery protocol, we performed a scalability analysis using Prowler [22], a simulator for WSN applications. We simulated both grid and uniform random topologies. For each, we measured the message overhead of the service discovery protocol by considering (i) the number of message transmissions, (ii) the number of nodes discovered, and (iii) the time required for completing the service discovery.

When queried, each sensor node replies with a list of the services it provides. For our analysis, we measured the number of unique replies, which is an implicit measure of the number of services discovered. After service discovery completed, the total number of messages sent by all the nodes was tallied, along with the total number of discovered nodes and the total time required for service discovery. Figure 8 shows the number of message transmissions for n-hop service discovery, figure 9 shows the number of sensor nodes discovered, and figure 10 shows the time taken for n-hop service discovery for each of the network topologies. As expected, the number of message transmissions and discovered nodes increases quadratically with the number of hops, while the time taken for service discovery increases linearly. In addition, the number of message transmissions and discovered nodes increases linearly with node density in the network, while time taken for service discovery remains approximately constant.

We define the *discovery ratio* as the ratio of service discovery messages to the number of discovered nodes. Figure 11 shows the discovery ratio for different network topologies. From the results above, we can make some general useful observations. The discovery ratio increases linearly with the number of hops (i.e. the protocol requires approximately n discovery messages per discovered node for n-hop service discovery). Interestingly, the discovery ratio remains mostly constant with respect to node density. These results indicate that the service discovery protocol performs linearly for the number of discovery messages per discovered node with respect to the number of hops. Hence, the optimal number of hops for service discovery can be selected based on the distribution and number of services in the network.

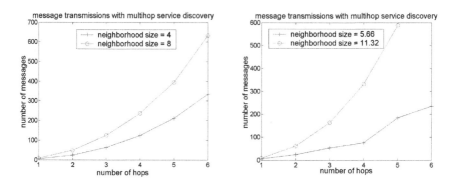

Fig. 8. Number of message transmissions for (a) grid and (b) random topology

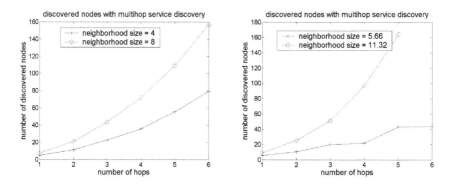

Fig. 9. Number of discovered nodes for (a) grid and (b) random topology

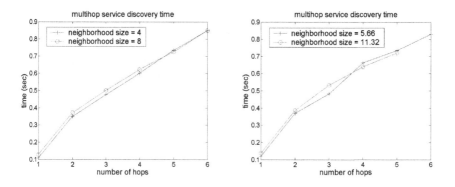

Fig. 10. Time taken for n-hop service discovery for (a) grid and (b) random topology

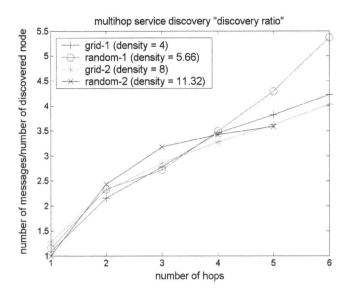

Fig. 11. Discovery ratio with number of hops for all four network topologies

7   Related Work

Design principles for traditional distributed computing middleware are not directly applicable to WSNs because sensor nodes are small-scale devices with limited resources, properties which directly affect computation, sensing, and communication. Recently, the WSN community has seen the emergence of a diverse body of macroprogramming languages, frameworks, and middleware that provide solutions to overcome these limitations (see [23] and the references therein). In the following, we focus on models and frameworks similar to OASiS.

SONGS [5] is a service-oriented programming model, similar to ours in many respects. However, unlike our object-centric approach to driving application behavior, SONGS dynamically composes a service graph in response to user-generated queries. While this technique works well as an information retrieval system, SONGS lacks the ability to alter its behavior based on a change in environmental conditions.

The object-centric paradigm has been successfully used in the EnviroSuite programming framework [6]. EnviroSuite and OASiS provide a similar level of network abstraction to the application developer, however by employing a service-oriented architecture, OASiS is able to incorporate aspects of modular functionality, resource utilization, and ambient-awareness more efficiently.

The Abstract Task Graph (ATaG) [24] is a macroprogramming model which allows the user to specify global application behavior as a series of abstract tasks connected by data channels for passing information between them. Currently, the ATaG is only a means for describing application behavior. A model interpreter must be employed to decompose this behavior to node-level executable code.

In addition, the ATaG provides no means for delegating tasks to sensor nodes which satisfy specific property or resource constraints.

The Agilla framework [25] adopts a mobile agent-based paradigm. However, unlike most other frameworks, Agilla does not require the sensor network application to be deployed statically. Instead, autonomous agents, each with a specific function, are injected into the network at run-time, a technique referred to as *in-network programming*. This approach allows the underlying network application to only be uploaded once onto the node hardware, after which applications can be swapped out or reconfigured at any time. The primary disadvantage of using an Agilla network, compared with our middleware, is that all nodes must be executing the Agilla run-time application. This rules out access to a variety of devices operating on different architectures.

Ambient-aware computing [26] is an emergent technology in which applications are given the ability to interact with their environment such that all devices and services within a fixed geographical range are known at all times. However, for sensor networks consisting of resource-constrained nodes, communication with neighboring devices is often costly. Hence a tradeoff exists between the rate at which a node can update its understanding of the surrounding environment and the amount of time the node can run before depleting its power supply.

Bridging a sensornet-based service-oriented architecture with the Internet has been realized with the CodeBlue project [27] in which sensors used for healthcare monitoring relay data to a Web service. This provides a convenient mechanism for transferring a patient's vital signs, obtained through an embedded sensor device, to a medical records system or monitoring station. CodeBlue's Gateway application is similar to our own, with the exception that it translates sensor data into the HL7v3 format, a standard used for communicating medical information.

Dynamic software reconfiguration in sensor networks has been achieved in [28] by expressing system requirements as constraints on design space quality-of-service parameters. A run-time search of the design space is made possible by situating the reconfiguration controller on a powerful base station, a strategy which cannot be realized in resource-constrained sensor nodes.

MiLAN [29] is a middleware for WSN application development that optimizes the trade-off between application QoS and network resource utilization. Quality of service constraints are specified in graphs, which MiLAN interprets and uses to maintain a minimum set of active devices which provide the functionality required by the application. Although MiLAN employs a dynamic service configuration mechanism similar to that of OASiS, it only assists the application developer in managing QoS, and is not a complete programming framework.

Spatial Programming [30] is a programming model for distributed embedded systems that abstracts the network into a single virtual address space. Nodes are referenced based on their location and provided functionality rather than ID, providing the application programmer with greater design flexibility in the presence of dynamic network topology. The authors implemented the spatial programming model using the Smart Messages [31] architecture in Java, and deployed the application on Linux PDAs. It is unclear how such a model will perform on sensor nodes with tighter resource constraints.

8   Conclusion

We have developed OASiS, an object-centric, service-oriented programming model and middleware for ambient-aware sensor network applications. Upon detection of an external event, the sensor network instantiates a unique logical object which then drives the application. Application functionality is bundled in modular, autonomous services distributed across the network, and dynamic service configuration is employed at run-time to locate and bind these services. This process involves an efficient search of the design space to ensure all constraints have been satisfied. In addition, a Gateway application, deployed on a base station, permits the sensor network to discover and access Web services. This capability provides a substantial benefit to WSN applications, as they are able to perform computations and access information using methods unavailable to resource-constrained sensor nodes. The utility of our programming model was demonstrated with a simple indoor heat-source tracking application. Our results indicate service-oriented architectures are feasible and can benefit the design of sensor network applications.

The ambient-aware behavior of our programming model can be further developed to react gracefully to communication failures and node dropout during application execution. This will involve failure detection, isolation, and recovery mechanisms that restore the network application to a stable configuration both quickly and efficiently.

References

1. Akyildiz, I., Su, W., Sankarasubramaniam, Y., Cayirci, E.: Wireless Sensor Networks: A Survey. IEEE Computer 38(4), 393–422 (2002)
2. Yarvis, M., Kushalnagar, N., Singh, H., Rangarajan, A., Liu, Y., Singh, S.: Exploiting Heterogeneity in Sensor Networks. In: INFOCOM. Proceedings of the 24th Annual IEEE International Conference on Computer Communiation (March 2005)
3. Duarte-Melo, E., Liu, M.: Analysis of Energy Consumption and Lifetime of Heterogeneous Wireless Sensor Networks. In: Globecom. Proceedings of the 45th Annual IEEE Global Communications Conference (2002)
4. Lazos, L., Poovendran, R., Ritcey, J.A.: Probabilistic Detection of Mobile Targets in Heterogeneous Sensor Networks. In: IPSN. Proceedings of the 6th International Conference on Information Processing in Sensor Networks (2007)
5. Liu, J., Zhao, F.: Towards Semantic Services for Sensor-rich Information Systems. In: BaseNets. Proceedings of the 2nd IEEE/CreateNet International Workshop on Broadband Advanced Sensor Networks (2005)
6. Luo, L., Abdelzaher, T., He, T., Stankovic, J.: EnviroSuite: An Environmentally Immersive Programming System for Sensor Networks. ACM Transactions on Embedded Computing Systems 5(3), 543–576 (2006)
7. Booth, D., Haas, H., McCabe, F., Newcomer, E., Champion, M., Ferris, C., Orchard, D.: Web Services Architecture, http://www.w3.org/TR/ws-arch/

8. Welch, G., Bishop, G.: An Introduction to the Kalman Filter. Technical Report TR 95-041, Department of Computer Science, University of North Carolina at Chapel Hill (2004)
9. Cheong, E., Liebman, J., Liu, J., Zhao, F.: TinyGALS: A Programming Model for Event-driven Embedded Systems. In: SAC. Proceedings of the 18th Annual ACM Symposium on Applied Computing (2003)
10. Engelstad, P., Zheng, Y.: Evaluation of Service Discovery Architectures for Mobile Ad Hoc Networks. In: WONS. Proceedings of the 2nd Annual Conference on Wireless On Demand Network Systems and Services (2005)
11. Johnson, D.B., Maltz, D.A.: Dynamic Source Routing in Ad Hoc Wireless Networks. In: Imielinski, T., Korth, H. (eds.) Mobile Computing, Kluwer Academic Publishers, Dordrecht (1996)
12. Regin, J.C.: A Filtering Algorithm for Constraints of Difference in CSPs. In: Proceedings of the 12th National Conference on Artificial Intelligence, vol. 1 (1994)
13. Guibas, L.J.: Sensing, Tracking, and Reasoning with Relations. IEEE Signal Processing Magazine (March 2002)
14. Baase, S., Gelder, A.V.: Computer Algorithms: Introduction to Design and Analysis, 3rd edn. Addison-Wesley, Reading (1999)
15. Universal Description, Discovery, and Integration, http://www.uddi.org
16. SOAP, http://www.w3.org/TR/soap/
17. Mica2, http://www.tinyos.net/scoop/special/hardware/#mica2
18. Levis, P., Madden, S., Gay, D., Polastre, J., Szewczyk, R., Woo, A., Brewer, E., Culler, D.: The Emergence of Networking Abstractions and Techniques in TinyOS. In: NSDI. Proceedings of the 1st Symposium on Networked Systems Design and Implementation (2004)
19. Cheong, E., Liu, J.: galsC: A Language for Event-driven Embedded Systems. In: DATE. Proceedings of the Conference on Design, Automation and Test in Europe (2005)
20. Gay, D., Levis, P., von Behren, R., Welsh, M., Brewer, E., Culler, D.: The nesC Language: A Holistic Approach to Networked Embedded Systems. In: PLDI. Proceedings of the ACM SIGPLAN Conference on Programming Language Design and Implementation (2003)
21. Apache Web Services, http://ws.apache.org/
22. Simon, G., Volgyesi, P., Maroti, M., Ledeczi, A.: Simulation-based Optimization of Communication Protocols for Large-scale Wireless Sensor Networks. In: IEEE Aerospace Conference (2003)
23. Hadim, S., Mohamed, N.: Middleware: Middleware Challenges and Approaches for Wireless Sensor Networks. IEEE Distributed Systems Online 7 (2006)
24. Bakshi, A., Prasanna, V., Reich, J., Larner, D.: The Abstract Task Graph: A Methodology for Architecture-independent Programming of Networked Sensor Systems. In: EESR. Workshop on End-to-end, Sense-and-respond Systems, Applications, and Services (2005)
25. Fok, C.L., Roman, G.C., Lu, C.: Rapid Development and Flexible Deployment of Adaptive Wireless Sensor Network Applications. In: ICDCS. Proceedings of the 25th International Conference on Distributed Computing Systems (2005)
26. Dedecker, J., Cutsem, T.V., Mostinckx, S., D'Hondt, T., Meuter, W.D.: Ambient-oriented Programming. In: OOPSLA. Proceedings of the 20th Annual Conference on Object-oriented Programming, Systems, Languages, and Applications (2005)

27. Baird, S., Dawson-Haggerty, S., Myung, D., Gaynor, M., Welsh, M., Moulton, S.: Communicating Data from Wireless Sensor Networks Using the hl7v3 Standard. In: BSN. International Workshop on Wearable and Implantable Body Sensor Networks (2006)
28. Kogekar, S., Neema, S., Eames, B., Koutsoukos, X., Ledeczi, A., Maroti, M.: Constraint-guided Dynamic Reconfiguration in Sensor Networks. In: IPSN. Proceedings of the 3rd International Symposium on Information Processing in Sensor Networks (2004)
29. Heinzelman, W.B., Murphy, A.L., Carvalho, H.S., Perillo, M.A.: Middleware to Support Sensor Network Applications. IEEE Network 18(1), 6–14 (2004)
30. Borcea, C., Iyer, D., Kang, P., Saxena, A., Iftode, L.: Spatial Programming Using Smart Messages: Design and Implementation. In: ICDCS. Proceedings of the 24th International Conference on Distributed Computing Systems (2004)
31. Borcea, C., Iyer, D., Kang, P., Saxena, A., Iftode, L.: Cooperative Computing for Distributed Embedded Systems. In: ICDCS. Proceedings of the 22nd International Conference on Distributed Computing Systems (2002)

Composing and Decomposing QoS Attributes for Distributed Real-Time Systems: Experience to Date and Hard Problems Going Forward

Richard Schantz and Joseph Loyall

BBN Technologies
March 31, 2007

Abstract. Distributed real-time embedded (DRE) systems combine the stringent quality of service (QoS) requirements of embedded systems and the dynamic conditions of distributed systems. In these DRE systems, QoS requirements are often critical, and QoS must be managed end-to-end, from the mission layer down to the resource layer, across competing applications, and dynamically as conditions change. In this paper, we discuss issues in providing QoS management in DRE systems and some middleware- and component-based solutions that we have developed to enable QoS management. We illustrate these in the context of a live flight demonstration of DRE systems, discuss the experience gained from the application of the technology to this context, and discuss some future directions for further research.

1 Introduction

Distributed real-time embedded (DRE) systems combine the stringent quality of service (QoS) requirements of traditional closed embedded systems with the challenges of the dynamic conditions associated with being widely distributed across an often volatile network environment. Traditionally, embedded systems have been able to rely on their closed environments and self-contained bus architectures to limit the dynamic inputs possible and could rely on static resource management techniques to provide the QoS and reliable performance they need. The environment of distributed, networked systems is more open with heterogeneous platforms, where inputs can come from external devices and platforms, and dynamic, in which conditions, resource availability, and interactions can change. Because of this, achieving the necessary predictable real-time behavior in these DRE systems has many diverse aspects and is a very large problem area. This places extra emphasis on both the decomposition of the problem space and the compositional approach toward solving it.

2 Issues in Providing QoS Management in DRE Systems

In DRE applications, quality of the service provided is as important as functionality, i.e., how well an application performs its function is as important as what it does. QoS

F. Kordon and O. Sokolsky (Eds.): Monterey Workshop 2006, LNCS 4888, pp. 150–167, 2007.
© Springer-Verlag Berlin Heidelberg 2007

management is a key element of the design and runtime behavior of DRE systems, but it is often defined in terms of management of individual resources, e.g., the admission control provided by network management or CPU scheduling mechanisms or services. While individual resource management is necessary, it is not sufficient in DRE systems. QoS management for DRE systems must derive and relate the individual QoS management to the specific mission requirements, simultaneously manage all the resources that could be or become bottlenecks, mediate varying and conflicting demands for resources, efficiently utilize allocated resources, and dynamically reconfigure and reallocate as conditions change.

We can decompose the discussion of issues in providing QoS management in DRE systems into the following four major separate, but related subissues:

- End-to-end QoS management – The management of QoS for an individual end-to-end information stream, from information sources to information consumers. That is, managing the resources associated with information collection, processing, and delivery to satisfy a particular use of information.
- Multi-layer, scaleable QoS management – The management of QoS for a mission or set of high-level operational goals, which includes the mapping of high-level, system-wide concepts into policies driving QoS at the lower levels, followed by enforcement at the lowest level.
- Aggregate QoS management – The mediation of demands and negotiation for resources between multiple end-to-end streams that are competing for resources.
- Dynamic QoS management – Adapting to changes in resource availability, mission and application needs, and environmental conditions (e.g., scale, number of elements under QoS management, failure and damage management, cyber attacks) to maintain, improve, or gracefully degrade delivered QoS.

With enough time and budget, intelligent engineers could likely produce a system with QoS management that fulfills each of these characteristics for a specific system. However, our vision is more ambitious. We need to develop QoS management not for a single instance of a specific system, but to develop commonly accepted and used tools and techniques that enable QoS management to be developed in many systems repeatedly, so that they are well designed, reusable, and maintainable. Accordingly, QoS management dovetails with and reinforces extended software engineering practices that support these goals:

- Separation of concerns, to support the separation of programming application code (which is the purview of a domain expert) and QoS code (which is the purview of a systems engineer).
- Components and composition, to support the encapsulation of QoS management code into reusable bundles and the construction of new systems by composing, specializing, and configuring existing components.
- Service orientation, supporting the loose integration of whole subsystems, enabling large DRE systems of systems to be constructed from existing DRE systems.

3   A Solution for Providing QoS Management in DRE Systems

3.1 Middleware for Dynamic QoS Management

Although it is possible to provide end-to-end QoS management by embedding QoS control and monitoring statements throughout a software system, such an approach leads to additional code complexity, reduced maintainability, and non-reusable software. A better approach is to separate the QoS concerns from the functional concerns of an application and combine the two into a QoS-managed software system through integration at a middleware layer.

An approach that we have taken to do this is providing extensions to standards based middleware that allow aspects of dynamic QoS management to be programmed separately and then integrated into distributed object or component-based systems. The solution is based in middleware, because QoS management largely falls in that space where the applications interact with the platforms and environments in which they are deployed, and can more easily be made part of a common infrastructure.

3.1.1 Quality Objects

Quality Objects (QuO) is a distributed object framework that supports the separate programming of (1) QoS requirements, (2) the system elements that must be monitored and controlled to measure and provide QoS, and (3) the behavior for controlling and providing QoS and for adapting to QoS variations that occur at runtime [26]. By providing these features, QuO separates the role of functional application development from the role of developing the QoS behavior of the system.

As shown in **Fig. 1**, a QuO application inserts additional steps in the path between elements of distributed applications. The QuO runtime monitors the state of QoS before remote operations through the use of System Condition Objects that provide a standard interface to observable and controllable parameters in a platform, such as CPU utilization or bandwidth usage. Delegates intercept remote operations and a QoS contract decides the appropriate behavior to apply. The contract defines the set of possible states of QoS in the system using predicates of system condition object values. Based upon the current QoS state, the contract could (1) allow the call to proceed as is; (2) specify additional processing to perform; or (3) redirect the invocation to a different method; or (4) invoke a callback on the application to alter its execution.

3.1.2 Qoskets and Qosket Components

One goal of QuO is to separate the role of QoS programmer from that of application programmer. A complementary goal of this separation of programming roles is that QoS management code can be encapsulated into reusable units that are not only developed separately from the applications that use them, but that can be reused by selecting, customizing, and binding them to an application program. To support this goal, we have defined *Qoskets* as a unit of encapsulation and reuse in QuO applications [20]. Qoskets are used to bundle in one place all of the specifications and objects for controlling systemic behavior, as illustrated in Fig. 2. Qoskets encapsulate the following QoS aspects:

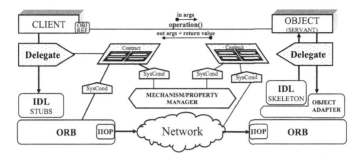

Fig. 1. QuO adds components to control, measure, and adapt to QoS aspects of an application

- Adaptation and control policies – As expressed in QuO contracts and controllers
- Measurement and control interfaces – As defined by system condition objects and callback objects
- Adaptive behaviors – Some of which are partially specified until they are specialized to a functional interface
- QoS implementation – Defined by qosket methods.

A Qosket Component [21] is an executable unit of encapsulation of Qosket code wrapped inside standards-compliant components, such as the CORBA Component Model (CCM) [16], which can be assembled and deployed using existing tools. They expose interfaces, so they can be integrated between functional components and services to intercept and adapt the interactions between them. Each Qosket component offers interception ports that can be used to provide in-band adaptation along the functional path. Qosket components can also provide ports to support out-of-band adaptation and interact with related QoS management mechanisms.

Qosket components provide all the features of Qoskets and all the features of components to provide lifecycle support for design, assembly, and deployment. Each qosket component can have as many adaptive behaviors as desired. However,

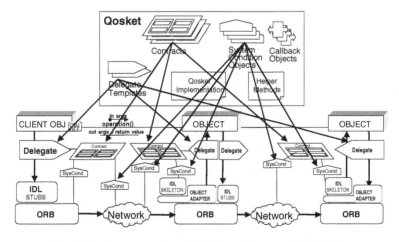

Fig. 2. Qoskets encapsulate QuO objects into reusable behaviors

encoding each qosket with one and only one adaptive behavior decouples different adaptive behaviors and increases the reusability of each. The tradeoff is between the assembly time flexibility allowed by the separation of QoS behaviors versus the performance overhead of having additional components to assemble. This is the same design versus performance tradeoff that exists in functional component based applications and which can be alleviated by assembly tools and component implementations that optimize component and container instantiations. Implementations that encapsulate a single QoS behavior in each qosket component can provide an aggregate, end-to-end behavior by combining qosket components. Additionally, there can be side effects associated with specific combinations of individual Qoskets.

3.2 Composition and Composition Patterns

A DRE application often consists of many components—both functional and QoS. In the rare case in which these components are independent, the order of assembly or composition can be unimportant. However, in the usual case, the order of execution of these components must be carefully crafted to achieve the desired end-to-end, aggregate behavior (ordering sensitivity is one of the component composition side-effects mentioned earlier which are under investigation). In some cases the way in which components are assembled is the difference between correct and incorrect behavior:

- Some qosket components must coordinate to implement a desired behavior. For example, a compression qosket must frequently be paired with a decompression qosket. These must be assembled in the correct order, since decompressing prior to compressing can result in undesired behavior. "Undo" QCs usually need to be composed in reverse order of the composition of their paired QCs.
- Some qosket components interfere with one another in a contradictory manner. For example, compressing or encrypting data might result in the inability to scale, crop, or tile data because it changes the data into a format that can no longer be manipulated. These qosket components must be composed in a compatible way, e.g., scale or crop prior to compression (a variant of order sensitivity), or composed using a decision, e.g., a contract determines whether to crop or compress, but not both.
- Some qosket components can affect the dynamics of one another. For example, any qosket component that includes processing, such as compression or encryption, can affect the dynamics of a CPU management qosket.

There are a few general composition techniques that we have extracted that serve as patterns of composition [22], illustrated in Fig. 3:

- Layered Composition – In this pattern, qosket components that make higher level decisions (such as a System Resource Manager, SRM, a QoS management component of larger scope and granularity) are layered upon qosket components that enforce these decisions (such as Local Resource Managers, LRMs, QoS management components of smaller scope and finer granularity), which in turn are

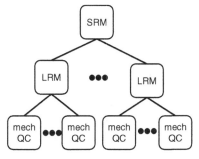

(a) *Hierarchical composition* – Each layer manages a set of QCs below it, pushing policy and control down and receiving status up.

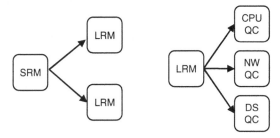

(b) *Parallel composition* – A set of QCs needs to be invoked in parallel.

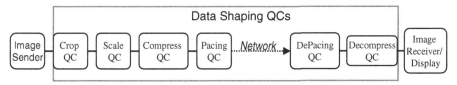

(c) *Sequential composition* – A set of QCs form a chain of composed QoS behavior.

Fig. 3. Composition patterns driving our uses of qosket components

layered upon mechanism qosket components that control resources and QoS behaviors. Key challenges with this composition pattern include selecting the appropriate abstraction and granularity for the layers, as well as the number of layers, under assumptions of system evolution and growth. Inevitably, what is today considered a "system" is often embedded into another context which often adds additional layering concerns. The ability to introduce and/or coordinate with additional scopes of control and/or decision making is a significant consideration for multi-layered design.

- Parallel Composition – When qosket components receive data simultaneously and perform their QoS behaviors independently, they can be composed in parallel. Key challenges with this composition pattern include the need to establish and maintain the independence, non-interference and/or coordination of the parallel branches. This is especially difficult under real-time conditions, when parallel patterns are of most value.

- Sequential Composition – In some cases, a set of components must be tightly integrated such that a set of QoS behaviors are performed sequentially, with the output of each component becoming the input to the next component. This is probably the simplest and most often used composition pattern, comparable to the simplicity of straightline code over more complex branching behavior. Key challenges with this pattern include selecting appropriate granularity of an individual component, merging/splitting individual components especially as new techniques emerge which may not exactly line up within existing boundaries, and identifying and managing side-effects of component order.

4   An Example of Providing and Integrating Elements of Dynamic QoS Management

As part of DARPA's Program Composition for Embedded Systems (PCES) program, BBN, Boeing, and Lockheed Martin developed a capstone flight demonstration of advanced capabilities for time critical missions [13]. It was a medium scale DRE application, consisting of several communicating airborne and ground-based heterogeneous nodes in a dynamic environment with changing mission modes, requirements, and conditions. It consisted of a set of Unmanned Air Vehicles (UAV) performing theater-wide surveillance and target tracking, and sending imagery to, and under the control of, a control center. Specific UAVs could be reconfigured on demand to effect different roles which in turn placed different QoS requirements on the delivery of their sensor output.

To manage the multiple dimensions of QoS in the PCES capstone demonstration, we developed a multi-layered, dynamic QoS management architecture [15], illustrated in Fig. 4. The System Resource Manager (SRM) is a supervisory controller responsible for allocating resources among the system participants and for disseminating system and mission wide policies to local resource managers. These policies include the resource allocation, the relevant mission requirements and parameters, and tradeoffs.

In order to determine which QoS behaviors to employ, the LRM uses a system dynamics model to predict the effect of employing each QoS behavior and combination of QoS behaviors. In Fig. 4, we separately indicate the control and prediction parts of the LRM, the former illustrated as a Controller and the latter as a QoS Predictor. The system dynamics (i.e., effect) of some QoS behaviors can be determined analytically, e.g., the results of cropping an image (i.e., the amount of data in the resulting image) or reserving an amount of bandwidth (i.e., the amount of bandwidth available to the application). Other behaviors have no analytical model (or less accurate ones), e.g., some compression algorithms or setting a network priority (the results of which are difficult to determine analytically without global knowledge of many other external factors). With the former, the QoS predictor contains the model, equation, or formula to predict the behavior. With the latter, the QoS predictor is initialized with experimental data produced in test runs, and updated at runtime with more accurate monitored information.

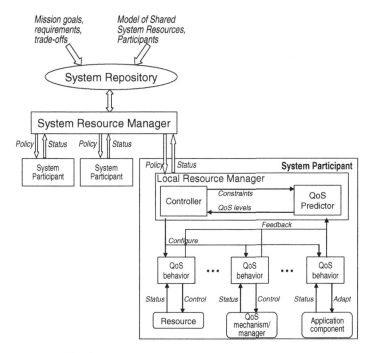

Fig. 4. Elements of Multi-Layer QoS Management

The QoS mechanism layer consists of encapsulated QoS behaviors that control and monitor the following:

- Resources, such as memory, power, or CPU, which can be monitored and controlled through knobs exposed by the resource.
- Specific QoS mechanisms, such as network reservation [25] or network priority services [10] that expose interfaces to resource monitoring and control; or QoS managers, such as bandwidth brokers [6] or CPU brokers [8], that provide higher level management abstractions.
- Application or data adaptation, such as changing the rate of tasks, algorithms or parameters of functional routines, or shaping the data used or produced by application components.

4.1 Construction Techniques

We constructed the multi-layered QoS management for the end-to-end imagery streams by composing it from reusable QoS and functional components. We implemented the elements of our end-to-end QoS management architecture as qosket components so that they can be assembled with the components of the functional application, as illustrated in Fig. 5. The SRM qosket component includes decision making code to decide how resources should be allocated among participants and wraps that allocation into a policy, with some monitoring code to determine the

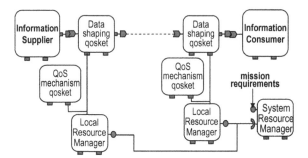

Fig. 5. End-to-end QoS management elements are instantiated as qosket components and assembled with the functional components

number of current participants, the amount and type of shared resources, and other information affecting the policy decision, such as mission states, requirements, and conditions.

The LRM qosket components include decision making code to decide local actions based on the policy, monitoring code to measure the effects of the QoS management, and control code to adjust levels to satisfy the policy. The LRM's control code is typically limited to setting the proper attributes on the QoS behavior for the lower level qosket components and invoking them in the proper order.

The assembly also includes as many QoS behavior qosket components as necessary. In the example in Fig. 5, we illustrate two types of QoS behavior qosket components, one that does data shaping and another that interfaces to an infrastructure QoS mechanism.

A DiffServ QoS mechanism qosket component is responsible for setting DiffServ codepoints (DSCPs) [10] on component containers. The LRM uses the network priority from the SRM policy to configure the Diffserv component to ensure that all packets going out have their DSCP set correctly. Routers configured to support Diffserv ensure that the packets get queued according to their DSCP priorities.

A CPU Broker QoS mechanism qosket component is responsible for reserving CPU cycles over a period of time for a component container. The LRM uses the minimum and maximum CPU reservation and the relative importance from the SRM policy to configure the CPU Broker component. The underlying CPU mechanisms (CPU Broker and TimeSys Linux) guarantee that the container gets at least the minimum CPU cycles it needs. In the case of CPU contention, no more than the maximum CPU cycles are allocated to the container.

Once the available CPU and network resources have been allocated across UAV streams, each stream must shape its data to use the allocated resources effectively. Data Shaping Qosket Components are a collection of individual data shaping capabilities. We assemble several data shaping qoskets that the LRM uses to accomplish matching available data transmission resources with effective use.

Assuming there are sufficient resources, the SRM ensures that every end-to-end image stream gets at least the minimum it needs and that the more important streams get the majority of the resources. In cases where there are not enough resources for all the streams, the SRM ensures that the most important streams get the resources that are available. The LRMs in turn ensure that the allocated resources for each end-to-end stream are used most effectively for the UAV's particular role in the system. They utilize specific lower level mechanism qoskets to affect, control, and enforce these behaviors.

5 Early Experience and Challenges with Applying and Using the QC Composition Approach

We successfully built, configured, ran and evaluated the demonstration system described briefly in the previous section. Here we briefly discuss aspects of what was accomplished against the QoS management issues articulated in section 2, evaluate the derived benefits of the compositional approach, and discuss new, more detailed issues that arose in the context of the evaluation..

Our evaluation exemplar incorporated elements of each of the aspects of QoS management.

End-to-end QoS management – Management of end-to-end chains was based on the principal of establishing specific roles for end users of QoS managed products. From these end user roles, we can derive the appropriate QoS specifications needed to meet those expectations. We propagate the QoS specifications to the source of the end-to-end chain and apply a control strategy to the production and delivery of information to enforce them. This is done for each end-to-end chain operational at the time.
.

Multi-layer, scaleable QoS management – Our multi-layer management solution approach calls for higher layers providing the allocation policy to the lower level configuration, monitoring and enforcement mechanisms. So, in effect, higher levels of management determine the constraints under which the end-to-end chains previously mentioned operate. Additionally it provides the lower layer enforcement components with the means to appeal to the higher levels when they are unable to sustain their objectives. Although our evaluation example used a 2 layer approach, we believe the general approach to be applicable to additional scopes and granularities associated with much larger systems.

Aggregate QoS management – When all current demands do not deplete available resources, meeting all role dependent expectations is feasible. However, when demand would exceed supply, high level policy components provide the means to determine who gets what, by estimating allocations that serve to maximize utility, according to pre-determined utility functions. Aggregation across these multiple competing end-to-end uses for shared resources is handled through the multi-layered design with high level components using estimating techniques to develop policies that share resources in accord with importance and utility measures driving those allocation policies. The lower level end-to-end components are then responsible for setting up and keeping within those bounds, or providing status indications that this is not feasible.

Dynamic QoS management – The principles of dynamic reconfiguration were applied to each of these three aspects of QoS management to address the changes and shortfall against expectations that regularly occurred or were induced in our exemplar. All of the aspects are wired together via status and control linkages to provide for the automated reconfiguration of all or parts of the process on selected events (e.g. additional users, loss of available resources, or significant changes in importance) Although quite complicated in its linkages, there are a number of heuristics which drive the process and are intended to prevent reconfiguration thrashing. Although maximizing utility is an important longterm goal, the emphasis of the experiments reported here had a focus on the software engineering aspects of tying together the diverse elements of the overall solution, while adequately and effectively meeting QoS demands in a domain consistent manner.

5.1 Observed Benefits of QC Composition

As expected, there were a number of benefits that were realized with our experience building systems using embedded QCs, rather than as a one-of-a-kind, custom crafted stove-piped system, including the following:

- *Reusability* – Many of the QCs that were used in this demonstration were reused or adapted from earlier contexts and are members of our QC library. Part of our ongoing work involves exploring the tradeoffs associated with decoupling a QC from functional interfaces (thereby increasing its reusability in different contexts) but increasing the work associated with composing it in a specific context.
- *Simplified development* – Using the embedded QC approach, providing QoS management in a DRE system becomes more of a configuration issue rather than a programming exercise. One can, therefore, assemble the components required for QoS management into an existing or developing component-based distributed application. In our demonstration system, this allowed us to rapidly prototype versions of the system with or without specific QoS behaviors and with specific combinations of QCs, simply by assembling the system using available CCM assembly tools
- *Supporting Integrated QoS management at different epochs* – Traditional embedded systems rely on static QoS provisioning, at design time or system configuration time. Our approach supports QoS provisioning at several different lifecycle epochs of an application as follows:
  - o At configuration time, one can set the default values of QC attributes. For example, the attributes of an LRM QC can be set to define the default strategy for selecting and activating a QC.
  - o At assembly time, one can compose QCs to provide a desired aggregate or end-to-end QoS.
  - o At deployment time, the placement of QCs and their monitoring sources affects the provided QoS. Prior knowledge of the host and network load can facilitate the process of selecting suitable hosts.
  - o At runtime, QCs facilitate the dynamic control of QoS and adaptation to changing conditions.

5.2 Continuing Challenges

While in the large we have had success in developing a significant working artifact using QCs and in composing them to create a real working example of a DRE system, there are still many short term "nuts and bolts" type issues that remain only partially addressed on the path toward more widespread practice and operational use.

Data-specific QCs. There is a tradeoff to be made in developing a QC that is specific to a particular data format versus one that is not. A QC that is not specific to a particular data format should be more widely reusable. However, this might not always be feasible. For example, an attempt to develop a format-neutral compression QC leads to the following pitfalls:

- *A useless QC* – Trying to remove code that understands specific data formats from a QC might result in an empty shell that contains little behavior and requires everything to be specified at assembly time or compensated for elsewhere.
- *A bloated QC* – Including a wide variety of algorithms that work with many different formats might create an unwieldy QC that is too heavyweight for any specific context.
- *An inefficient QC* – There are format neutral compression algorithms, such as gzip, that could be used. However, in many cases, data specific algorithms are more useful. JPEG compression, for example, is more useful for imagery because it compresses efficiently and comes with display software. Over time, emerging standards, de facto or de jure, are likely to help alleviate some of these issues, if for no other reason than to reduce the space of acceptable choices.

In much of our work we have made QCs as format-neutral as possible, even while continuing to work on additional solutions, such as QC interface templates. This can lead to the problem of QC *data incompatibility*, in which data emitted from one set of QCs may not be compatible as input to another set of QCs. Currently, we have no way to specify this or annotate the QCs to aid the assemblers. The assemblers need knowledge of the domain's data types and functional components, and therefore must either work with domain experts or possess domain expertise. This problem does not propagate to application code because each QC that alters the output data is paired with a QC that undoes the alteration.

Need for hardware and system support. QCs that provide system-level controls and monitoring require support from the system infrastructure to work correctly. For instance, a DiffServ QC that provides network prioritization requires universal support for DiffServ capabilities at all intermediate routers. This becomes difficult over an uncontrolled network, such as the Internet. A solution to this problem is to use only more controlled subsets, to emphasize traffic shaping techniques instead, or to use a reactive approach that adjusts to the provided QoS, even in a "best effort" environment such as the Internet.

Maintaining QoS while integrating with other middleware services. It is tricky to provide end-to-end QoS dynamically when the QCs need to interoperate with other middleware services such as the Joint Battlespace Infosphere (JBI) [1], a publish/subscribe oriented service or the CORBA Notification Service [17]. While these other middleware services are individually compliant with the standards, there is, as yet, no uniform protocol for communicating among them, or maintaining QoS while doing so. Our solution has been to provide as much QoS as possible, up to the boundaries of entering uncontrolled services and introducing QCs that react to the observed QoS in uncontrolled environments, while at the same time promoting and helping to develop QoS management awareness and capabilities for these other middleware services.

Exposing and Resolving Explicit and Implicit Dependencies – There are dependencies between QCs that can be useful to guide the composition or that can restrict the circumstances in which they can be usefully composed. Explicit dependencies can be reflected in QC interfaces, such as the policy interface provided by the LRM and used by the SRM, or type matching, such as the cropping QC working only with specific, uncompressed data types. Other implicit dependencies can be due to semantic or algorithmic factors, and can be more difficult to detect and manage. For example, some encryption and compression algorithms might not compose well, since encrypting might restrict the ability to compress data very much and compressing data might produce a result that cannot be properly encrypted. We are still investigating methods to incorporate this type of information so that automated tools can verify appropriate composition.

Effective and Optimized Configuration and Placement of QCs – The host boundaries on which QCs are deployed can play a crucial role in the effectiveness of the aggregate QoS management. Placing data shaping QCs closest to the data source makes the most sense *unless* the data is used by multiple consumers demanding different qualities. Some QCs are only effective when separated by host boundaries. For example, compression can only reduce network traffic if the compression and decompression QCs are placed on different hosts. In addition, because our demonstration was based on a military scenario, there was a defined central authority in the C2 center and, therefore, an obvious place to put the SRM managerial QC. A peer-to-peer or ad hoc system, however, might need a different number and placement of managerial QCs. We are still experimenting with understanding and how to express the relationships between placement of QCs and outcome of the end-to-end compositions.

6 Related Work

A key area of related work is in providing QoS support in component models and instantiations of CCM. The Component Integrated ACE ORB (CIAO) [5] is an open-source implementation of the CCM standard based upon the open-source TAO ORB [23]. There are efforts underway to include QoS support in OMG component and specification standards [18, 2]. We have utilized CIAO extensively in the work described in this paper. Containers in component-based middleware frameworks provide a means for inserting QoS enforcement and control in component middleware, as described in [24]. de Miguel [7] enhances EJB containers to support the exchange of QoS-related information with component instances. This differs from our approach in that our approach assembles the QoS control transparently to the component implementations. In their dynamicTAO project, Kon and Campbell [11] apply adaptive middleware techniques to extend TAO so it can be reconfigured at runtime by dynamically linking selected modules. Their work is similar to ours in that both support realizing dynamic QoS provisioning with middleware, but ours offers a more comprehensive QoS provisioning abstraction, whereas Kon and Campbell's work concentrates on configuring middleware capabilities.

Other research projects have tackled the issues of end-to-end QoS management. Many of these concentrate only on network QoS, where end-to-end means managing the reservations or queues along network paths [3, 19]. Others look at the problem more broadly, as we do, from the middleware and application perspective. The BRENTA architecture [14] describes contract-based negotiation of network QoS, but with the addition that applications should adapt to the available resources, even while realizing that some legacy applications might not have that flexibility. QARMA [9] is a centralized QoS architecture, including a resource manager and system repository, provided as CORBA services. Li et al [12] propose a task control model approach in which they add a monitoring task and an adaptation task for each functional task in the system. The monitoring task recognizes QoS violations and the adaptation task adjusts application behavior to compensate. The Adapt project [4] provides middleware that supports the dynamic reconfiguration and composition of object implementations. It includes support for QoS properties, management, and monitoring. Adapt proposes a new middleware, whereas our approach is applied to existing middleware standards.

7 Moving Forward from Here

The work described here has already gone beyond the laboratory setting and has been used in demonstrations, field tests and systems for military and industrial organizations. Applying the QoS management middleware research to these transitions has served to validate the research results and encourage its use as a base for further increasing the capabilities while reducing the risk associated with developing the complex DRE systems emerging in real-world domains.

However, there is still a long way to go before the concepts developed and described here can become standard operating procedure or normal best practice for constructing DRE systems. In addition to the short range issues mentioned earlier, there are a number of longer range issues as well. Among these are the following:

- Easy to use tools to automate the design process
- Expanded shelves of reusable QoS mechanisms and management components and policies that can reasonably cover the common situations
- Automated conflict identification and resolution across various QoS dimensions
- Approaches and tools for evaluating, verifying and certifying correct dynamic decision making operation

- Methods and techniques for combining and analyzing different (integrated) QoS aspects with sufficient flexibility to manage simultaneous requirements for guaranteed service and safe operation.

7.1 New Branches: Assessment and Certification of Dynamic Behavior in DRE Systems

Many DRE systems serve mission critical needs and domains which have in place careful evaluation procedures before they can be deployed. These procedures are currently deeply wedded to static design approaches. We have observed first hand the autonomic avoidance reaction to many/any forms of dynamic resource management from those involved with the certification process. This represents another critical hurdle for the general acceptance of the dynamic behavior approaches to constructing real-time systems.

The goal of certification is to document (to the satisfaction of the certification authority) that the system exhibits correct behavior during all operational situations and in all operational environments. Traditionally, certification has involved a combination of adherence to documented processes, testing, and formal analysis. Established approaches to software certification commonly involve exhaustive state exploration and code coverage. Certification standards based on exhaustive testing and evaluation are generally infeasible for distributed real-time embedded systems because the size of the state space of a composed system can be exponential in the number of components. Distributed real-time embedded systems typically have a richer set of extensible inputs (including environment conditions and nondeterministic decisions) that affect dynamic system behavior that can be difficult to quantify formally, and hence affect certifiability. Additionally, a particular certification problem focus area involves the large scale systems of systems approaches being taken today. Much of the focus is on certification of an individual part, operating in isolation. No attention (or at best little) is focused on the problems of certifying the aggregate, integrated package, which of necessity shares some common base, and on recertifying a complete package when only a single (or a few) elements have actually changed.

We are integrating a focus on these subproblems around the design of multi-layered resource management (MLRM) capabilities, similar to that previously described. An MLRM allows for the dynamic adjustment of the allocation of resources provided to computational tasks. It is a hierarchical resource control system that uses the system's measured application utility as a feedback control signal to dynamically adjust the system's allocation of resources at multiple levels of abstraction.

We define a utility function, called the *Application Utility* function, which is focused on user-perceived elements of derived external value to assess the ability of the system to effectively allocate resources. The utility function is computed in real-time as the system performs its diverse computation jobs. Every computation job that is completed successfully causes an increase in the system's utility, while every failure to complete a computation job causes a decrease in the system's utility. Hence, when partial system failures or a change in operating mode occurs, in order to avoid decreases in the computed utility, the system should make adjustments to the resource allocation.

Decreases in the calculated utility can be an indication that failures have occurred which cause the current resource allocation to be insufficient and the system may need to redeploy its resources to accommodate possible failures. By redeploying resources, the system utility would increase if the new allocation allows the system to better accomplish its computation tasks. Consequently, we are using the utility measure as an evidentiary artifact to evaluate how well the system dynamically adjusts system resources.

There is a discernable relation between the assessment utility measures we are developing, their use in control of DRE systems, and certification processes for these systems. Traditional testing and formal analysis methods face difficulties when being applied to dynamic systems because it is more difficult to identify a finite set of tests that would cover system operation. We believe that utility measures and utility-driven control functions can be used as a tool for certification of dynamic systems.

- Utility functions can capture all the attributes (or a large set of them) of higher or lower utility, without needing to capture all the factors contributing to them. For example, a utility measure can recognize that utility is negatively affected by missing deadlines, without needing to identify what can cause missed deadlines (such as network outages, denial of service attacks, improper scheduling, resource overload, hardware or software failures, and so on). This provides a quantitative measure for certification that is achievable even in highly open and dynamic environments.
- Feedback controllers driven by system utility lend themselves to Monte Carlo simulations to gain statistical evidence of the system's ability to maintain correct behavior under different conditions.
- Application utility is a measure of the user-perceived value derived from using the MLRM and gives evidence for how well the MLRM can respond to changes in system operating modes. We can combine that with mission-derived limits on system operating modes, which focuses the certification effort on verifying the controller's ability to enforce correct behavior within these limits. A controller based design provides convenient and easy to understand places within the architecture to implement simplified control "limiters" which may be amenable to be certified by inspection or formal methods.
- Evidence of properly restricted feedback interactions between a controller and a system ease the difficulty of certifying the overall controlled system.

References

1. AFRL JBI Reference Implementation 1.2.6, http://www.rl.af.mil/programs/jbi/
2. ARTIST, http://www.artist-embedded.org/artist/QoS-Aware-Components.html
3. Bai, H., Atiquzzaman, M., Ivancic, W.: Achieving End-to-End QoS in the Next Generation Internet: Integrated Services Over Differentiated Service Networks. NASA/TM-2001-210755 (March 2001)

4. Blair, G., Coulson, G., Robin, P., Papathomas, M.: An Architecture for Next Generation Middleware. In: Proceedings of the IFIP International Conference on Distributed Systems Platforms and Open Distributed Processing, The Lake District, England (1998)
5. CIAO, http://www.cs.wustl.edu/ schmidt/CIAO.html
6. Dasarathy, B., Gadgil, S., Vaidyanathan, R., Parmeswaran, K., Coan, B., Conarty, M., Bhanot, V.: Network QoS Assurance in a Multi-Layer Adaptive Resource Management Scheme for Mission-Critical Applications using the CORBA Middleware Framework. In: RTAS 2005. 11th IEEE Real Time and Embedded Technology and Applications Symposium, pp. 246–255 (2005)
7. deMiguel, M.: QoS-Aware Component Frameworks. In: IWQoS. Proceedings of the 10th International Workshop on QoS, Miami Beach, Florida (May 2002)
8. Eide, E., Stack, T., Regehr, J., Lepreau, J.: Dynamic CPU Management for Real-Time, Middleware-Based Systems. In: RTAS. 10th IEEE Real-Time and Embedded Technology and Applications Symposium, Toronto, ON (May 2004)
9. Fleeman, D., Gillen, M., Lenharth, A., Delaney, M., Welch, L., Juedes, D., Liu, C.: Quality-based Adaptive Resource Management Architecture (QARMA): A CORBA Resource Management Service. In: International Parallel and Distributed Processing Symposium, Santa Fe, NM (April 2004)
10. IETF, An Architecture for Differentiated Services, http://www.ietf.org/rfc/rfc2475.txt
11. Kon, F., Costa, F., Blair, G., Campbell, R.: The Case for Reflective Middleware. In: CACM (June 2002)
12. Li, B., Xu, D., Nahrstedt, K., Liu, J.: End-to-End QoS Support for Adaptive Applications Over the Internet. In: SPIE Proceedings on Internet Routing and Quality of Service, Boston, Massachusetts (November 1-6, 1998)
13. Loyall, J., Schantz, R., Corman, D., Paunicka, J., Fernandez, S.: A Distributed Real-time Embedded Application for Surveillance, Detection, and Tracking of Time Critical Targets. In: RTAS. Real-time and Embedded Technology and Applications Symposium, pp. 88–97 (March 2005)
14. Mandato, D., Kassler, A., Valladares, T., Neureiter, G.: Handling End-To-End QoS in Mobile Heterogeneous Networking Environments. In: International Symposium on Personal, Indoor and Mobile Radio Communications (October 2001)
15. Manghwani, P., Loyall, J., Sharma, P., Gillen, M., Ye, J.: End-to-End Quality of Service Management for Distributed Real-time Embedded Applications. In: WPDRTS 2005. The Thirteenth International Workshop on Parallel and Distributed Real-Time Systems, Denver, Colorado (April 4-5, 2005)
16. Object Management Group, CORBA Component Model, V3.0 formal specification, http://www.omg.org/technology/documents/formal/components.htm
17. Object Management Group, Notification Service Specification, Version 1.1, formal/04-10-11 (October 2004)
18. Object Management Group, UML Profile for Modeling Quality of Service and Fault Tolerance Characteristics and Mechanisms, OMG document ptc/2005-05-02 (May 20, 2005)
19. Sander, V., Adamson, W., Foster, I., Roy, A.: End-to-End Provision of Policy Information for Network QoS. In: HPDC. 10th IEEE Symposium on High Performance Distributed Computing (August 2001)
20. Schantz, R., Loyall, J., Atighetchi, M., Pal, P.: Packaging Quality of Service Control Behaviors for Reuse. In: ISORC 2002. Proceedings of the 5th IEEE International Symposium on Object-Oriented distributed Computing, Washington DC (April 29-May 1, 2002)

21. Sharma, P., Loyall, J., Heineman, G., Schantz, R., Shapiro, R., Duzan, G.: Component-Based Dynamic QoS Adaptations in Distributed Real-Time and Embedded Systems. In: DOA. International Symposium on Distributed Objects and Applications, Agia Napa, Cyprus (October 25-29, 2004)

22. Sharma, P., Loyall, J., Schantz, R., Ye, J., Manghwani, P., Gillen, M., Heineman, G.: Using Composition of QoS Components to Provide Dynamic, End-to-End QoS in Distributed Embedded Applications - A Middleware Approach. IEEE Internet Computing 10(3), 16–23 (2006)

23. Schmidt, D., Levine, D., Mungee, S.: The Design and Performance of the TAO Real-Time Object Request Broker. Computer Communications 21(4) (April 1999)

24. Wang, Schmidt, Kircher, Parameswaran.: Towards a Reflective Middleware Framework for QoS-enabled CORBA Component Model Applications. IEEE Distributed Systems Online 2 (July 2001)

25. Zhang, L., Deering, S., Estrin, D., Shenker, S., Zappala, D.: RSVP: A New Resource ReSerVation Protocol. IEEE Network (September 1993)

26. Zinky, J., Bakken, D., Schantz, R.: Architectural Support for Quality of Service for CORBA Objects. Theory and Practice of Object Systems (April 1997)

Recent Additions on the Application Programming Interface of the TMO Support Middleware

K.H. (Kane) Kim, Juan A. Colmenares*, Liangchen Zheng, Sheng Liu, Qian Zhou, and Moon-Cheol Kim

DREAM Lab
Department of Electrical Engineering and Computer Science
University of California, Irvine
Irvine, CA, USA
{khkim,jcolmena,lzheng,shengl,qianz,mckim}@uci.edu

Abstract. Developing distributed real-time systems with high degrees of assurance on the system reliability is becoming increasingly important, yet remains difficult and error-prone. The Time-triggered Message-triggered Object (TMO) scheme is a high-level distributed object-oriented programming approach that has proved to be effective in developing such systems. The TMO programming scheme allows real-time application developers to explicitly specify temporal constraints in terms of global time in simple and natural forms. TMOSM is a middleware model that provides the execution support mechanisms for TMOs and TMOSL is a C++ class library that provides a convenient application programming interface (API) for developing TMO applications. The TMO scheme, TMOSM, and TMOSL have evolved during these years in order to support complex distributed real-time applications more effectively. This paper presents some recent additions on the TMOSM API that resulted from this evolution.

1 Introduction

In the last decade distributed real-time applications have become common and essential, but the state of the art in engineering large-scale distributed real-time computing application systems remains inadequate. Such application systems are still produced without accompanying any tight bounds on the service or response time that the system will yield. In addition, the real-time distributed computing programs are implemented using low-level languages which dictate the developers to directly manipulate low-level program constructs such as threads, task priorities, and sockets [1,2,3]. Extensive research has been performed on timing analysis of simple single-threaded programs running on hardware without intervention of an operating systems [4,5,6,7,8,9,10,11,12]. However, such research

---

* Also with the Applied Computing Institute, School of Engineering, University of Zulia.

F. Kordon and O. Sokolsky (Eds.): Monterey Workshop 2006, LNCS 4888, pp. 168–186, 2007.

has not been extended yet to cover the cases of real-time distributed computing programs.

A major challenge is the difficulty of programming such applications while maintaining timing guarantees. The first co-author established the initial skeleton of a distributed real-time computing object programming model, called TMO (*Time-Triggered Message-Triggered Object*) [13,14,15,16,17], 15 years ago and since then he and his collaborators have been enhancing the model and support tools.

TMO is a syntactically simple and natural but semantically powerful extension of the conventional object structure. It is also considered one of the most ambitious real-time programming approaches in terms of the *level of abstraction* at which programmers are allowed to exercise their logic. TMO combines the complexity management benefits of the object-oriented structuring paradigm with the ability of explicitly specifying temporal constraints in terms of *global time* [18] in natural forms.

To enable programming and execution of TMOs, the *TMO Support Middleware* (TMOSM) was developed [19,16,20]. TMOSM is a middleware model that provides the execution support mechanisms for TMOs and can be easily adapted to a variety of commercial, industry standard kernel, and hardware platforms. Prototype implementations of TMOSM currently exist for Windows XP, Windows CE, and Linux 2.6.[1] Along with TMOSM, the *TMO Support Library* (TMOSL) has been developed [15,14,17,21]. It provides a friendly application programming interface (API) that wraps the execution support services of TMOSM. TMOSL defines a number of C++ classes and enables convenient high-level programming by approximating a programming language directly supporting TMO as a basic building block. Other research teams have also developed TMO execution engines based on different kernel platforms [22,23].

The TMO programming scheme and supporting tools have been used in a broad range of basic research and application prototyping projects in a number of research organizations [24,25,26,27,28]. They have also been used in an undergraduate course on real-time distributed computing programming at UCI for some years.[2] Since its first introduction, the TMO programming model has been enhanced in several steps along with TMOSM and TMOSL. In the last few years, new-generation application demos have also been developed, e.g., cars that can be driven by drivers located thousands of miles away, tiled display capable of playing high-definition movies, digital music ensemble, and high-QoS multimedia streaming synchronization. These applications have required: i) enabling the activation and deactivation of time-triggered methods, ii) the specification of the *release time* of service requests, iii) a more adequate interaction mechanism between threads outside TMOSM and TMO methods, iv) an enhanced multicast communication scheme among TMOs, and v) the use of the local time-stamp counter in addition to global time. Thus, this paper presents the improvements on the TMOSM API that resulted from these efforts.

---

[1] Available at: `http://dream.eng.uci.edu/TMOdownload/`
[2] `http://dream.eng.uci.edu/eecs123/learn.htm`

The paper is structured as follows. Section 2 gives an overview of the TMO programming scheme and the TMOSM. Section 3 describes the improvements on the API of TMOSM. Finally, the paper concludes in Section 4.

2   Overview of the TMO Programming Scheme

TMO is a natural, syntactically minor, and semantically powerful extension of conventional object structure. As depicted in Fig. 1, the basic TMO structure consists of four parts:

1. **ODS-sec** (*Object-data-store section*). This section contains the data-container variables shared among methods of a TMO. Variables are grouped into *ODS segments* (ODSSs), which are units that can be locked for exclusive use by a TMO method in execution. Access rights of TMO methods for ODSSs are explicitly specified and the execution engine (a composition of networked hardware, node OS, and middleware) analyzes them to exploit maximal concurrency.

2. **EAC-sec** (*Environment access capability section*). This section contains "gate objects" that provide efficient call-paths to remote TMO methods,

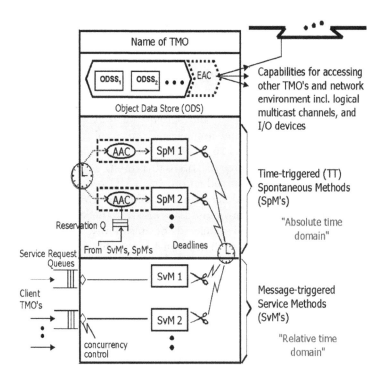

Fig. 1. Basic TMO structure (adapted from [13]).

logical multicast channels called *Real-time Multicast and Memory Replication Channels* (RMMCs) [14,17], and I/O device interfaces.

3. **SpM-sec** (*Spontaneous method section*). It contains *time-triggered (TT) methods* whose executions are initiated within user-specified time-windows.
4. **SvM-sec** (*Service method section*). It contains service methods which can be called by other TMOs.

The major features of the TMO programming scheme are reviewed below.

- **Use of a Global Time Base.** All time references in a TMO are references to *global time* [18] in that their meaning and correctness are unaffected by the location of the TMO. If GPS receivers are incorporated into the TMO execution engine, then a global time base of microsecond-level precision can easily be established. Within a cluster computer or a LAN-based distributed computing system a master-slave scheme, which involves time announcements by the master and exploitation of the knowledge on the message delay between the master and the slave, can be used to establish a global time base of sub-millisecond level precision [29].

- **Distributed Computing Component.** A TMO is a distributed computing component and thereby TMOs distributed over multiple nodes may interact via *remote method calls*. Non-blocking remote method calls are supported to allow concurrent execution of client methods in one node and server TMO methods in different nodes or the same node.

  TMOs can use another interaction mode in which messages are exchanged over logical multicast channels. The channel facility is called the *Real-time Multicast and Memory-replication Channel* (RMMC) [14,17]. The RMMC scheme facilitates real-time publisher-subscriber channels in a versatile form. It supports not only conventional *event messages* but also *state messages* based on distributed replicated memory semantics [18].

- **Autonomously Activated Distributed Computing Component.** The autonomous-action capability of the TMO stems from one of its unique parts, called the *time-triggered (TT) methods* or *spontaneous methods* (SpMs), which are clearly separated from the conventional *service methods* (SvMs). The SpM executions are triggered upon reaching of the global time at specific values determined at design time whereas the SvM executions are triggered by service request messages from clients. For example, the triggering times of an SpM may be specified as:

```
FOR t = FROM 10:00am TO 10:50am
  EVERY 30min
  START-DURING (t,t+5min)
  FINISH-BY (t+10min)
```

This specification of the execution-time window of an SpM is called the *Autonomous Activation Condition* (AAC) of the SpM and has the same effect as the following does:

```
{[START-DURING (10:00am,10:05am) FINISH-BY 10:10am],
 [START-DURING (10:30am,10:35am) FINISH-BY 10:40am]}
```

By using SpMs, *global-time-based coordination of distributed computing actions* (TCoDA), a principle pioneered by Kopetz [30,18], can be easily designed and realized.

- **Basic Concurrency Constraint (BCC).** BCC is a major execution rule intended to reduce the designer's efforts in guaranteeing timely service capabilities of TMOs and it prevents potential conflicts between SpMs and SvMs. Basically, *activation of an SvM triggered by a message from an external client is allowed only when potentially conflicting SpM executions are not in place*. The full set of data members in a TMO is called an *object data store* (ODS). An ODS is declared as a list of *ODS segments* (ODSSs), each of which is thus a subset of the data members in the ODS and is accessed by concurrently running object-method executions in either the *concurrently-reading* mode or the *exclusive-writing* mode. Thus, an SvM is allowed to execute only if no SpM that accesses the same ODSSs to be accessed by this SvM has an execution time-window that will overlap with the execution time-window of this SvM. However, the BCC rule does not stand in the way of either concurrent SpM executions or concurrent SvM executions.

- **Natural-form Specification of Timing Requirements and Guarantees.** TMO has been devised to contain only high-level intuitive and yet precise expressions of timing requirements. *Start-time-windows* and *completion deadlines* for object methods are used but no specification in indirect terms (e.g., priority) are required. A completion deadline may be specified in the form of a global time instant (e.g., 09:45am) or a bound on execution time (e.g., 130 milliseconds) spent after a signal triggering the method execution activation arrives at the host node. The latter bound is called the *guaranteed execution duration bound* (GEDB). GEDBs associated with a TMO are taken as guaranteed service-time bounds by the designers of the clients of the TMO. *Deadlines for result arrivals* can also be specified in the client's calls for service methods.

- **Power of TMO Network Structuring.** An underlying design philosophy of the TMO scheme is that an real-time computing application system will always take the form of a network of TMOs, which may be produced in a top-down multi-step fashion [13]. All conceivable practical real-time and non-real-time applications can be built as TMO networks.

3   Improvements on the TMOSM API

3.1   Activation and Deactivation of Spontaneous Methods

In the last few years the TMO programming scheme was extended to enable dynamic activation and deactivation of execution of SpMs at runtime. Such dynamic control of SpM executions allows application programs to easily adapt to changing functional and temporal requirements as the execution environment changes, which is an important requirement for many real-time distributed computing applications. For instance, in a multi-party video-conferencing application, a local participant receives video frames from other remote participants and plays them. Video playback can be naturally realized by an SpM (e.g., Video_Play_SpM). The local participant may stop or resume video playback at any time responding to an application user's input or on-line control commands from the remote participants. If the local participant is supposed to stop playing, executions of the Video_Play_SpM can be deactivated at run-time. Similarly, when the local participant wants to resume playing, executions of the Video_Play_SpM can be dynamically activated.

Furthermore, this feature allows TMO applications to support: i) transitions between different operation modes initiated either automatically or by an operator (e.g., passage between autonomous mode, manual mode, and tele-operation mode of an autonomous vehicle [31]), and/or ii) different levels of quality of service (QoS) under various network conditions characterized by performance metrics such as bandwidth, delay, jitter, and packet-loss rate.

Two different mechanisms are provided by TMOSM for supporting dynamic activation and deactivation of SpM executions. The mechanism introduced most recently to the TMO scheme defines two SpM execution modes: *active mode* and *idle mode*. When the mode of an SpM execution is set to "active", which is the default mode for every SpM execution, the execution of the SpM is scheduled according to the timing specifications of its AACs. If the mode of an SpM execution is set to "idle", TMOSM does not schedule executions of the SpM.

TMOSL provides four methods for changing the mode of SpMs; they are:

- BOOL PutSpMinIdleMode(int SpM_ID, tms& idling_start_time, tms& idling_end_time), which puts the SpM with SpM_ID into the idle mode from idling_start_time to idling_end_time.
- BOOL PutSpMinIdleMode(int SpM_ID, tms& idling_start_time), which puts the SpM with SpM_ID into the idle mode from idling_start_time until the method WakeSpMfromIdleMode is called to wake the SpM from the idle mode.
- BOOL WakeSpMfromIdleMode(int SpM_ID), which wakes the SpM with SpM_ID from the idle mode.
- BOOL WakeSpMfromIdleMode(int SpM_ID, tms& idling_end_time), which wakes the SpM with SpM_ID from the idle mode at the time specified by idling_end_time.

All these methods return SUCCESS when they succeed; otherwise, they return FAIL.

Thus, in the the multi-party video-conferencing application described above, when a user orders the application to stop video playback, the TMO method handling user commands will call the method:

```
PushSpMinIdleMode(Video_Play_ID, TMO::now());
```

to put the method Video_Play_SpM into idle mode. Similarly, when the user tells the application to resume video playback, the TMO method handling user commands will invoke the method:

```
WakeSpMfromIdleMode(Video_Play_ID);
```

to wake `Video_Play_SpM` up back in active mode. Here `Video_Play_ID` is an integer variable that represents the identifier of `Video_Play_SpM` and it is obtained when the SpM is registered to TMOSM.

In addition, the TMO programming scheme already has the mechanism for allowing application programs to dynamically activate and deactivate *candidate AACs* of an SpM. An SpM can have two different types of AACs: *permanent* and *candidate*. A permanent AAC is always used for triggering an SpM. Permanent AACs, as the name implies, cannot be dynamically activated or deactivated at runtime whereas candidate AACs can. Another difference is that every candidate AACs has a name (or label) whereas permanent AACs do not. Based on this difference TMOSM is able to discriminate among permanent and candidate AACs. Thus, an AAC created with a name will be a candidate AAC, and an AAC created with its name equal to `NULL` will be a permanent AAC.

Run-time activation and deactivation of candidate AACs provide greater control over specifying temporal behavior of SpM executions than the active/idle mechanism that only allows for a binary execution mode selection of SpMs (i.e., active or idle). This versatility in specifying various timing requirements comes in two-fold. First, because each SpM can have multiple candidate AACs, the range of timing specification selections has been broadened. Second, multiple instances of the same SpM can be execute according to the currently active candidate AACs of the SpM. However, application programmers must be aware of any possibility of resource contention or anomaly due to concurrent executions of the same SpMs with different AAC specifications.

Two methods for supporting dynamic activation and deactivation of candidate AACs are provided by TMOSL; they are:

- `BOOL activate_AAC(TCHAR* cand_label, tms& activation_time)`,
  which activates the candidate AAC identified by the name `cand_label` at the time specified by `activation_time`. The `cand_label` of an AAC in the same TMO must be unique.
- `BOOL deactivate_AAC(TCHAR* cand_label, tms& deactivation_time)`,
  which deactivates the candidate AAC identified by the name `cand_label` at the time specified by `deactivation_time`.

Both methods return `SUCCESS` when succeed, and `FAIL` otherwise.

For example, the following code fragment of the `main` function of a TMO application creates a candidate AAC, called `aac1`, with the label `CAND-AAC`, and a permanent AAC, called `aac2` (with no label). The constructor of `MyTMO` class receives both `aac1` and `aac2` as parameters in order to create the object `myTMO` and register its SpM along with the AACs to TMOSM.[3]

Fragment

```
#include "TMOSL.h"
#include "MyTMO.h"
```

---

[3] The registration is not shown in the code.

```
using namespace TMO;
  . . .
const MicroSec MILLISECOND = 1000;
const MicroSec SECOND = 1000 * 1000;
const MicroSec MINUTE = 60 * 1000 * 1000;
  . . .
int main(int argc, char* argv[]) {
    StartTMOengine();
    tms tmoStartTime = tm4_DCS_age(2*SECOND);
      . . .
    // Candidate AAC
    AAC aac1(_T("CAND-AAC"),
        tm4_DCS_age(2 * SECOND),        // from
            tm4_DCS_age(60 * MINUTE),   // until
            1 * SECOND,                 // every
            100 * MILLISECOND,          // est
            150 * MILLISECOND,          // lst
            200 * MILLISECOND);         // by
    // Permanent AAC
    AAC aac2(NULL,
        tm4_DCS_age(2 * SECOND),   // from
        tm4_DCS_age(60 * MINUTE),  // until
        . . . );
    MyTMO myTMO(_T("TMO1"), aac1, aac2, tmoStartTime);
    MainThrSleep();
    return 0;
}
```

Then, aac1 can be deactivated by invoking the method:

```
deactivate_AAC(_T("CAND-AAC"), TMO::now());
```

3.2 Use of the Local Time-Stamp Counter in Addition to Global Time

Coordination of distributed actions in a real-time distributed computing environment can extensively benefit from a global time base established among distributed computing nodes. Several ways of establishing global time bases with various degrees of precision are currently available. These days commercial global positioning systems (GPS) provide sub-microsecond accuracy. Alternatively, clock synchronization protocols among cooperating distributed computing nodes (e.g., [32,29,33]) can create a global time base among themselves with the precision of tens of microseconds without using special hardware equipment such as GPS.

TMOSM provides a global time base to TMO applications. TMOSL defines four types for representing time in TMOSM [21]:

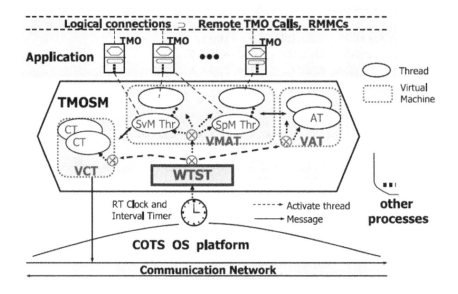

Fig. 2. TMOSM Architecture (adapted from [20])

- `MicroSec` is a 64-bit integer that represents a number of microseconds.
- `C21_age` is the same as `MicroSec` except that it represents the number of microseconds past since January 1, 2000 in UTC.
- The `tms` class is a wrapper class of the `C21_age` type.
- The `tml` class is derived from `tms` class and represents calendar time.

The precision of the global time base provided by TMOSM can be set by application programmers in the variable `CredibleGPPrecision` in the configuration file `config.ini`. The unit of the `CredibleGTPrecision` variable is microsecond. When a TMO application obtains a time value from TMOSL (e.g., by calling `now()`), the time value is truncated and returned with significant bits matching with the specified precision. TMO applications can obtain the `CredibleGTPrecision` value by calling the function

```
MicroSec GetGTprecision();
```

One execution engine model that we have adopted for enabling programming and execution of TMOs is based on the TMO Support Middleware (TMOSM). TMOSM has been implemented to be easily adapted to a variety of commercial, industry standard OS kernel + hardware platforms. As shown in Fig. 2, our TMOSM implementation includes 3 virtual machines (VMs) [20], each managing a set of threads and using them to perform certain specialized functions as parts of executing TMOs. The VMs are:

1. **VMAT** (*VM for Main Application Threads*), which maintains the application threads dedicated to executing methods of TMOs (i.e., SpMs and SvMs) with maximal exploitation of concurrency.

2. **VCT** (*VM for Communication Threads*), which maintains the application threads dedicated to sending and receiving middleware messages.
3. **VAT** (*VM for Auxiliary Threads*), which maintains a pool of threads called *auxiliary threads*. Some auxiliary threads are designed to be devoted to controlling certain peripherals under orders from TMO methods (executed by main application threads). Others wait for orders for executing certain application program-segments and such orders come from main application threads in execution of TMO methods.

The processor and memory resources are leased to VMAT, VCT, and VAT in a time-sliced and periodic manner. Thus, each VM can be viewed conceptually as being periodically activated to run for a time-slice. For example, VCT-VMAT-VAT-VMAT can be an iteration of the specified execution cycle of the VMs, called *TMOSM cycle*.

With the advent of dual-core processors as de facto standard hardware platform for desktop and laptop computers, we can dedicate one CPU core to VMAT. If there is only a TMO method active at a certain time, that method can monopolize the CPU core and finer-precision real-time control activities can be performed inside the method, even at precision greater than that of the global time base. This is particularly useful for controlling special hardware devices that require high-frequency control signals. Therefore, we believe that it is convenient for TMO applications to be able to determine the elapsed time during the execution of a piece of code by reading the processor's Timestamp Counter (TSC) and obtaining the frequency of the TSC, both in a standard manner. Thus, TMOSL currently provides the function

```
__int64 Read_LTSC();
```

for reading the value of TSC. The TSC's frequency is also specified by application programmers in the variable LTSCFrequency of the configuration file config.ini. The type of the LTSCFrequency variable is int and its unit is *MHz*. TMO applications can call the function

```
int Get_LTSC_Frequency();
```

to obtain the LTSCFrequency value.

3.3 Service Requests with Official Release Time

A TMO can invoke methods in another TMO executing on the same or a different node. These methods are called *Service Methods* (SvMs) and client TMOs send *service requests* (carried in the form of messages by TMOSM) when invoking SvMs in server TMOs.

SvMs are declared as ordinary member functions of a TMO class (i.e., a class inherited from the CTMOBase class). In order for a server TMO to make an SvM available to other TMOs, the server TMO must register the SvM to TMOSM with at least the following parameters:

- The external *name* of the SvM, which is a globally recognized symbolic name to the world outside the enclosing TMO.
- The *guaranteed execution duration bound* (GEDB) of the SvM (in microseconds).
- Set of *identifiers* and *access modes* (i.e., read-only and read-write) of the ODSSs that the SvM intends to use.

TMO application developers can also provide: i) the maximum allowed number of concurrent executions of the SvM (pipeline_degree), and ii) the maximum invocation rate of the SvM, in terms of the maximum number of service requests (max_invocations) in a specified period of time (basic_period), that the SvM will honor. If TMO application developers do not specify the parameters pipeline_degree, max_invocations and basic_period, they are assigned default values.

A client TMO must invoke an SvM through a locally accessible proxy called *SvM gate*, which is an SvMGateClass instance. An SvMGateClass object is created with three parameters: i) the *name of the server TMO*, ii) the *external name of the SvM* to be invoked, and iii) a tms object[4] that represents the service start time. For example, the following line of code:

```
SvMGateClass mySvMGate(_T("MyTMO"), _T("MySvM"),
                tm4_DCS_age(7*1000*1000));
```

creates the object mySvMGate, which a SvM gate for sending service requests to the SvM with the external name MySvM of the TMO called MyTMO. The service start time is 7 seconds after the instant the distributed computing system started operating. The tms object that represents the service start time is obtained from the function tm4_DCS_age.

Once an SvM gate is created and the service start time elapses, the SvM gate is able to send service requests to the specified SvM. The SvMGateClass provides different methods for invoking an SvM; some examples are:

- int BlockingSR(void* pParam, int size, MicroSec dra1, MicroSec ort1), which sends a service request to the SvM and waits until the reply returns from the server or the deadline for result arrival (dra1) expires. The method returns SUCCESS if the service request was sent successfully and the the server's reply arrives before the expiration of the deadline for result arrival (DRA). If the DRA expires and the server's reply has not arrived yet, then the method returns DRA_MISSED. If the operation fails on sending the service request, the method returns FAIL.
- int OnewaySR(void* pParam, int size, MicroSec ort1), which sends a service request to the SvM and immediately returns the control to the caller; there is no reply from the server. The method returns SUCCESS if the service request was sent successfully; FAIL otherwise.
- int NonBlockingSR(void* pParam, int size, tmsp& timestamp, MicroSec ort1), which sends a service request to the SvM and immediately returns the control to the caller. The parameter timestamp is returned

---

[4] The tms type is described briefly in Section 3.2.

and can be used later in the methods specifically defined to check the result of the service request (e.g., `BlockingGetResultOfNonBlockingSR`). The method `NonBlockingSR` returns `SUCCESS` if the service request was sent successfully; `FAIL` otherwise.

In these methods, the parameter `pParam` is a pointer to the data structure that contains the input and output parameters of the SvM, and `size` indicates the size of that structure. Additionally, there are variations of those methods whose time parameters (i.e., `ort1` and `dra1`) are of `tms` type. Note that local and remote client TMOs call an SvM exactly in the same way.

The addition of the *Official Release Time* (ORT) as an input parameter in the methods above is a refinement in the API of the `SvMGateClass` that was adopted some time ago. The ORT of a service request indicates that *the service request message will be read at the server side at or after the ORT and the invoked SvM will be subject to the deadline of ORT+GEDB.*

The ability to specify the release time of an SvM allows us to delay and synchronize the execution of the SvM with some other events. For example, in distributed real-time fault-tolerant applications TMOs are replicated in different nodes. A client that sends a service request to an SvM of a server TMO should also send an identical service request to the same SvM of each replica of the server TMO.[5] By specifying the same ORT in the service requests sent to the TMO replicas, the TMO execution engine guarantees that the execution of the SvM of each replica will start at or after the time, ensuring replica consistency.

Moreover, the ORT can sometimes be used to control the order of execution of different SvMs.

3.4 Interaction between Non-TMO Threads and TMO Methods

There are TMO applications requiring that non-TMO programs running on threads not managed by TMOSM interact with TMO methods. An example is a TMO-based two-party video conference application. In each node, a TMO method needs to get the video data from a web camera and transfer the data to the other node via an RMMC (Real-time Multicast and Memory Replication Channel). However, the video data can only be obtained by a *device callback function* running on a non-TMO thread and cannot be passed to the TMO method directly. Therefore, a communication mechanism between non-TMO programs and TMO methods is needed.

TMOSL provides the class `CGate_4_NonTMO` that has the following member function for passing messages from non-TMO threads to TMO methods:

- `BOOL OnewaySR(TCHAR* tmoName, TCHAR* svmName, void* pParam, int size)`. This method is invoked from a non-TMO thread to send a service request to the specified SvM of the specified TMO. The parameters `tmoName` and

---

[5] An alternative approach that enables the invocation of SvMs via a multicast channel is discussed in Section 3.5.

svmName indicate the names of the target TMO and the target SvM, respectively. The parameter pParam is a pointer to the buffer that contains the message to be sent, and the parameter size specifies the size of the message. The method returns TRUE if the service request was sent successfully; FALSE otherwise.

The next fragments of C++ code exemplify the use of this function on TMOSM running on Microsoft Windows XP. This simple TMO program contains a TMO class, called TMO1, that implements an SvM, called SvM1. SvM1 sends video frames captured by a web camera to other TMOs executing in remote nodes. A callback function, called videoCallBack, is registered to a video library which only contains non-TMO threads. The callback function executing on a non-TMO thread gets the video raw data and then sends the data to SvM1 through a non-TMO-to-TMO service call.

- Fragment 1 contains the definition of the data structure VideoFrame that represents the format of the message sent by videoCallBack to SvM1. It also includes the implementation of the TMO1 class. The constructor of TMO1 class registers SvM1 and the TMO1 instance to TMOSM. Moreover, the TMO1 class includes the member function Init_Capture_Device which initializes the web camera and registers videoCallBack to the video library in order to obtain the video data.

Fragment 1

```
#include "TMOSL.h"

// Message
struct VideoFrame {
    unsigned int nBytes;
    unsigned int nID;
    char data[MAXIMUM_FRAME_SIZE];
    . . .
}

// Definition of the TMO class
class TMO1: public CTMOBase {
private:
    int SvM1(VideoFrame* pFrame) {
        . . .
        char* frame_data = pFrame->data;
        // Send the video frame to remote TMOs
        . . .
        return 1;
    };
public:
    TMO1(TCHAR* TMO_name, TCHAR* SvM_name,
```

```
            const tms& TMO_start_time) {
            // Register SvM1 to TMOSM
            SvM_RegistParam svm_regist_param;
            _tcscpy(svm_regist_param.name, SvM_name);
            RegisterSvM((PFSvMBody)&TMO1::SvM1, &svm_regist_param);

            // Register this TMO instance to TMOSM
            TMO_RegistParam tmo_regist_param;
            _tcscpy (tmo_regist_param.global_name, TMO_name);
            tmo_regist_param.start_time = TMO_start_time;
            RegisterTMO(&tmo_regist_param);
        };

        void Init_Capture_Device() {
            . . .
            // Create a window for video capturing
            . . .
            // Set parameters for video capturing
            . . .
            // Register the callback function
            // to the video library
            capSetCallbackOnVideoStream(m_hWnd, videoCallBack);
            . . .
        };
    };
```

– Fragment 2 first includes the files TMOSL.h and NonTMO2TMO.h and creates a CGate_4_NonTMO instance. Then it defines the callback function videoCallBack. Fragment 2 also contains the main function of the program. This function first starts the TMO execution engine, next creates a TMO1 instance, and finally makes the main application thread sleep to prevent early termination of the program.

Fragment 2

```
#include "TMOSL.h"
#include "NonTMO2TMO.h"

CGate_4_NonTMO gate;

LRESULT CALLBACK videoCallBack(HWND hWnd, LPVIDEOHDR lpVHdr) {

    VideoFrame currentVideoFrame;

    // Get video frame data and copy the data
    // in currentVideoFrame.data
    . . .
```

```
        // Set the other fields of currentVideoFrame
        . . .
        gate.OnewaySR(_T("TMO1"),
                      _T("SvM1"),
                      (void*)&currentVideoFrame,
                      sizeof(VideoFrame));
        return (LRESULT)TRUE;
    }

    void main() {
        StartTMOengine();
        tms TMO_start_time1 = tm4_DCS_age(3*1000*1000);
        // Create the TMO instance
        TMO1 tmo1(_T("TMO1"),_T("SvM1"),TMO_start_time1);
        . . .

        MainThrSleep();
    }
```

3.5   Invocation of Service Methods Via RMMC

A number of real-time distributed applications fits very naturally into the publisher-subscriber model; in these applications the constituent nodes exchange event messages over (logical or actual) multicast channels. For example, in a multi-party video-conferencing application each node multicasts the video and audio streams to the nodes participating in the session.

The TMO programming scheme provides a multicast facility called the *Real-time Multicast and Memory-replication Channel* (RMMC) [17]. RMMC supports not only conventional *event messages* but also *state messages* based on distributed replicated memory semantics [18].

Very often TMO subscribers are implemented using an SpM that periodically checks whether new event messages have been received through the RMMC or not. If there are new messages the current execution of the SpM processes them; otherwise, the SpM execution (possibly does other job) and finishes, and another SpM execution will re-attempt in the next period. Moreover, to avoid buffer overflow subscriber SpMs usually execute at a frequency somewhat higher than that at which the publishers sends the messages. Thus, under these circumstances executions of subscriber SpMs will recurrently find no new message and will be in vain.

In the last few years we have incorporated in TMOSM another multicast scheme that allows for more efficient implementation of RMMC subscribers. This new multicast scheme, called *RMMC2SvM*, enables the invocation of SvMs via a multicast channel.

A TMO must access the RMMC2SvM channel through a local proxy called *RMMC2SvM gate*, which is an instance of a derived class of the

RMMC2SvM_GateBaseClass. After being created, the gate must be registered to TMOSM by invoking the method:

  BOOL RegisterRMMC2SvM_gate(const TCHAR* rmmcName);

Two distinctive methods of the RMMC2SvM_GateBaseClass are:

- void build_register_info_SvM(TCHAR* svnName), which allows a subscriber TMO to bind an SvM (with the name svnName) to the multicast channel. Thus, the specified SvM will be executed upon the reception of a message on the channel. This method must be invoked before registering the RMMC2SvM gate to TMOSM.
- int SRmulticast(void* pParam, int size, MicroSec ort1), which is used by a TMO to announce (i.e., multicast) a message. The parameter pParam is a pointer to the message to be announced and size indicates the size of the message. The parameter ort1 is the *Official Release Time* (ORT) and indicates that the announced message will be read by the receiver TMOs at or after the ORT and the invoked SvMs of the receiver TMOs will be subject to the deadline of ORT+GEDB. This method returns SUCCESS if the message was sent successfully; FAIL otherwise.

A message sent by the method SRmulticast creates the effect of a one-way call on the SvM that has been bound to the RMMC2SvM channel in each subscriber TMO (including the announcing subscriber).

Subscribers which receive SRmulticast messages must go through BCC checks before activating called SvMs. Therefore, application designers must be aware of the possible effects of the BCC rule on the application's response time. That is, the execution of a subscriber SvM may be delayed by a conflicting SpM execution when both need write-access to a common ODSS. This means that the application's response time may increase.

Finally, note that the support for state messages in RMMC2SvM is identical to the original RMMC.

4 Conclusion

In recent years the TMO programming model and the TMO Support Middleware (TMOSM) have been enhanced along with the extension of the TMO Support Library (TMOSL). The newly-introduced classes and methods of TMOSL reinforce TMOSM by providing more flexibility and convenience via dynamic activation and deactivation of time-triggered methods, an interaction mechanism between threads outside TMOSM and TMO methods, an enhanced multicast communication scheme among TMOs, the specification of the release time of service requests, and the standardized access to the CPU's time-stamp counter.

The recent additions on the TMOSM API have proved to be effective in facilitating the development of prototype implementations of new-generation distributed real-time applications (e.g., digital music ensemble, cars controlled by drivers located thousands of miles away, and high-definition tiled display). In the future, we will continue demonstrating the power of the TMO programming model and TMOSM by developing more complex distributed real-time applications. This effort will also help validate and refine even more the TMOSM API.

Acknowledgments

The work reported here was supported in part by the NSF under Grant Numbers 03-26606 (ITR) and 05-24050 (CNS) and under Cooperative Agreement ANI-0225642 to the University of California, San Diego for "The OptIPuter". Juan A. Colmenares also thanks the University of Zulia (LUZ) for supporting his participation in this research. No part of this paper represents the views and opinions of any of the sponsors mentioned above.

References

1. Audsley, N.C., Burns, A., Davis, R.I., Tindell, K.W., Wellings, A.J.: Fixed priority pre-emptive scheduling: An historical perspective. Real-Time Systems 8(2), 173–198 (1995)
2. Fay-Wolfe, V., DiPippo, L.C., Cooper, G., Johnson, R., Kortmann, P., Thuraisingham, B.: Real-time CORBA. IEEE Transactions on Parallel and Distributed Systems 11(10), 1073–1089 (2000)
3. Object Management Group: RealTime-CORBA Specification, v 2.0. Object Management Group. OMG Document formal/03-11-01 edn (November 2003)
4. Lim, S.S., Bae, Y., Jang, C., Rhee, B.D., Min, S., Park, C., Shin, H., Park, K., Ki, C.: An accurate worst-case timing analysis for risc processors. IEEE Transactions on Software Engineering 21(7), 593–604 (1995)
5. Puschner, P., Schedl, A.: Computing maximum task execution times - a graph-based approach. Real-Time Systems 13(1), 67–91 (1997)
6. Li, Y.T.S., Malik, S.: Performance analysis of embedded software using implicit path enumeration. IEEE Transactions on Computer-aided Design of Integrated Circuits and Systems 16(12), 1477–1487 (1997)
7. Li, Y.T.S., Malik, S., Wolfe, A.: Performance estimation of embedded software with instruction cache modeling. ACM Transactions on Design Automation of Electronic Systems 4(3), 257–279 (1999)
8. Burns, A., Edgar, A.: Predicting computation time for advanced processors architectures. In: ECRTS 2000. Proceedings of the 12th Euromicro Conference on Real-Time Systems, p. 89 (June 2000)
9. Stappert, F., Ermedahl, A., Engblom, J.: Efficient longest executable path search for programs with complex flows and pipeline effects. In: CASES 2001. Proceedings of the 4th Int'l Conference on Compilers, Architecture, and Synthesis for Embedded Systems, pp. 132–140 (November 2001)
10. Colin, A., Bernat, G.: Scope-Tree: a program representation for symbolic worst-case execution time analysis. In: ECRTS 2002. 14th Euromicro on Real-Time Systems, pp. 50–59 (June 2002)
11. Ermedahl, A., Stappert, F., Engblom, J.: Clustered worst-case execution-time calculation. IEEE Transactions on Computers 54(9), 1104–1122 (2005)

12. Burguière, C., Rochange, C.: History-based schemes and implicit path enumeration. In: WCET 2006. Proceedings of the 6th Workshop on Worst-Case Execution Time Analysis, pp. 17–22 (July 2006)
13. Kim, K.H.: Object structures for real-time systems and simulators. IEEE Computer 30(9), 62–70 (1997)
14. Kim, K.H.: APIs for real-time distributed object programming. IEEE Computer 33(6), 72–80 (2000)
15. Kim, K.H.: Real-time object-oriented distributed software engineering and the tmo scheme. International Journal of Software Engineering and Knowledge Engineering 9(2), 251–276 (1999)
16. Kim, K.H.: Commanding and reactive control of peripherals in the TMO programming scheme. In: ISORC 2002. Proceedings of the 5th IEEE International Symposium on Object-Oriented Real-time Distributed Computing, pp. 448–456 (May 2002)
17. Kim, K.H., Li, Y., Liu, S., Kim, M.H., Kim, D.H.: RMMC programming model and support execution engine in the TMO programming scheme. In: ISORC 2005. Proceedings of the 8th IEEE International Symposium on Object-Oriented Real-Time Distributed Computing, pp. 34–43 (May 2005)
18. Kopetz, H.: Real-Time Systems: Design Principles for Distributed Embedded Applications. Kluwer Academic Publishers, Dordrecht (1997)
19. Kim, K.H., Ishida, M., Liu, J.: An efficient middleware architecture supporting time-triggered message-triggered objects and an NT-based implementation. In: ISORC 1999. Proceedings of the 2nd IEEE International Symposium on Object-Oriented Real-time Distributed Computing, pp. 54–63 (May 1999)
20. Jenks, S.F., Kim, K.H., Henrich, E., Li, Y., Zheng, L., Kim, M.H., Lee, K.H., Seol, D.M., Youn, H.Y.: A linux-based implementation of a middleware model supporting time-triggered message-triggered objects. In: ISORC 2005. Proceedings of the 8th IEEE International Symposium on Object-Oriented Real-Time Distributed Computing, pp. 350–358 (May 2005)
21. Kim, K.H.: TMO Support Library (TMOSL): Facilities for C++ TMO Programming. Version 4.2.1. DREAM Laboratory, University of California, Irvine (January 2007)
22. Kim, H.J., Park, S.H., Kim, J.G., Kim, M.H., Rim, K.W.: TMO-Linux: A linux-based real-time operating system supporting execution of TMOs. In: ISORC 2002. Proceedings of the 5th IEEE International Symposium on Object-Oriented Real-Time Distributed Computing, pp. 288–294 (April 2002)
23. Kim, J.G., Kim, M.H., Kim, K., Heu, S.: TMO-eCos: An eCos-based real-time micro operating system supporting execution of a TMO structured program. In: ISORC 2005. Proceedings of the 8th IEEE International Symposium on Object-Oriented Real-Time Distributed Computing, pp. 182–189 (May 2005)
24. Kim, M.H., Kim, J.G., Kim, K.H., Lee, M.S., Park, S.Y.: Time-triggered message-triggered object modeling of a distributed real-time control application for its real-time simulation. In: COMPSAC 2000. Proceedings of the 24th Annual Int'l Computer Software and Applications Conference, pp. 549–556. IEEE Computer Society, Los Alamitos (2000)
25. Jo, E.H., Kim, M.H., Kim, J.G.: Modeling of multimedia streaming services based on the TMO structuring scheme. In: ISORC 2001. Proceedings of the 4th IEEE Int'l Symposium on Object-Oriented Real-Time Distributed Computing, pp. 420–427. IEEE Computer Society Press, Los Alamitos (2001)

26. Kim, M.H., Lim, S.H., Kim, J.G.: Modeling of a real-time distributed network management based on TMN and the TMO model. In: WORDS 2003. Proceedings of the 8th Int'l Workshop on Object-Oriented Real-Time Dependable Systems, pp. 56–63. IEEE Computer Society Press, Los Alamitos (2003)

27. Kim, K.H., Henrich, E., Im, C., Kim, M.C., Kim, S.J., Li, Y., Liu, S., Yoo, S.M., Zheng, L.C., Zhou, Q.: Distributed computing based streaming and play of music ensemble realized through tmo programming. In: WORDS 2005. Proceedings of the 10th IEEE Int'l Workshop on Object-Oriented Real-Time Dependable Systems, pp. 129–138 (February 2005)

28. Lee, H., Hwang, J., Lee, J., Park, S., Lee, C., Nah, Y., Jeon, S., Kim, M.H.: Long-term location data management for distributed moving object databases. In: ISORC 2006. Proceedings of the 9th IEEE Int'l Symposium on Object and Component-Oriented Real-Time Distributed Computing, IEEE Computer Society, Los Alamitos (2006)

29. Kim, K.H., Im, C., Athreya, P.: Realization of a distributed OS component for internal clock synchronization in a LAN environment. In: ISORC 2002. Proceedings of the 5th IEEE Int'l Symposium on Object-Oriented Real-Time Distributed Computing, pp. 263–270. IEEE Computer Society, Los Alamitos (2002)

30. Kopetz, H., Ochsenreiter, W.: Clock synchronization in distributed real-time systems. IEEE Transactions on Computers 36(8), 933–940 (1987)

31. Kemner, C.A., Peterson, J.L.: Remote control system and method for an autonomous vehicle. US Patent No. 5448479 (September 1995)

32. Veríssimo, P., Rodrigues, L.: A posteriori agreement for fault-tolerant clock synchronization on broadcast networks. In: FTCS 1992. Proceedings of the 22th Int'l Symposium on Fault-Tolerant Computing, pp. 527–536. IEEE Computer Society Press, Los Alamitos (1992)

33. Elson, J., Girod, L., Estrin, D.: Fine-grained network time synchronization using reference broadcasts. In: OSDI 2002. Proceedings of the 5th USENIX Symposium on Operating Systems Design and Implementation, pp. 147–163. ACM Press, New York (2002)

Integrating Automotive Applications Using Overlay Networks on Top of a Time-Triggered Protocol

Roman Obermaisser

Vienna University of Technology, Austria
`romano@vmars.tuwien.ac.at`

Abstract. The integration of multiple automotive subsystems (e.g., powertrain, safety, comfort) on a single distributed computer system can significantly reduce the number of Electronic Control Units (ECUs) and networks for in-vehicle electronic systems. The benefits of this integration include reduced hardware cost and reliability improvements due to fewer connectors. However, a major challenge in such an integrated automotive architecture is the management of access to the shared communication resources (i.e., the common network). In order to support a seamless integration of application subsystems from different vendors and to permit the integration of application subsystems with different criticality levels, a fault in one application subsystem should not have an adverse affect on the resources that are available to other application subsystems. For this reason, we devise a solution for encapsulating the communication activities of application subsystems in this paper. Each application subsystem is provided with a dedicated overlay network on top of an underlying time-triggered network. Such an overlay network has predefined temporal properties (i.e., latencies, bandwidths), which are independent from the communication activities on the overlay networks of other application subsystems. An exemplary configuration of the overlay networks in a prototype implementation demonstrates that the encapsulated overlay networks can handle the communication load of a present day car with the additional time-triggered traffic of future X-by-wire subsystems.

1   Introduction

A steady increase in automotive electronics has occurred during the past years. While this trend has lead to significant improvements concerning safety and comfort, a side-effect has been a growth of the deployed in-vehicle hardware and software. In conjunction with the prevalent "1 Function – 1 ECU" strategy [1], present day luxury cars can contain more than 70 ECUs and multiple networks with different communication protocols (e.g., CAN, MOST, ByteFlight) [2]. Furthermore, the increase in automotive electronics is likely to continue its growth due to customers expectations. Cars are no longer simple means of transportation but rather need to convince customers with respect to design, performance, driving behavior, safety, infotainment, comfort, maintenance, and cost.

F. Kordon and O. Sokolsky (Eds.): Monterey Workshop 2006, LNCS 4888, pp. 187–206, 2007.

To circumvent the increase of ECUs and networks, the automotive industry is currently evolving towards integrated system architectures [3, 4]. Integrated system architectures promise a reduction of ECUs, networks, and connectors by using the ECUs and networks as shared resources for multiple application subsystems. Each ECUs can execute jobs from multiple application subsystems and different vendors. Likewise, a network supports message exchanges of more than one application subsystem.

The challenge in moving from today's federated automotive architectures to this new architectural paradigm is the management of the increasing complexity in the emerging integrated automotive systems. In order to manage this complexity, system architects are forced to follow a divide-and-conquer strategy that enables a reduction of the mental effort for understanding a large system by structuring the system into smaller subsystems that can be developed and analyzed in isolation.

Composability is a concept that refers to the stability of component properties across integration, thus enabling the correctness-by-construction of component-based systems [5]. A system is composable with respect to a particular property, if the integration does not invalidate the property when it has already been established at the subsystem level. For example, *temporal composability* is an instantiation of the general notion of composability. A system is temporally composable, if timeliness is not refuted by the system integration [6]. Temporal composability facilitates the construction of temporally predictable systems, because the temporal properties of subsystems can be analyzed in isolation. Temporal composability can be supported at the communication system by controlling the possible interactions of subsystems in order to prevent unintended side effects. An example for an unintended side effect is resource contention between subsystems on the communication system. Consider for example an exemplary scenario with two application subsystems. If the two application subsystems share a common CAN bus [7], then both application subsystems must be analyzed and understood in order to reason about the correct behavior of any of the two application subsystems. Since the message transmissions of one application subsystem can delay message transmissions of the other application subsystem, arguments concerning the correct temporal behavior must be based on an analysis of both application subsystems.

A federated architecture (e.g., as used in present day automotive systems [8]) trivially rules out unintended side effects by assigning to each application subsystem separate computational and communication resources, i.e., ECUs and networks for the exclusive use by the application subsystem. In an integrated architecture (without encapsulation mechanisms), however, the communication system could extend the inherent complexity of application subsystems with an additional accidental complexity [9] due to integration-induced interference at the communication system. Therefore, the communication system of an integrated architecture should ensure that interactions between subsystems occur only via the specified message-based interfaces.

Motivated by the need to avoid accidental complexity as a side-effect of integration, this paper presents a solution for providing to each application subsystem its own protected communication infrastructure that is free of interference with other application subsystems. The communication infrastructure of an application subsystem is realized as an encapsulated overlay network on top of a time-triggered communication protocol, thus exploiting the upcoming time-triggered communication networks that will be deployed in the automotive domain [10]. Based on the Time Division Multiple Access (TDMA) scheme of a time-triggered communication network (e.g., FlexRay [11], Time-Triggered Protocol (TTP) [12], or Time-Triggered Ethernet (TTE) [13]), temporal partitioning mechanisms ensure predefined temporal properties (i.e., latency, bandwidth) of each overlay network.

The paper is structured as follows. Section 2 describes the construction of time-triggered and event-triggered overlay networks on top of a time-triggered communication network. A prototype implementation based on a TDMA-controlled Ethernet network is presented in Section 3. Section 4 shows an exemplary configuration of the prototype implementation for handling the communication requirements of a future X-by-wire car. An overview of related work is the content of Section 5. The paper concludes with a discussion in Section 6.

2 Overlay Networks on Top of a Time-Triggered Physical Network

Based on the requirements and functional coherence of automotive applications, the functionality of the electronic systems aboard a car can be structured into a set of application subsystems (e.g., powertrain subsystem, comfort subsystem, passive safety subsystem, etc.). On its behalf, each application subsystem consists of smaller functional elements called jobs (e.g., in the powertrain subsystem: engine control job, automatic gear job, etc.).

Today, the implementation of automotive electronic systems typically follows the "1 Function – 1 ECU" philosophy [1], where each ECU exclusively hosts a single job from a respective application subsystem. In contrast, we focus on integrated system architectures, where each ECU supports the coexistence of multiple jobs from one or more application subsystems.

In order to provide the communication infrastructure for the exchange of messages between the jobs of an application subsystem, this section describes the construction of event-triggered and time-triggered overlay networks on top of a time-triggered physical network. After defining the required services of the underlying time-triggered communication network, the allocation of communication resources based on a hierarchic subdivision of TDMA slots is explained. Finally, this section explains the exploitation of the communication resources on the time-triggered communication network for the exchange of state and event messages.

2.1   Time-Triggered Physical Network

Time-triggered networks (e.g., SafeBus [14], the Time-Triggered Protocol [12], FlexRay [11]) have become generally preferred for safety-critical systems [15,16]. For example, in the automotive industry a time-triggered network will provide the ability to handle the communication needs of by-wire cars [17]. In addition to hard real-time performance, time-triggered networks help in managing the complexity of fault-tolerance and corresponding formal dependability models, as required for the establishment of ultra-high reliability (failure rates in the order of 10^{-9} failures/hour). The predetermined points in time of the periodic message transmissions allow error detection and establishing of membership information. Redundancy can be established transparently to applications [18], i.e., without any modification of the function and timing of application systems. A time-triggered network also supports replica determinism [19], which is essential for establishing fault-tolerance through active redundancy.

Since the presented system architecture with its overlay networks targets mixed-criticality applications with application subsystems up to the highest considered criticality class (e.g., level A in RTCA DO-178B [20] or SIL4 in EN ISO/IEC 61508 [21]), we use a time-triggered physical network as the basis for the establishment of the encapsulated overlay networks. The time-triggered physical network provides a *clock synchronization service* in order to establish a global time base. In addition, the time-triggered network offers a *time-triggered message transport service* for the periodic exchange of state message at predefined instants with respect to the global time base. At each ECU the communication controller (e.g., TTP controller C2 [22], FlexRay Controller MFR4200 [23]) provides a memory element with outgoing state messages that are written by the application and read by the communication controller prior to broadcasting them on the time-triggered network. In addition, the memory element contains incoming state messages that are read by the application and updated by the communication controller with state messages read from the time-triggered network (i.e., information broadcast by other ECUs). This memory element, which is denoted Communication Network Interface (CNI) in TTP and Controller Host Interface (CHI) in FlexRay, is provided by most time-triggered networks with syntactic differences of state messages (e.g., header format) and protocol-specific constraints (e.g., only one message sent by an ECU per communication round in TTP [12], same size for all state messages in FlexRay [11]).

2.2   Hierarchic Subdivision of Communication Slots

For the realization of overlay networks, we use the time-triggered physical network and perform a hierarchic temporal subdivision of the communication resources (see Figure 1). The media access control strategy of the time-triggered physical network is TDMA. TDMA statically divides the channel capacity into a number of slots and controls access to the network solely by the progression of time. Each ECU is assigned a unique ECU slot that periodically recurs at a priori specified global points in time. An ECU sends messages during its ECU

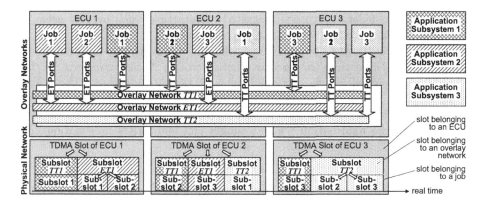

Fig. 1. Hierarchic Subdivision of Communication Resources

slot and receives messages during the ECU slots of other ECUs. A sequence of ECU slots, which allows every ECU in an ensemble of ECUs to send exactly once, is called a TDMA round.

We further subdivide each ECU slot in correspondence to the functional structuring of the overall system. In a first step, the ECU's slot is subdivided into subslots for the overlay networks. Such a subslot contains those messages that are produced by the jobs in the ECU that are connected to a particular overlay network. By using a one-to-one mapping between overlay networks and application subsystems, these subslots are also specific to a particular application subsystem. On its part, a slot belonging to an overlay network consists of smaller subslots belonging to individual jobs. When an ECU hosts multiple jobs of an application subsystem that send messages to the overlay network, then each of these jobs is assigned a corresponding slot carrying the messages sent by that job.

The assignment of the slots within a TDMA round to ECUs, as well as the further subdivision into slots for overlay networks and jobs is fixed at design time. This static allocation ensures that the network resources are predictably available to jobs. In particular, this static strategy facilitates complexity management, because for understanding the behavior of a job, the consumption of network resources by other jobs need not be considered.

2.3   Time-Triggered and Event-Triggered Overlay Networks

An overlay network is a network which is built on top of another network. For the Internet, several solutions for overlay networks have been designed in the past. For example, Virtual Private Networks (VPNs) [24] have been realized in order to improve security. Another example of overlay networks is the resilient overlay network described in [25], which aims at improving robustness of Internet applications in the presence of path outages and periods of degraded performance.

In this paper, we build overlay networks for encapsulating the communication activities of application subsystems in an integrated embedded system. When moving from a federated to an integrated architecture, each overlay network serves as a substitute for a respective physical network.

We distinguish between two fundamentally different types of overlay networks: event-triggered and time-triggered overlay networks. A *time-triggered overlay network* is designed for the periodic exchange of state messages. The access point between a time-triggered overlay network and a job is a memory element denoted as a *time-triggered port*. As depicted in Figure 2, the sender job acts according to the information push paradigm [26] and writes information into

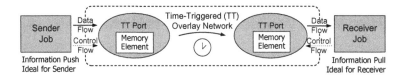

Fig. 2. Message Exchange between two Jobs through a Time-Triggered Overlay Network

the memory element at its output port (update-in-place). The receiver job must pull information out of the input port by reading the memory element in the input port. Using the job slot of the sender, the time-triggered overlay network autonomously carries the state information from the memory element of the sender to the memory element(s) of the receiver(s) at a priori determined global points in time. Since no control signals cross the ports, temporal fault propagation is prevented by design. Time-triggered overlay networks employ implicit flow control [27]. A job's ability for handling received messages can be ensured at design time, i.e., without acknowledgment messages. Implicit flow control makes time-triggered overlay networks well-suited for multicast communication relationships, because ports offer elementary interfaces [28], i.e., a unidirectional data flow involves only a unidirectional control flow.

Event-triggered overlay networks are designed for the sporadic exchange of event messages, combining event semantics with external control [27]. In order to support exactly-once processing of event messages, the access point between an event-triggered overlay network and a job is a message queue (denoted as an *event-triggered port*). Thereby, the overlay networks provides bandwidth elasticity. Due to the queues at the output ports, a job can pass more message to the overlay network than can be transmitted in a single TDMA round using the underlying time-triggered network. Overlay networks can handle such a burst as long as the average bandwidth consumption can be bounded to dimension the job slots in the TDMA scheme, and the maximum message load of a burst is known in order to dimension the queue sizes.

The interactions between a sender and a receiver via an event-triggered overlay network are depicted in Figure 3. At the sender side, event messages are inserted into the message queue at the output port via an explicit transmission request from the job (information push with external control) or as a result of

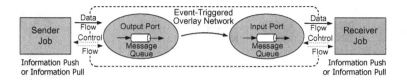

Fig. 3. Message Exchange between two Jobs through an Event-Triggered Overlay Network

the reception of a request message (information pull, e.g., a client/server interaction). The event-triggered overlay network exploits the bandwidth available via the sender's job slot for transporting the event messages to the message queue at the receiver. At the receiver side, the job either fetches the incoming message from the input port (information pull via polling for messages) or the event-triggered overlay network presses received messages into the job (information push via interrupt mechanism).

2.4   Encapsulation of Overlay Networks

Encapsulation confines the effects of a job failure that results in the transmissions of incorrect messages. In case of such a job failure, one can distinguish between message timing and message value failures. A message sent at an unspecified time is denoted as a *message timing failure*. Examples for specific message timing failures are crash/omission failures and babbling idiot failures [29, 30]. A *message value failure* occurs in case the contents of a transmitted message do not comply with the interface specification. In general, the detection of message value failure requires application-specific knowledge either through a priori knowledge or redundant computations. An example for the latter case is active redundancy (e.g., Triple Modular Redundancy (TMR) [31]), which supports the detection and masking of message value failures by majority voting. In the scope of this work, we focus on the encapsulation in the time domain by means of temporal partitioning.

Providing a dedicated port for each overlay network at all receivers and the reservation of dedicated slots in the underlying TDMA scheme are the two key elements for temporal partitioning of overlay networks.

In case of event ports, *separate ports* and thus separate queues ensure that the queuing delays for messages received from one job do not depend on the communication activities of other jobs (see Figure 4). In addition, separate message queues prevent a sender job that violates its message interarrival time specification [32] from causing the loss of messages sent by other jobs. A message omission failure caused by a queue overflow at an input port only affects the messages sent by a single job.

In addition to providing separate ports, we also need to prevent interference between messages from different senders prior to the arrival at the respective ports. For this purpose, the overlay network performs a separation of application subsystems and jobs via statically reserved slots in the underlying TDMA

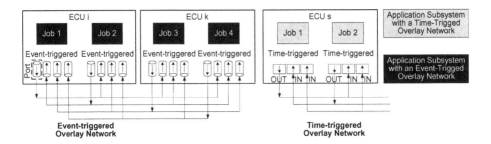

Fig. 4. Encapsulation of Overlay Networks

scheme. Thereby, guardians can protect the access to these slots based on the a priori knowledge concerning the delimiting points in time of TDMA slots and the associations between TDMA slots and the structural elements of the integrated system (i.e., application subsystems and jobs). While several solutions for the protection of ECU slots on a time-triggered network are already available (e.g., [33, 34, 35]), middleware services for the protection of the subslots for application subsystems, and jobs have been realized in the scope of this work.

Due to encapsulation, developers need not look at all possible interactions between jobs and application subsystems in order to understand the temporal behavior of an overlay network. In particular, upon the occurrence of faults of individual jobs and application subsystems, the encapsulation of overlay networks preserves the modularization of the overall system. The primary purpose of encapsulation is the prevention of adverse effects on the message exchanges of a particular overlay network induced by the message exchanges on overlay networks of other application subsystems. In addition, overlay networks are designed for encapsulation at the level of jobs by preventing adverse effects on the message exchanges of a job induced by the message exchanges of other jobs in the same application subsystem.

3   Communication Middleware for the Realization of Overlay Networks

This section describes a realization of encapsulated time-triggered and event-triggered overlay networks on top of an exemplary time-triggered physical network. The time-triggered physical network is a TDMA-controlled Ethernet network that interconnects a set of five ECUs (see Figure 5). Each ECU is implemented on a Soekris net4801 [36] embedded single-board computer, which contains the 586 class processor SC1100 clocked at 266 MHz. The software within an ECU encompasses a real-time operating system, a real-time Ethernet driver, communication middleware for the establishment of overlay networks, and multiple jobs of one or more application subsystems.

Although the prototype implementation uses a TDMA-controlled Ethernet network, the presented solution of a communication middleware for the estab-

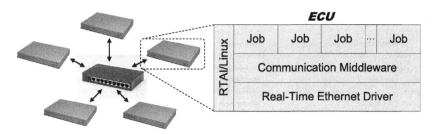

Fig. 5. Setup for Implementation of Encapsulated Overlay Networks

lishment of overlay network is also compatible with other time-triggered communication protocols. For example, the ECUs can be deployed with FlexRay or TTP communication controllers and the real-time Ethernet driver can be replaced with a driver for interfacing FlexRay or TTP. Except for protocol-specific constraints (e.g., maximum message size), these time-triggered communication protocols offer the same type of interface to the host: a memory element that contains state messages that are sent or received by the communication system at predefined global points in time.

3.1 Operating System

The real-time Linux variant RTAI/LXRT [37] serves as the operating system of the ECUs. Each job executes as a Linux Real-Time (LXRT) user mode task and the Memory Management Unit (MMU) of the SC1100 processor provides memory protection. Furthermore, a time-triggered task scheduler ensures that jobs cannot delay other jobs by blocking the CPU. A static round-robin schedule uses predefined time intervals for the execution of all jobs on an ECU.

3.2 Real-Time Ethernet Driver

Time-triggered communication on top of Ethernet is a solution capable of ensuring predictable real-time behavior, while employing Commercial-Off-The-Shelf (COTS) hardware [13]. For the implementation of overlay networks, we have employed a software-based implementation of a TDMA-controlled Ethernet network. In each ECU a real-time Ethernet driver performs a master/slave clock synchronization and periodic time-triggered transmissions and receptions of state messages. The real-time Ethernet offers to the higher layers (i.e., communication middleware and application) a global time base with a precision of $50\,\mu s$. In addition, the real-time Ethernet driver provides a memory region with five state messages. One state message can be written by the communication middleware and is broadcast on the TDMA-controlled Ethernet network. The other four state messages contain information received from the TDMA-controlled Ethernet network and can be read by the communication middleware.

We have used a homogeneous configuration with a communication round consisting of five communication slots. The communication round allows each of the

```
1   S = ⟨O[] ⟩                                              // system : the overall system provides multiple overlay networks
2   O = ⟨M[] , id_network, paradigm : < tt | et > ⟩          // overlay network : comm. infrastructure for the jobs of an appl. subsystem
3   M = ⟨P_out, P_in[], id_job⟩                              // job : associated with input and output ports
4   P_out = ⟨buffer: ⟨variable | queue⟩, msg_partial ⟩       // output port : access point of an overlay network for a job to send msgs.
5   P_in = ⟨buffer: ⟨variable | queue⟩, sender_job, msg_partial ⟩  // input port : access point of an overlay network for a job to receive msgs.
6   N = ⟨msg_Eth [] ⟩                                        // time-triggered physical network : provides a msg. for each node
7   msg_Eth = ⟨segment_overlay-network [] ⟩                  // msg. on time-triggered physical network : data segments for overlay networks
8   segment_overlay-network = ⟨segment_job[] , id_network⟩   // overlay network segment : data segment belonging to a specific overlay network
9   segment_job = ⟨data , id_job⟩                            // job segment : data segment that belongs to a specific job

10  // pre-transmission invocation : transfer msgs. from output ports to data segments
11  pretransmit(id_node ) :
12  ∀x ∈ msg_Eth[id_node].segment_overlay-network,  ∀y ∈ x.segment_job :
13      if (x.paradigm = TT)                                // time-triggered overlay network
14          y.data = S.O[x.id_network].M[x.id_job].P_out.buffer  // update-in-place of data segment with data from port
15      else                                                // event-triggered overlay network
16          y.data = empty msg.                             // dequeue as many msgs. from output ports as fit into the segment
17          while (space available in y.data)
18              if (msg_partial = empty)  msg_partial = dequeue(S.O[x.id_network].M[x.id_job].P_out)
19              extract packet p from msg_partial
20              y.data | p
21          end
22      end

23  // post-reception invocation : transfer received msgs. into input ports
24  postreception(id_node) :
25  ∀x ∈ msg_Eth[id_node].segment_overlay-network,  ∀y ∈ x.segment_job :
26      if (x.paradigm = TT)                                // time-triggered overlay network
27          ∀z ∈ S.A[x.id_network].M[].P_in with z.sender_job = id_job : z.buffer = y.data  // update-in-place of port with data from segment
28      else                                                // event-triggered overlay network
29          ∀z ∈ S.A[x.id_network].M[].P_in with z.sender_job = id_job :  // assemble msgs. and enqueue in input ports
30              ∀p ∈ y.data:
31                  z.msg_partial | p
32                  if (msg_partial completely assembled)
33                      z.data ← msg_partial
34                      msg_partial = empty message
35              end
36      end
```

Fig. 6. Pseudo Code Description of Communication Middleware

five ECUs to send exactly once and has a duration of 2 ms. The size of a state message that is broadcast within a communication slot has been set to 1500 bytes. Note, however, that the size of a message on the time-triggered physical is configurable, i.e., the size of 1500 bytes is only an example configuration. Using the hierarchical subdivision of the communication resources (as described in Section 2.2), the 1500 bytes per message are used by the communication middleware for disseminating information from multiple jobs attached to one or more overlay networks.

3.3 Communication Middleware

The communication middleware is a Linux kernel module that establishes the ports, which enable the jobs to access the overlay network of the respective application subsystem. As introduced in Section 2, a port is either a memory element storing a single state message (i.e., with updates-in-place) or a queue for multiple event messages. The ports of each job are located in a corresponding shared memory between the communication middleware in Linux kernel mode and the jobs in user mode. Each shared memory has a unique shared memory identifier. A job possesses only knowledge of the identifier of the shared memory containing the job's own ports. In contrast to the jobs, the communication middleware possesses all shared memory identifiers, because a single communication middleware on each ECU serves all jobs on the ECU.

Figure 6 describes the behavior of the communication middleware in pseudo code. Lines 1 to 9 capture the configuration information that parameterizes the communication middleware according to a specific application. The overall system S provides a set of overlay networks O, each serving as the communication infrastructure of a respective application subsystem. An overlay network exhibits a corresponding control paradigm (i.e., time-triggered or event-triggered) and is connected to a set of jobs via output and input ports (Lines 3ff). Both types of ports contain a buffer, which is either a message queue for an event-triggered overlay network or a state variable with update-in-place semantics for a time-triggered overlay network. Ports, which are attached to an event-triggered overlay network, also contain a partially transmitted or received message msg_{partial} for message fragmentation. In addition, an input port stores an identification of the sending job, i.e., the job from which messages are stored in the input port.

The structure of the messages that are exchange on the TDMA-controlled Ethernet work is defined in Lines 6–9. An Ethernet message exchanged on the TDMA-controlled Ethernet network is a compound structure, which results from the hierarchic subdivision of the TDMA slots. At the finest granularity in Line 9, each data segment is uniquely associated with an overlay network and a sending job.

After the configuration data structures, the reception and transmission handlers follow in Figure 6. The activation of the communication middleware occurs time-triggered, either prior to the periodic transmission of an Ethernet message (Line 10) or after the a priori known receive instants of Ethernet messages (Line 23). Both handlers go through the segments of all overlay networks and all jobs (Lines 12 and 24). The processing of such a data segment depends on the control paradigm of the overlay network.

- **Data segment of a time-triggered overlay network.** Prior to the periodic transmission of an Ethernet message, the communication middleware overwrites the data segment in the Ethernet message with the contents of the state variable at a job's port (Line 14). Consequently, the communication middleware samples the current value of the port and causes the dissemination of the value at the sampling point.

  After the reception of a periodic Ethernet message, each data segment belonging to a time-triggered overlay network is used for an update-in-place in the ports of the jobs. In order to determine which input ports need to be updated, the communication middleware exploits the a priori knowledge concerning the identity of the sender that is uniquely associated with each data segment in the Ethernet message. For each job, which is located on the ECU and possesses an input port that accepts messages from the sender of the data segment, the communication middleware overwrites the state variable at the port with the contents of the data segment (Line 27).

- **Data segment of an event-triggered overlay network.** Prior to the periodic transmission of an Ethernet message, the communication middleware fills each data segment with event messages retrieved from the queue at the ports of the respective job (Lines 16ff). To efficiently use the bandwidth, the communication middleware not only transfers complete messages, but also fragments messages into slices so they fit into the data segment. Depending on the size of the event messages relative to the size of the data segment, it can be possible for multiple event messages to fit into the data segment or it may be necessary to fragment an event message into packets to be sent during multiple consecutive rounds.

  After the reception of a periodic Ethernet message, the communication middleware reads event messages from the data segment and forwards them to corresponding ports of the jobs (Lines 29ff). For each job, which is located on the ECU and possesses an input port that accepts messages from the sending job of the data segment, the communication middleware inserts the event messages from the data segment into the port's message queue. If messages are fragmented over multiple rounds, the communication middleware reassembles the event messages out of the parts retrieved from the data segment.

4 Exemplary Overlay Networks based on Automotive Communication Requirements

This section describes an exemplary configuration of overlay networks for the prototype implementation, which is based on the requirements of present day automotive network infrastructures. In addition, the configuration provides a time-triggered overlay network, e.g., for X-by-wire functionality [38,39].

Table 1. SAE Network Classes

Network Class	Exemplary Protocols	Bandwidth	Exemplary Application Domains
Class A	LIN	< 10 kbps	sensor/actuator access
Class B	CAN	10kbps-125kbps	comfort domain
Class C	CAN	125kbps-1Mbps	powertrain domain
Class D	FlexRay, Byteflight	> 1 Mbps	multimedia, X-by-wire

4.1 Present Day Network Infrastructure

Based on the performance four classes of in-vehicle networks can be distinguished (see Table 1) according to the Society of Automotive Engineers (SAE) [40]. In present-day luxury cars, networks belonging to all four classes can be found. For example, in the BMW 7 series [2] two class B networks (peripheral CAN and body CAN) interconnect the ECUs of the comfort domain. A class C network

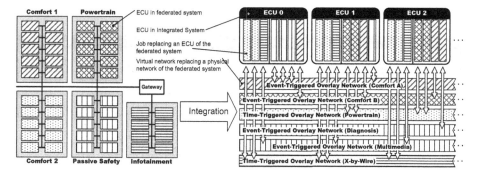

Fig. 7. Mapping Physical Networks to Overlay Networks in the Integrated Architecture

(powertrain CAN with 500 kbps) serves as the communication infrastructure of the powertrain domain. In addition, the BMW 7 series is equipped with class D networks for multimedia (MOST [41]) and safety functions (Byteflight [42]). LIN fieldbus networks [43] for accessing low-cost sensors/actuators belong to SAE class A. Similarly, the communication architecture of the Volkswagen Phaeton comprises LIN fieldbus networks, two class B CAN networks for the comfort domain, a class C CAN network for drivetrain, and a class D network for multimedia [44].

4.2 Exemplary Configuration of Overlay Networks

The exemplary overlay networks are based on the communication architecture of a typical present day automotive system. The overlay network configuration, which is depicted in Figure 7, enables the transition from a collection of physical networks towards an integrated architecture with overlay networks. Each overlay network serves as a substitute for a respective physical network.

The overlay network configuration supports two class B networks, one class C network, and two class D networks (see Table 2). Two overlay networks with a bandwidth of 117 kbps (named comfort A and comfort B) support on-demand event message exchanges, e.g., as deployed as medium-speed CAN networks for the comfort subsystem in a car. An overlay network with a bandwidth of 492 kbps provides the communication infrastructure of the powertrain subsystem of a car, thus replacing a high-speed CAN network.

Since CRC checks are handled by the underlying time-triggered communication protocol, the net bandwidths of the overlay networks exceed the net bandwidths of physical CAN networks with a raw bandwidth of 125 kbps or 500 kbps respectively. A further difference to a physical CAN network is that the 117 kbps or 492 kbps are simultaneously available to all jobs. Effectively, the entire overlay network has the ten-fold bandwidth (1170 kbps or 4920 kbps) in case of the 10 jobs in the overlay network configuration. The reason for this bandwidth multiplication is that in a physical CAN network, the total system-wide bandwidth is available to a single ECU. In an overlay network, however, the available band-

Table 2. Overlay Network Configuration

Overlay Network	Node 0	Node 1	Node 2	Node 3	Node 4
Comfort A	Job 0 (117kbps)	Job 1 (117kbps)	Job 2 (117kbps)	Job 3 (117kbps)	Job 4 (117kbps)
	Job 5 (117kbps)	Job 6 (117kbps)	Job 7 (117kbps)	Job 8 (117kbps)	Job 9 (117kbps)
Comfort B	Job 0 (117kbps)	Job 1 (117kbps)	Job 2 (117kbps)	Job 3 (117kbps)	Job 4 (117kbps)
	Job 5 (117kbps)	Job 6 (117kbps)	Job 7 (117kbps)	Job 8 (117kbps)	Job 9 (117kbps)
Powertrain	Job 0 (492kbps)	Job 1 (492kbps)	Job 2 (492kbps)	Job 3 (492kbps)	Job 4 (492kbps)
	Job 5 (492kbps)	Job 6 (492kbps)	Job 7 (492kbps)	Job 8 (492kbps)	Job 9 (492kbps)
Diagnosis	Job 0 (70kbps)	Job 1 (70kbps)	Job 2 (70kbps)	Job 3 (70kbps)	Job 4 (70kbps)
Multimedia	Job 0 (1496kbps)	Job 1 (1496kbps)	Job 2 (492kbps)	Job 3 (492kbps)	Job 4 (492kbps)
X-by-Wire	Job 0 (617kbps)	Job 1 (617kbps)	Job 2 (617kbps)	Job 3 (617kbps)	Job 4 (617kbps)
	Job 5 (617kbps)	Job 6 (617kbps)	Job 7 (3117kbps)	Job 8 (3117kbps)	Job 9 (3117kbps)

width via a job slot is not shared and only available to a single ECU. However, in case of a priori knowledge of the fraction of the overall bandwidth used by a job, this overhead can be significantly reduced.

An overlay (named diagnosis) with a bandwidth of 70 kbps serves for the exchange of event messages carrying diagnostic information. Such a diagnostic overlay network is required for the online analysis of observed errors, which is a promising strategy for reducing the numbers of cannot duplicate failures in future car generations [45].

The multimedia cluster is frequently based on a protocol with support for streaming audio and video (e.g., MOST [41]). For this purpose, we have provided an overlay network (named multimedia) with a bandwidth of 492 kbps or 1496 kbps (depending on the job). A non-uniform bandwidth allocation is chosen, since some jobs may only transmit audio information, while other jobs also transmit audio and video information. Finally, the configuration includes an overlay network (named X-by-wire) for the time-triggered exchange of state messages as required for safety-critical application subsystems.

No overlay networks are provided for class A networks, because low-cost fieldbus networks (e.g., LIN) are assumed to remain as separate physical networks despite the shift to an integrated architecture.

5   Related Work

This section describes related work on integrated architectures in the automotive domain. In addition, we point out the differences of the proposed overlay networks compared to other solutions for the integration of event-triggered and time-triggered communication.

5.1   Integration of Automotive Application Subsystems

The Automotive Open System Architecture (AUTOSAR) [46] is a system architecture and development methodology for automotive electronic systems, which also addresses the sharing of communication resources among application subsystems and software components. For interactions between software components,

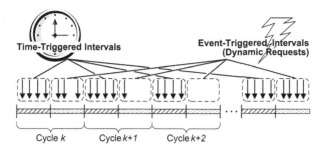

Fig. 8. Integration of Control Paradigms at MAC Layer: Time Intervals for Event-Triggered and Time-Triggered Communication

AUTOSAR provides a so-called *Virtual Function Bus (VFB)* with support for unidirectional message exchanges (called sender-receiver communication) and bidirectional interactions (called client-server communication).

The implementation of the virtual function bus occurs using the runtime environment, which acts as a communication switch and ensures location transparency. Communication between software components on the same ECU is realized by passing arguments directly to the respective runnables. Communication between software components on different ECUs exploits the services layer of the ECU in order to establish a mapping to the communication network (e.g., CAN).

In contrast to the proposed solution of overlay networks on top of a time-triggered physical network, AUTOSAR currently does not specify mechanisms for encapsulation of the communication activities of application subsystems and software components.

Nevertheless, the presented overlay networks for an integrated architecture can also serve for improving the communication system in an AUTOSAR system. Encapsulated overlay networks could provide the communication infrastructure of AUTOSAR software components. To accomplish this goal, future work will have to address the mapping of the proposed overlay network to the VFB interface that is part of the AUTOSAR runtime environment.

5.2 Integration of Control Paradigms

The proposed solution of layering event-triggered and time-triggered overlay networks on top of an underlying time-triggered physical network significantly differs from other solutions that combine these two communication paradigms. For example, event-triggered and time-triggered communication have been integrated at the MAC layer using two types of periodically recurring time intervals in the protocols FlexRay [11], TTCAN [48], and FTT-Ethernet [47]. These protocols employ a MAC layer that supports both event-triggered and time-triggered message transmissions. The start and end instants of the periodic time-triggered message transmissions, as well as the sending ECUs are specified at design time. For this class of messages, contention is resolved statically. Within each cycle, the time that is not reserved for time-triggered message exchanges is available for event-triggered communication. Consequently, time is divided into two types of intervals: event-triggered and time-triggered intervals. In event-triggered intervals, message exchanges depend on external control and the start instants of message transmissions can vary. This difference with respect to the start instants of event-triggered and time-triggered intervals is depicted in Figure 8 (arrows mark the start instants of the message transmissions in Figure 8). Furthermore, event-triggered intervals can be assigned to multiple (or all) ECUs of the system. For this reason, the MAC layer needs to support the dynamic resolving of contention when more than one ECU intends to transmit a message. During event-triggered intervals a sub-protocol (e.g., CSMA/CA, CSMA/CD) takes over that is not required during time-triggered intervals in which contention is prevented by design.

The main benefit of the two types of intervals at the MAC layer is the ability to combine temporal predictability in the time-triggered intervals with resource efficiency and flexiblity in the event-triggered intervals. Within the latter type of interval, ECUs can dynamically share communication resources since bandwidth that is not used by one ECU becomes available to other ECUs.

On the negative side, the event-triggered intervals at the MAC layer can introduce dependencies in the temporal domain between ECUs. The message transmission latencies at an ECU can no longer be computed in isolation. Upon system integration, the addition of ECUs will lead to more messages competing for transmission in the event-triggered intervals, thus increasing the transmission latencies. In addition, at run-time the latencies of the messages transmitted by a ECU can vary depending on the transmission behavior of the other ECUs. This variability of the transmission latency is disadvantageous for jitter-sensitive applications, e.g., in control loops where jitter impairs the quality of control.

In contrast to these MAC layer solutions, the presented overlay networks exhibit an invariant temporal behavior (i.e., bandwidth, latency, latency jitter) during system integration. The layering of event-triggered and time-triggered overlay networks on top of an underlying time-triggered physical network ensures that the temporal properties of independently developed components (i.e., jobs) remain invariant upon integration, thus enabling a seamless system integration without unintended side effects (i.e., temporal composability [6]).

Furthermore, the use of an underlying time-triggered physical network facilitates replica determinism [19] by preventing the occurrence of race conditions between jobs at the communication system.

Finally, the static schedule of the time-triggered physical network can be exploited for error detection and error containment, e.g., using bus guardians [33, 34,35]. Thereby, the communication system improves the robustness of the overall system by providing error containment for the consequences of physical faults (e.g., single event upsets, single event transients) and software faults (e.g., design fault of a job).

On the negative side, this rigid design with a static communication schedule results in lower resource efficiency. Firstly, large communication loads that dynamically vary between ECUs can lead to an inefficient use of the overall bandwidth. The presented overlay networks support no global sharing of bandwidth, i.e., communication slots that are not used by one ECU do not become available to the other ECUs. Secondly, the static resource allocation decreases flexibility w.r.t. extensions and modifications of the communication system. For the addition of messages or ECUs, either free slots need to be reserved at design time or a new time-triggered communication schedule needs to be computed and programmed into the ECUs.

6 Discussion

This paper has shown that a time-triggered physical network is an effective foundation for establishing multiple overlay networks, each tailored to a respective application subsystem via its control paradigm (event-triggered vs. time-triggered). Overlay networks exhibit predefined temporal properties for the messages transmitted by a job, independently from the transmission behavior of other jobs and other application subsystems. A prototype implementation has yielded evidence that the inherent mechanisms for encapsulation do not prevent the overlay networks from meeting the bandwidth requirements imposed by present-day automotive applications and those envisioned for the future (e.g., X-by-wire).

Encapsulation is particularly important in the context of the increasing complexity of embedded systems. System architects are forced to follow divide-and-conquer strategies that permit a reduction of the mental effort for developing and understanding a large system by partitioning the system into smaller subsystems that can be developed and analyzed in isolation.

The temporal encapsulation of the communication resources belonging to subsystems, such as application subsystems or jobs, is a key requirement for the constructive integration of integrated computer systems. By ensuring guaranteed temporal properties (e.g., bandwidth, latencies) for the messages transmitted by each job, prior services are not invalidated by the behavior of newly integrated jobs at the communication system. This quality of an architecture, which is denoted as temporal composability, relates to the ease of building systems out of subsystems. A system, i.e., a composition of subsystems, is considered temporally composable, if the temporal correctness is not invalidated by the integration provided that temporal correctness has been established at the subsystem level.

Overlay networks on top of a time-triggered network support temporal composability by ensuring that temporal properties at the communication system are not invalidated upon system integration. Furthermore, in the context of upcoming time-triggered technology in the automotive domain, the availability of a time-triggered communication network with high bandwidth (e.g., FlexRay [11]) enables the elimination of some of the physical networks deployed in present day cars. The communication resources of a single time-triggered network can be shared among different application subsystems. In conjunction with integrated ECUs, i.e., ECUs for the execution of application software from different application subsystems, the sharing of communication and computational resources not only reduces the number of ECUs, but also results in fewer connectors and wires. Fewer connectors and wires not only decrease hardware cost, but also lead to improved reliability.

Acknowledgments

This work has been supported in part by the European IST project ARTIST2 under project No. IST-004527 and the European IST project DECOS under project No. IST-511764.

References

1. Bouyssounouse, B., Sifakis, J. (eds.): Embedded Systems Design. LNCS, vol. 3436. Springer, Heidelberg (2005)
2. Deicke, A.: The electrical/electronic diagnostic concept of the new 7 series. In: Convergence Int. Congress & Exposition On Transportation Electronics, Detroit, MI, USA, SAE (October 2002)
3. Heinecke, H., Schnelle, K.-P., Fennel, H., Bortolazzi, J., Lundh, L., Leflour, J., Maté, J.-L., Nishikawa, K., Scharnhorst, T.: AUTomotive Open System ARchitecture - An Industry-Wide Initiative to Manage the Complexity of Emerging Automotive E/E-Architectures. In: Proceedings of the Convergence Int. Congress & Exposition On Transportation Electronics, Detroit, MI, USA, SAE (October 2004)
4. Obermaisser, R., Peti, P., Huber, B., El Salloum, C.: DECOS: An integrated time-triggered architecture. e&i journal (journal of the Austrian professional institution for electrical and information engineering) 3, 83–95 (2006), http://www.springerlink.com
5. Sifakis, J.: A framework for component-based construction. In: SEFM 2005. Proc. of 3rd IEEE Int. Conference on Software Engineering and Formal Methods, pp. 293–300 (September 2005)
6. Kopetz, H., Obermaisser, R.: Temporal composability. Computing & Control Engineering Journal 13, 156–162 (2002)
7. Robert Bosch Gmbh, Stuttgart, Germany. CAN Specification, Version 2.0 (1991)
8. Leen, G., Heffernan, D., Dunne, A.: Digital networks in the automotive vehicle. Computing & Control Engineering Journal 10(6), 257–266 (1999)
9. Brooks, F.P.: The Mythical Man-Month. Addison-Wesley, Reading (1975)
10. Analysis of the European automotive in-vehicle network architecture markets. Technical report, Frost & Sullivan (October 2004)
11. FlexRay Consortium. BMW AG, DaimlerChrysler AG, General Motors Corporation, Freescale GmbH, Philips GmbH, Robert Bosch GmbH, and Volkswagen AG. FlexRay Communications System Protocol Specification Version 2.1 (May 2005)
12. TTTech Computertechnik AG, Schönbrunner Strasse 7, A-1040 Vienna, Austria. Time-Triggered Protocol TTP/C – High Level Specification Document (July 2002)
13. Kopetz, H., Ademaj, A., Grillinger, P., Steinhammer, K.: The Time-Triggered Ethernet (TTE) design. In: ISORC. Proc. of 8th IEEE Int. Symposium on Object-oriented Real-time distributed Computing (May 2005)
14. Hoyme, K., Driscoll, K.: SAFEbus. IEEE Aerospace and Electronic Systems Magazine 8, 34–39 (1993)

15. Rushby, J.: Bus architectures for safety-critical embedded systems. In: Henzinger, T.A., Kirsch, C.M. (eds.) EMSOFT 2001. LNCS, vol. 2211, pp. 306–323. Springer, Heidelberg (2001)

16. Kopetz, H.: Why time-triggered architectures will succeed in large hard real-time systems. In: Proc. of the 5th IEEE Computer Society Workshop on Future Trends of Distributed Computing Systems, Cheju Island, Korea (August 1995)

17. Bretz, E.: By-wire cars turn the corner. IEEE Spectrum 38(4), 68–73 (2001)

18. Bauer, G., Kopetz, H.: Transparent redundancy in the time-triggered architecture. In: DSN 2000. Proc. of the Int. Conference on Dependable Systems and Networks, NY, USA, pp. 5–13 (June 2000)

19. Poledna, S.: Fault-Tolerant Real-Time Systems: The Problem of Replica Determinism. Kluwer Academic Publishers, Dordrecht (1995)

20. Radio Technical Commission for Aeronautics, Inc. (RTCA), Washington, DC. DO-178B: Software Considerations in Airborne Systems and Equipment Certification (December 1992)

21. IEC: Int. Electrotechnical Commission. IEC 61508-7: Functional Safety of Electrical/Electronic/Programmable Electronic Safety-Related Systems – Part 7: Overview of Techniques and Measures (1999)

22. TTTech Computertechnik AG, Schönbrunner Strasse 7, A-1040 Vienna, Austria. TTP/C Controller C2 Controller-Host Interface Description Document, Protocol Version 2.1 (November 2002)

23. Freescale Semiconductor. MFR4200 datasheet FlexRay communication controllers. Technical report (August 2005)

24. Venkateswaran, R.: Virtual private networks. IEEE Potentials 20(1), 11–15 (2001)

25. Andersen, D., Balakrishnan, H., Kaashoek, F., Morris, R.: Resilient overlay networks. In: SOSP 2001. Proceedings of the eighteenth ACM symposium on Operating systems principles, pp. 131–145. ACM Press, New York (2001)

26. Deline, R.: Resolving Packaging Mismatch. PhD thesis, Computer Science Department, Carnegie Mellon University, Pittsburgh (June 1999)

27. Kopetz, H.: Real-Time Systems, Design Principles for Distributed Embedded Applications. Kluwer Academic Publishers, Dordrecht (1997)

28. Kopetz, H.: Elementary versus composite interfaces in distributed real-time systems. In: Proc. of the 4th Int. Symposium on Autonomous Decentralized Systems, Tokyo, Japan (March 1999)

29. Cristian, F.: Understanding fault-tolerant distributed systems. Communications of the ACM 34(2), 56–78 (1991)

30. Temple, C.: Avoiding the babbling-idiot failure in a time-triggered communication system. In: Proc. of 28th Int. Symposium on Fault-Tolerant Computing, Munich, Germany, pp. 218–227 (1998)

31. Randell, B., Lee, P., Treleaven, P.C.: Reliability issues in computing system design. ACM Computing Surveys 10(2), 123–165 (1978)

32. Kleinrock, L.: Queuing Systems Volume I: Theory. John Wiley and Sons, New York (1975)

33. Ferreira, J., Pedreiras, P., Almeida, L., Fonseca, J.: Achieving fault tolerance in FTT-CAN. In: Proc. of the 4th IEEE Int. Workshop on Factory Communication Systems (2002)

34. Bauer, G., Kopetz, H., Steiner, W.: The central guardian approach to enforce fault isolation in a time-triggered system. In: ISADS 2003. Proc. of the 6th Int. Symposium on Autonomous Decentralized Systems, Pisa, Italy, pp. 37–44 (April 2003)

35. FlexRay Consortium. BMW AG, DaimlerChrysler AG, General Motors Corporation, Freescale GmbH, Philips GmbH, Robert Bosch GmbH, and Volkswagen AG. Node-Local Bus Guardian Specification Version 2.0.9 (December 2005)
36. Soekris Engineering. net4801 series boards and systems. Technical report (April 2004), www.soekris.com
37. Beal, D., Bianchi, E., Dozio, L., Hughes, S., Mantegazza, P., Papacharalambous, S.: RTAI: Real-Time Application Interface. Linux Journal (April 2000)
38. Hedenetz, B., Belschner, R.: Brake-by-wire without mechanical backup by using a TTP-communication network. In: Proceedings of SAE Congress, Daimler-Benz AG (1998)
39. Heitzer, H.D.: Development of a fault-tolerant steer-by-wire steering system. Auto Technology 4, 56–60 (2003)
40. Leen, G., Heffernan, D.: Expanding automotive electronic systems. Computer 35(1), 88–93 (2002)
41. MOST Cooperation, Karlsruhe, Germany. MOST Specification Version 2.2 (November 2002)
42. Berwanger, J., Peller, M., Griessbach, R.: Byteflight a new protocol for safety critical applications. In: Proc. of the FISITA World Automotive Congress, Seoul (2000)
43. Audi AG, BMW AG, DaimlerChrysler AG, Motorola Inc., Volcano Communication Technologies AB, Volkswagen AG, and Volvo Car Corporation. LIN specification and LIN press announcement. SAE World Congress Detroit (1999)
44. Leohold, J.: Communication requirements for automotive systems. In: Keynote Automotive Communication – 5th IEEE Workshop on Factory Communication Systems, Vienna, Austria (September 2004)
45. Peti, P., Obermaisser, R.: A diagnostic framework for integrated time-triggered architectures. In: Proc. of the 9th IEEE Int. Symposium on Object-oriented Real-time distributed Computing (April 2006)
46. AUTOSAR GbR. AUTOSAR – Technical Overview V2.0.1 (June 2006)
47. Pedreirasand, P., Gai, P., Almeidaand, L., Buttazzo, G.C.: Ftt-ethernet: a flexible real-time communication protocol that supports dynamic qos management on ethernet-based systems. IEEE Transactions on Industrial Informatics 1(3), 162–172 (2005)
48. Führer, T., Müller, B., Dieterle, W., Hartwich, F., Hugel, R.: Time-triggered CAN - TTCAN: Time-triggered communication on CAN. In: ICC6. Proc. of 6th Int. CAN Conference, Torino, Italy (2000)

Reliability Properties of Models for Flexible Design and Run-Time Analysis

Luqi, V. Berzins, and P.M. Musial

Naval Postgraduate School
Monterey, CA 93943, USA
luqi@nps.edu

Abstract. Development and analysis of complex systems embedded in physical environments requires special modeling techniques. Development aids involve abstraction on multiple levels of representation in order to connect cross-cutting constraints and facilitate involvement of various stakeholders. Alternatively, run-time analysis requires type of modeling that is based on representation of interactions and behaviors. We discuss the Documentation Driven Development (DDD) approach for software development and Agent Based Systems for run-time analysis. We show that despite differences in architectures and functions both approaches possess important properties of reliability and flexibility and allow easy upgrading of their elements.

1 Introduction

The design and implementation process and run-time analysis of contemporary software are accompanied by numerous assisting development tools. The functions of these tools include facilitation of system design and satisfaction of multiple constraints from disparate stakeholders. Further development of embedded systems and *systems of embedded systems* (SoES) require even greater supporting capabilities. First, SoES demand a new type of programming aids that are capable of representing physical devices with which software interacts; second, development of SoES demonstrates the shortcomings of existing software tools: poor means of representation of interactions in the system, lack of support for managing concurrency, as well as interoperability and scalability issues. To cope with these problems contemporary means of design and analysis of SoES incorporate modeling of the system under development and its interactions with the external environment.

The process of modeling inextricably involves some degree of abstraction. Abstraction as any simplification has its own pros and cons, but if properly managed can lead to a good compromise between efficiency and reliability. In this work, we examine how two types of modeling affect robustness, reliability and flexibility of complex systems. In particular, we consider a Documentation Driven Development (DDD) [1] approach to development and Agent Based System (ABS) approach [9,15] for run-time analysis of SoES.

The structure of this paper is as follows. Section 2 provides an overview of the state of the art on model-driven development and analysis. Section 3 describes on the

F. Kordon and O. Sokolsky (Eds.): Monterey Workshop 2006, LNCS 4888, pp. 207–219, 2007.

Documentation Driven Approach (DDD) as an example of a method for development of safety critical embedded systems. Section 4 reviews the Agent Based System (ABS) methodology. Finally, Section 5 concludes the paper.

2 Model-Driven Development and Analysis

The aforementioned context is characterized by increased complexity of tasks, communication throughput, multiplicity of software platforms and protocols, as well as complexity of embedded physical devices. These complexities contribute to qualitatively new requirements for modern software design and analysis practices. In short, the challenge is to find a good compromise between various constraints and requirements that have different scope, timescale, and priority. Since it is hard to express all these constraints and requirements on an equal footing, a framework is needed that is able to express and connect constraints and requirements. Model-driven approaches are an example of such a framework and are widely applied to both design and analysis of complex systems. Fig. 1 summarizes the common functions of modeling.

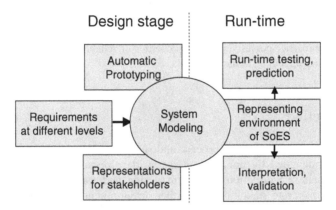

Fig. 1. Various functions of modeling

In system design, multi-level representations play a crucial role. For example, large systems are usually described hierarchically and composite component can be viewed at two levels: as a single component, or as a subsystem composed of interacting lower level components. In this context, requirements from the higher level are allocated to some subset of the lower level components, and reformulated in terms of concepts that match the principles of operation at the lower level, but that may not be visible or meaningful at the higher level of abstraction. In general, multi-level representation allows presentation of software elements to stakeholders at different levels of abstraction. In addition, a multi-level approach facilitates means for imposing constraints of various scopes and means for automated prototyping. In comparison, more dynamic types of modeling may be appropriate for run-time analysis. Exploring the parameter space of a system and testing various deployment scenarios against all possible input domains can be quite tedious if at all computationally feasible. Thus a simplified model of interactions that limits the number of behaviors and groups events in a fixed set of categories streamlines the analysis process. An architecture consists of a connection pattern that identifies system's components and their interactions, together with a set of constraints that define the intended behavior of the system as a whole and the standards and properties to which the components and their interactions must conform to ensure they will work together to realize the intended behavior of the system as a whole. In particular, the preferable architectures are ones that manage interactions and are suited for describing system behaviors. In such architectures, the complexity of the principles of operation is manageable since the architecture description addresses the interplay of well-specified behaviors in addition to system structure. This allows easy experimentation with run-time models and clear understanding of their properties, hence making experimentation with run-time models easier and at the same time makes interpretation of the results easier. As depicted in Fig. 1 a run-time analysis includes testing, predicting, and interpretation of the results. In the following two sections we describe two modeling approaches that are applied to the design and analysis of complex embedded systems.

3 Documentation Driven Approach (DDD)

Documentation is an integral part in software and system engineering. Although significant effort has been applied toward improving documentation technology [1, 2, 3, 4], there are still open challenges that hinder use of documentation as means for providing efficient support for complex real-time systems development. Documentation formats are numerous, for instance diagrams, informal natural language descriptions, multi-media presentations are only a few examples. Maintaining consistency of information across the different documentation representations is still an unresolved problem. A related and equally challenging issue is the extraction of information relevant to the stakeholders and its presentation in a comprehensive and concise way. Extraction of information from the various documentation formats requires transformations that are tedious and error prone when carried out manually. Some rigorous formal representations are conducive to machine manipulation, but are difficult for human understanding. Informal representations such as natural language are comfortable for the human stakeholders, but are too vague and ambiguous for direct use by computer tools [13]. To guarantee software quality in the end product, the information in documents of successive development phases must be kept consistent. Traditional documentation technologies do not solve this problem. In the description that follows, we present our approach to solve the aforementioned problems.

We propose an approach where models and simulations are included as documentation that is used to directly drive computer-aided design tools, and to provide information needed by human stakeholders. Typically system models include computational models and design models, where these serve as the basis to support development activities such as requirements analysis, architecture design, validation, and verification. Simulation and prototyping are examples of computer aided processes used to validate the correctness of the requirements for the system under development. With this shift from passive to active representations, documentation can provide more effective support for the entire development process. The DDD approach addresses needs to promptly adapt to new requirements and support participation of diverse stakeholders, while preserving high confidence and timing constraints. This significantly improves the agility of software development and supports partial automation.

All of the above concerns will become more prominent as systems of systems become increasingly integrated and serve even more complex purposes. It is possible that software components are deployed in dynamic systems where hardware, peripheral systems, and communication networks may change over time. In such domains the idea that system requirements can be determined once and then remain unchanged is unrealistic. Hence, a successful integration of the system components depends on being able to accommodate requirements changes and system extensions to address the emerging requirements that could not be anticipated in the original design. In particular, as systems become more integrated, subsystems impact larger groups of stakeholders in larger numbers of contexts. This multiplies the number of viewpoints affecting requirements and constraints, complicates analysis, and makes it potentially error prone. However, this flexibility must not compromise the dependability of the system.

In DDD, documentation is computationally active structured information with automated decision support and representations in multiple formats. Documentation can be classified into two categories: documentation for tools and documentation for humans. Formats of documentation for tools include mathematical notations, design languages, programming languages, system models, requirements/design specifications, source code, test cases, and application data (such as biomedical databases, results of measurements, medical records, financial databases, tables of properties of physical materials, and any other reference information relevant to system design). Formats of documentation for humans are typically graphical or in easily understood text annotations in natural language, decision tables, spread sheets, or computed attributes. In addition the documentation formats can be expanded to include video and audio clips, live simulations, queries, etc.

The DDD approach uses a *Document Management System* (DMS) and a *Process Measurement System* (PMS). Next we describe the two systems in more detail.

3.1 Document Management System (DMS)

DMS creates, organizes monitors, analyzes, manipulates, and displays documentation. These are the basic operations on documents associated with system development. In addition, DMS must handle many types of documentation including requirement specifications, abstracted models, stakeholder input, design rationale, project management information, source code, etc. Moreover, it extracts relevant information from all development activities such as requirements analysis, prototyping, architectural design, software composition, system verification and validation, and system deployment. DMS has three main components, see Fig 2.

1. The Documentation Repository (DR) stores the information in a structured format with a well defined meaning, which enables finding appropriate subsets and projections of the documents for particular purposes, and extracting computed attributes of documents.

2. The Representation Converters are used to transform and present documentation in DR to different stakeholders and tools.
3. The transition drivers transform information from one development process into forms suitable for the next.

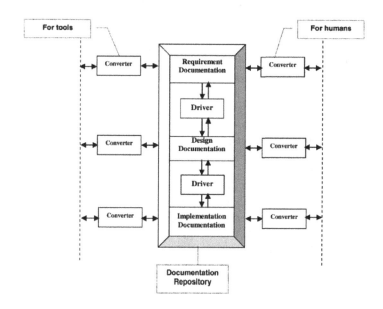

Fig. 2. Structure of documentation management system

To give a concrete example of one of the DMS's components, consider a Representation Converter that works on the level of software requirements and facilitates requirement management for various stakeholders. Requirement specifications that are written in *natural language* (NL) are converted into *resource description framework* (RDF) representations. This conversion is accomplished by NL processing tools and includes several stages: syntactic parsing, reference resolution and construction of object-predicate-subject triples. Terms and relations in the triples are standardized according to W3C recommendations for URI (universal resource identifier) with possible employment of user-defined terminology. Importantly RDF representations constitute a basis for creating semantic networks that not only represent formal relations between system's components but also provide functionalities for flexible search, summarization and prioritization of information encoded [14]. The automated conversion to RDF is followed by validation processes that use multiple representations for human review, to find and correct errors and resolve ambiguities.

To close the loop in software development, we have introduced a set of metrics to measure the effort and the risk in an evolutionary software project [5, 6]. These metrics can be automatically obtained early in the requirements phase, based on information contained in the DMS. They accommodate changes in requirements, process, technology, and resources of a project. Based on the set of metrics, a measurement model for effort and risk of failure of a project has been proposed [7]. With respect to the high confidence measurement model, we developed an Instantiated Activity Model (IAM) that supports a formal approach for safety analysis by providing precise metrics [8].

3.2 Process Measurement System (PMS)

The functions of PMS are to monitor the frequent changes in system requirements, assess the effort and success possibility of the project, and measure the high confidence properties of the system. PMS obtains necessary information from the documentation repository. The analysis results are intended to provide feedback to the developers, managers and users as feedback. Note that quick communication and analysis are the key factor for agile system development. Feedback is most useful when it can be delivered while the relevant aspect of the system is still in the process of being created, rather than after it has been completed and other system decisions have been made based on a faulty version of that aspect.

PMS consists of two parts: (i) a measurement model for effort and risk of a project, and (ii) a measurement model for high confidence. We introduced a set of metrics to measure the effort and risk in a software project design phase [16, 18]. These metrics can be automatically obtained early in the requirements phase, and accommodate changes in requirement, process, technology, and resources allocated for the project. Following is a list of the defined metrics [1]:

1. Requirements volatility characterizes fluctuations in project's requirements. This metric measures the rate at which existing requirements are removed and new ones are added to the specification of the developing system.
2. Organization efficiency is an estimated measure of the correspondence between the involved in the project and their roles in the software process. Specifically, for each individual what is the skill match between the job requirements and the ability of the individual to process the provided information and the rate of expectations fulfillment.
3. A product complexity metric is based on the requirements phase and is defined by a hybrid complexity measure that properly accounts for data flow and the properties associated with each operator and data stream.
4. Technology maturity is measured for each technology utilized in project's design to determine its degree of diffusion. Specifically, these metrics indicate where the given technology is on the spectrum between innovation and routine engineering practice.

In addition to the above metrics, project indicators for risk assessment [19] are computed. For example, project risk is affected by organizational, operational, managerial, and contractual parameters, such as outsourcing, personnel, time, and budget.

We proposed a measurement model that is based on Weibull distribution [1], where parameters in this distribution are matched with the quantitative metrics described above. The matching was calibrated via a large number of empirical experiments. The model works well for real-time applications [19]. Based on the provided input, the development effort and success probability of the project can be estimated by our model.

3.3 Application Example

An example of implementation and application of the DDD approach is the CAPS-PC system [1]. CAPS-PC is composed of five parts: Software Specification Editors, Software Project Management, Automatic Code Generation, Software Quality Facilities, and Software Execution Support. Each part is supported by extended facilities. The interface of the CAPS-PC system is depicted in Fig 3.

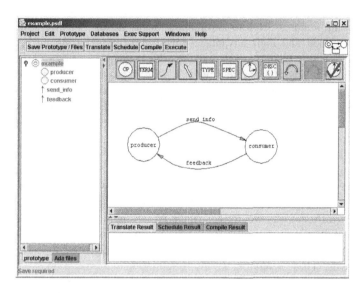

Fig. 3. The interface of the CAPS-PC environment

In CAPS-PC, a unified internal knowledge representation of software requirements is formalized and designed for supporting automatic materialization of multiple views for different purposes. To the extent that the processes supported by documentation are performed manually, its representation should be understandable by humans. To the extent the processes are performed by tools, the representation should be tractable by software. CAPS-PC provides both kinds of views.

The internal representation used in CASP-PC can be transformed into a graphical view of a prototype design that is suitable for designers and for supporting explanations of the system structure in review meetings. Designers can use this representation, illustrated in Fig. 2, to make adjustments to the prototype behavior using declarative control constraints. The system can automatically transform this representation into executable code that can support prototype demonstrations and it is capable of simulating execution on specified hardware configurations in linearly scaled real time. Such simulations can be used to assess whether the design will meet its timing requirements in the target execution environment. The system also provides tools that can generate graphical user interfaces suitable for demonstrating the behavior of the prototype to the system stakeholders and gathering feedback to adjust and firm up the requirements. A comprehensive description of DDD and CAPS-PC are found in [1].

4   Agent Based Systems (ABS)

Software agents have been studied by the research community, where agents are viewed as semi-autonomous software components that can be used in a distributed information environment. A comprehensive survey of the ABS area can be found in [15]. Representation of software components as agents allows modeling of complex systems and interaction between its components.

There are different definitions of agents some of which emphasize behavioral and some structural features. Before introducing further details, we briefly describe why agents are needed and their advantages over conventional software programs are. Decomposing a system into agents has the advantages of: (i) clarity in mapping between agents and physical entities/concepts with improved understanding of system dynamics; (ii) simple and well defined information exchange inherited in autonomous agents makes them structurally simple; and (iii) universal character of agent services can be used by many other agents and thus contributes to effective decomposition of tasks and problems.

The challenge of testing software is that it is often done in multidimensional space and thus is computationally difficult. To cope with the curse of dimensionality, one may use agents that autonomously (independently) deal with well defined and simple actions/tasks and effectively reduce the dimensionality of a system.

There are different ways to define agents. According to DARPA [9], agents should possess the following behaviors: (i) agents act autonomously to accomplish objectives, (ii) agents adapt to their environment, and (iii) agents cooperate to achieve common goals. These behaviors are illustrated in Fig. 4.

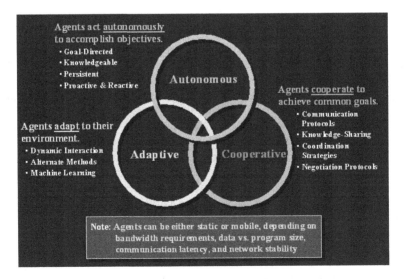

Fig. 4. Characteristics of Software Agents

4.1 Real-Time System Design

Design of real-time systems where scheduling of events is imperative can benefit from use of agents in the following ways. There are two possible options for to schedule activities of agents: (i) a global schedule, or (ii) a distributed schedule. In (i) agents perform local actions while considering collaboration with external resources and the global schedule is obtained through the merging of local schedules. Alternatively [20, 21, 22, 23], in (ii) where agents may act as a single resource, each agent is responsible for negotiation deadlines with other agents [24, 25, 26, 27].

4.2 IMPACT Development Platform

IMPACT [10], is a software development platform for creating and deploying autonomous, collaborating agents. This platform is useful for development of real-time systems as it supports constraint annotation on the agents. These annotations can express constraints on deadlines, geographical locations, concurrency restrictions, etc.

A structural description used in IMPACT specifies agents as consisting of (i) a set of data types, (ii) a set of API functions implemented in any language manipulating those types, (iii) a set of actions implemented in any language, (iv) a notion of concurrency, (v) a set of action constraints, (vi) a set of integrity constraints, and (vii) an agent program. Examples of actions that agents can perform include: execute request, modify request and execute, send message(s), clone agent, move to remote site, donothing, post web page, create file, create bar graph, construct route, and update database. The ABS advantages include [11]:

1. *Rich mathematical foundation.*
2. *Hierarchical development.* Agents can be built on legacy data/code and specialized data structures. The general structure of an ABS involves two parts: a set of agents and a platform for their interaction and execution (e.g., applications on Army Logistics data, Army JANUS simulation data, ARL CIP servers, Oracle data, etc.).
3. *Dynamic execution.* ABS can couple arbitrary actions to changes in agent environment (e.g., features based on coupling of send-mail, creation of Web pages, and file synthesis actions to changes in agent state when new messages are received.).
4. *Open interaction.* ABS can interact with other agent platforms. For example, IMPACT can connect to arbitrary IBM Aglets, and IMPACT security agents can interact with security agents built by Lockheed (ATIRP Consortium) and ARL's LTC.
5. *Security.* IMPACT agents can be used to make other applications more secure (e.g., ARL-ATIRP-IMPACT security agents).
6. *Intelligence.* IMPACT agents are capable of the following actions:
   - Collaborating with one another as well as agents in other agent platforms (e.g., bookstore procurement features).
   - Creating sophisticated plans. For example, noncombatant evacuation
   - Reasoning about time and uncertainty.
   - Making decisions based on agent objectives (expressed via objective functions).

7. *Heterogeneous information integration.* IMPACT agents support heterogeneous information integration (e.g., Army War Reserves Logistics application integrating Oracle and LOGTAADS data).
8. *Rapid generation and deployment.* IMPACT agents can be rapidly created and deployed via AgentDE, the IMPACT agent development environment.
   - Meta agent programs allow agents to reason about other agents' states (what does the other agent know?) and actions (what is the other agent going to do?)
   - Temporal agent programs allow agents to make commitments over time.
   - Probabilistic agent programs allow agents to make decisions in the presence of uncertainty.
   - Secure agent programs give the methods by which agents may provide data/services only to authorized agents.

Examples of types of agents include:

1. *Meta Agents.* Agents that reason about the beliefs and actions of other agents.
2. *Temporal Agents.* Agents that execute actions that have temporal extent and schedule actions for the future; those agents may reason about the past.
3. *Probabilistic Agents.* Agents that reason about uncertainty in the world.

As indicated in [28] use of agents is a good way of building complex software systems. Although use of agents as wrappers for legacy software is theoretically appealing, there are some documented limitations [29] to this approach.

Since agents are abstract entities with specified characteristics, testing of agents' state evolution and messaging behavior patterns can be done off line using any of the established formal methods, such as Hoare logic [30], Lambda Calculus[31], TIOA [32], provided that the agent representation can be successfully translated into targeted formal model.

4.3 Department Store Example

The following example is from the e-commerce domain; however, it is a much simpler vehicle to describe use of ABS than a more complicated real-time example.

Consider a large department store that uses a web-based marketing site. Today, the Internet contains a whole host of such sites, offering on-line shopping services.

As illustrated in [12], intelligent agent technology may be used to accomplish these goals through a simple architecture. This architecture is shown in Fig. 5 and involves the following agents:

1. *A Credit Database Agent*: This agent provides access to a credit database.
2. *Product Database Agent*: This agent provides access to product databases reflecting the merchandise that the department store sells. The agent may be used to retrieve tuples associated with a product description (e.g., "leather shoes").
3. *A Profiling Agent*: This agent takes as input the identity of a user (who is interacting with the Department Store Interface agent described below). It then requests the credit database agent for information on the user's credit history. Using the credit information on individual's spending habits, the profiling agent may classify the user as a "high", "average", or "low" spender. More detailed classifications are also possible (e.g., "high" spender on clothing).

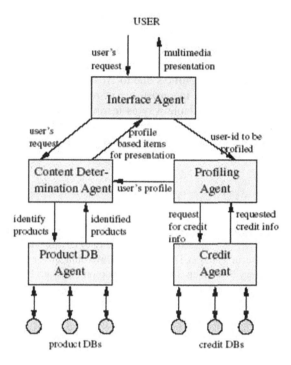

Fig. 5. Interactions between agents in the STORE example, adapted from [12]

4. *A Content Determination Agent*: This agent tries to determine what to show to the user by analyzing and filtering the information provided by the profiling agent to show key data (e.g., if the user is classified as a "high spender," it may select the ten most expensive pairs of leather shoes).
5. *Interface Agent*: This agent weaves a multimedia presentation using objects identified by the Content Determination Agent. This might be accompanied by focused advertising information.

Note that implementation details of each agent are irrelevant, as the system design is based on the interaction between agents. Hence, the agent paradigm provides a level of abstraction and reduces complexity of the overall system design.

5 Conclusion

In this paper we considered reliability and flexibility properties of DDD and ABS architectures. DDD that serves to design and upgrade complex systems emphasizes hierarchical representations and is well suited for satisfaction of a range of constraints. Alternatively, the function of ABS is to model system performance with an emphasis on interactions and behaviors of independent entities. Both architectures are well suited for upgrading either through automatic prototyping (DDD) or through rewriting certain agents without changing the overall system (ABS). Also, both architectures introduce some redundancy which makes them robust in the case of requirement conflict or uncertainty/incomplete information. In particular, multi-level DDD architecture duplicates constraints on at least three levels, so that certain inconsistencies on the lower level can be tolerated by the virtue of satisfaction high-level constraints. In such a way external conflicts due to cross-cutting constraints can be managed in the same way as internal inconsistency of requirements. Analogously, ABS agents handle uncertainty in the same way as incomplete information, namely using simple probabilistic reasoning and maintaining a system of beliefs. All these properties make DDD and ABS architectures well suited for the purposes of SoES design and analysis.

References

1. Luqi, Zhang, L., Berzins, V., Qiao, Y.: Documentation Driven Development for Complex Real-Time Systems. IEEE Transaction on Software Engineering 30(12), 936–952 (2004)
2. Luqi, Zhang, L.: Documentation Driven Agile Development for Systems of Embedded Systems. In: Monterey Workshop Series: Workshop on Software Engineering for Embedded Systems: From Requirement to Implementation, Chicago, IL (September 24-26, 2003)
3. Luqi, Liang, X., Zhang, L., Berzins, V.: Software Documentation-Driven Manufacturing. In: COMPSAC 2003. Proceedings of The 27th Annual International Computer Software and Applications Conference, Dallas, Texas (November 3-6, 2003)
4. Berzins, V., Qiao, Y., Luqi: Information Consistency Checking for Documentation Driven Development for Complex Embedded Systems. In: Monterey Workshop Series: Workshop on Software Engineering for Embedded Systems: From Requirement to Implementation, Chicago, IL (September 24-26, 2003)
5. Jacoby, G., Luqi: Intranet Portal Model and Metrics: A Strategic Management Perspective, IT Professional (January/February 2005)
6. Luqi, Zhang, L.: Quantitative Metrics for Risk Assessment in Software Projects. In: SEA 2003. Proceedings of IASTED International Conference on Software Engineering and Applications, Marina del Rey, pp. 76–81 (2003)
7. Jacoby, G., Luqi: Critical Business Requirements Model and Metrics for Intranet ROI. Journal of Electronic Commerce Research 6(1), 1–30 (2005)
8. Luqi, Liang, X., Brown, M.: Formal Approach for System Safety Analysis and Assessment via an Instantiated Activity Model. In: Proc. of 21st International System Safety Conference, Ottawa, Canada, August 4-8, 2003, pp. 1060–1069 (2003)
9. AFRL/IF, Control of Agent Based Systems (CoABS), AFRL/IF Information Directorate, http://www.rl.af.mil/tech/programs/coabs/coabs.html
10. Arisha, K., Ozcan, F., Ross, R., Subrahmanian, V.S., Eiter, T., Kraus, S.: IMPACT: A Platform for Collaborating Agents. IEEE Intelligent Systems 14, 64–72 (1999)
11. Shen, W., Norrie, D.H.: Agent-Based Systems for Intelligent Manufacturing: A State-of-the-Art Survey, http://198.20.44.104/wshen/papers/survey-abm.htm
12. Subrahmanian, V.S., Bonatti, P., Dix, J., Eiter, T., Kraus, S., Ozcan, F., Ross, R.: Heterogeneous Agent Systems. The MIT Press, Cambridge (2000), http://mitpress.mit.edu/catalog/item/default.asp?ttype=2&tid=3370&mode=toc
13. Charniak, E.: Statistical parsing with a context-free grammar and word statistics. In: Proceedings of the Fourteenth National Conference on Artificial Intelligence, AAAI Press, MIT Press, Menlo Park (1997)

14. Leskovec, J., Grobelnik, M., Milic-Frayling, N.: Learning Sub-structures of Document Semantic Graphs for Document Summarization. In: LinkKDD. Workshop on Link Analysis and Group Detection, Seattle, WA, USA (2004)

15. Shen, W., Norrie, D.H.: Agent-Based Systems for Intelligent Manufacturing: A State-of-the-Art Survey. Knowledge and Information Systems, an International Journal 1(2), 129–156 (1999)

16. Boehm, B.: Software Engineering Economics. Prentice-Hall, Englewood Cliffs (1981)

17. Karolak, D.: Software Engineering Management. IEEE CS Press, Los Alamitos (1996)

18. Garlan, D., Khersonsky, S., Kim, J.: Model Checking Publish-Subscribe Systems. In: Proc. of 10th Int'l SPIN Workshop Model Checking of Software, pp. 166–180 (2003)

19. Murrah, M.: Enhancements and Extensions of Formal Models for Risk Assessment in Software Projects. PhD Thesis, Naval Postgraduate School (September 2003)

20. Sadeh, N., Fox, M.S.: CORTES: An Exploration into Micro-Opportunistic Job-Shop Scheduling. In: IJCAI 1989. Proc. of Workshop on Manufacturing Production Scheduling (1989)

21. Sycara, K.P., Roth, S.F., Sadeh, N., Fox, M.S.: Resource Allocation in Distributed Factory Scheduling. Intelligent Scheduling, pp. 29–40. Morgan Kaufman Publishers, San Francisco (1991)

22. Murthy, S., Akkiraju, R., Rachlin, J., Wu, F.: Agent-Based Cooperative Scheduling. In: Proc. of AAAI Workshop on Constrains and Agents, pp. 112–117 (1997)

23. McEleney, B., O'Hare, G.M.P., Sampson, J.: An Agent Based System for Reducing Changeover Delays in a Job-Shop Factory Environment. In: Proc. of PAAM 1998 (1998)

24. Smith, R.G.: The Contract Net Protocol: High-Level Communication and Control in a Distributed Problem Solver. IEEE Transactions on Computers C-29(12), 1104–1113 (1980)

25. Fordyce, K., Sullivan, G.G.: Logistics Management System (LMS): Integrating Decision Technologies for Dispatch Scheduling in Semiconductor Manufacturing. In: Intelligent Scheduling, pp. 473–516. Morgan Kaufman Publishers, San Francisco

26. Saad, A., Biswas, G., Kawamura, K., Johnson, M.E., Salama, A.: Evaluation of Contract Net-Based Heterarchical Scheduling for Flexible Manufacturing Systems. In: IJCAI 1995. Proc. of Intelligent Manufacturing Workshop, pp. 310–321 (1995)

27. Ouelhadj, D., Hanachi, C., Bouzouia, B.: Multi-Agent System for Dynamic Scheduling and Control in Manufacturing Cells. In: Working Notes of the Agent-Based Manufacturing Workshop (1998)

28. Jennings, N.R.: An Agent-based Approach for Building Complex Software Systems. Communications ofthe ACM 44(4), 35–41 (2001)

29. Gawinecki, M., Kruszyk, M., Paprzycki, M., Ganzha, M.: Pitfalls of agent system development on the basis of a Travel Support System. In: BIS 2007, vol. 4439, pp. 488–499. Springer, Heidelberg (2007)

30. Hoare, C.A.R.: An axiomatic basis for computer programming. Communications of the ACM 12(10), 576–585 (1969)

31. Church, A.: The Calculi of Lambda Conversion. Princeton University Press, Princeton (1941)

32. Kaynar, D.K., Lynch, A., Segala, R., Vaandrager, F.: The Theory of Timed I/O Automata. In: Series Synthesis Lectures on Computer Science. Morgan and Claypool Publishers (2006)

Author Index

Lecture Notes in Computer Science

Sublibrary 2: Programming and Software Engineering

For information about Vols. 1– 4227
please contact your bookseller or Springer